EXPLORING GEOGRA

2 *The UK within Europe*

Ann Beckwith and Anne Sutcliffe

eries editor Simon Ross

 LONGMAN

Pearson Education Limited
Edinburgh Gate, Harlow,
Essex, CM20 2JE, England
and Associated Companies throughout the World.

First published 1991
Sixth impression 1999
ISBN 0 582 06795 2

Set in 11/13pt Palatino (Lasercomp)
Printed in China.
SWTC/06

Illustrations by Peter Edwards, Hardlines and Lynn Williams

British Library Cataloguing in Publication Data
Beckwith, Ann
    Exploring geography.
    2: the UK within Europe
    1. Geography
    I. Title   II. Sutcliffe, Anne
    910

ISBN 0-582-06795-2

Our thanks to Brian and Paul.

We should like to thank family,
friends and colleagues for encouragement,
support and inspiration throughout the
preparation of this book.

The publisher's policy is to use paper
manufactured from sustainable forests.

Contents

1 Sense of place and global location   *1*

1.1 What is Europe?   *1*
1.2 The formation of the European community   *3*
1.3 The EC and the world   *5*
1.4 Variety in the EC   *6*

2 Understanding maps   *8*

2.1 Recognising shapes   *8*
2.2 Measuring area on a map   *9*
2.3 Relief and cross-sections   *10*
2.4 Sketch maps   *12*

3 Weather and atmosphere   *16*

3.1 Weather and climate in Europe   *16*
3.2 European air masses   *20*
3.3 Depressions and anticyclones   *21*
3.4 Climatic hazards in Europe   *24*
3.5 Acid rain in Europe   *26*

4 Landscape and processes   *28*

4.1 The physical geography of Europe   *28*
4.2 Weathering and limestone scenery   *29*
4.3 Glaciated landscapes   *33*
4.4 River processes and landforms   *36*
4.5 Rivers and human activity   *39*

5 Ecosystems   *42*

5.1 Biomes, the environment and ecosystems   *42*
5.2 The Mediterranean biome   *44*
5.3 Trees and forests   *46*
5.4 Conservation and environmental protection   *48*

6 Population   *52*

6.1 Where do people live in the EC?   *52*
6.2 Population change   *54*
6.3 Migration   *56*
6.4 The quality of life   *60*

7 Settlement   *64*

7.1 The early siting of settlements   *64*
7.2 Shops and services   *65*
7.3 Case study – conurbations   *68*
7.4 Planning in urban areas   *72*
7.5 Settlements in remote parts of the EC   *74*
     Case study – rural Greece   *75*

8 Resources and energy   *78*

8.1 The resources of Europe   *78*
8.2 Energy – keeping Europe going   *80*
8.3 Case study – energy in the UK   *82*
8.4 Case study – the North Sea   *84*
     1 Fishing   *84*
     2 Oil and gas in the North Sea   *85*
     3 The North Sea or the Dead Sea?   *86*
8.5 Mineral resources in the EC   *89*
     Case study – quarrying dolomite
     in Ferryhill in the UK   *90*
     Case study – quarrying bauxite in France   *91*

9 Transport and communications   *93*

9.1 What are networks?   *93*
9.2 Motorways   *97*
9.3 Railways   *98*
9.4 Waterways and ports   *101*
9.5 Airports   *105*

10 Farming in the EC   *110*

10.1 Where does our food come from?   *110*
10.2 Farming patterns in the UK and the EC   *112*
10.3 Mixed farming in the UK   *114*
10.4 Mediterranean agriculture   *116*
10.5 Mixed farming in Denmark   *119*
10.6 The Common Agricultural Policy   *122*

11 Industry   *124*

11.1 What is industry?   *124*
11.2 The manufacturing industry system   *125*
11.3 The location of manufacturing industry in the EC   *127*
11.4 Case study – the heavy industrial triangle   *129*
11.5 Industry in the UK   *131*
     Case study – the North East of England   *132*
11.6 Case study – hi-tech and service industries
     in the UK   *136*

12 Leisure and recreation   *138*

12.1 More time, more money, more leisure   *138*
12.2 Holidays in the UK   *140*
12.3 Choosing a holiday abroad   *143*
12.4 Case study 1: Sea and sand, The Algarve, Portugal   *144*
         2: Cultural holiday, Venice, Italy   *146*
12.5 Case study – winter holiday, The Alps   *149*
12.6 European tourism in the future   *152*

Map symbols   *155*

Acknowledgements

We are grateful to the following for permission to reproduce copyright material;

The European Ltd for extracts from the articles 'Dutch tackle pollution head-on' by Rommert Kruithof from *The European* Weekend June 22–24, 1990 and 'Provence defends itself against high-speed train' by John Moynihan from *The European* Weekend May 25–27, 1990; Express Newspapers plc for an extract from the article 'Floods as Britain battered by wind and heavy rain' by Michael Shanahan and Oonagh Blackman from *Sunday Express* 17.12.89; The Journal, Newcastle upon Tyne, for the article 'Japanese to create 900 new North jobs' by Ian Cameron from *The Journal* 12.4.89; the author, Han J Lindeboom for extracts from his article 'How trawlers are raking the North Sea to death' from *Daily Telegraph* 19.3.90; Ewan MacNaughton Associates for extracts from the article 'Gatwick needs 2nd runway' by John Harlow from *Daily Telegraph* 27.2.89, the article 'Green tourist sites in favour' by John Harlow from *Daily Telegraph* 11.12.89, the article 'Project to harness geothermal power' by Roger Highfield from *Daily Telegraph* 6.12.89, the article '£6m visitor centre is planned at Stonehenge' by Kenneth Powell from *Daily Telegraph* 2.11.89, all (c) The Daily Telegraph plc, 1989, and extracts from the article 'Green menace chokes Venice' by Tim Jepson in *Sunday Telegraph*, (c) The Sunday Telegraph Ltd, 1989; Thomas Nelson & Sons Ltd for an abridged extract from *Cristo si e fermato a Eboli (Christ stopped at Eboli)* by Carlo Levi (pub Nelson Harrap); Newspaper Publishing plc for extracts from the article 'Put out more Blue Flags' by Frank Barrett from *The Independent* 8.6.91, an adaptation of the article 'Turning the Alps into a rocky desert' by Patricia Clough from *The Independent* 16.1.88 and extracts from the article 'Set for a meeting in mid-Channel' by Andy Glinecki from *The Independent* 26.5.89; north of England Newspapers for the article 'Consett 10 Years On' from *Durham Advertiser* 26.10.89; Solo Syndication & Literary Agency Ltd for extracts from the article 'Cool it! Rain is on its way' by Fiona Barton from *Mail on Sunday*.

We would like to thank the following for permission to reproduce photographic material:

ARC Southern (8.5 fig 6); BACMI (8.5 fig 5); British Airports Authority and IDA Advertising (9.5 fig 3); J. Allan Cash (4.1 fig 1, 6.4 fig 2, 7.2 fig 1, 7.3 figs 6 & 7, 7.5 figs 2 & 3, 8.2 fig 4, 9.3 fig 1, 10.4 figs 1, 4a & 5, 12.4 fig 3); (c) John Cleare (3.4 fig 4b); Earth Satellite Corporation/Science Photo Library (12.4 fig 3); European Commission/UK Press and Information Office (1.2 fig 2); (c) Euro Disney, Paris (12.6 fig 2); European Space Agency/Science Photo Library (3.3 fig 3); Forestry Commission (5.4 fig 1); Gateshead Metropolitan Borough Council (7.4 fig 2); Robert Harding Picture Library (Geoff Renner) (9.4 fig 5); Holt Studios Ltd (3.4 fig 2, 10.2 fig 1, 10.4 fig 4b, 10.6 fig 2); The *Journal*, Newcastle upon Tyne (7.4 fig 2); KLM/Aviation Picture Library (9.5 fig 4); KLM Luchtfotografie (5.3 fig 5); London Transport Museum (9.1 fig 3); London Tourist Service (12.2 fig 5); MetroCentre, Gateshead (7.2 fig 2); National Remote Sensing Centre (4.2 fig 9); Powergen (8.3 fig 4); Redland Aggregates Ltd (8.5 figs 7 & 8); Simon Ross (3.4 fig 4c, 4.1 fig 1, 4.4 fig 3, 10.2 fig 1); Sefton Photo Library (8.4 fig 5); Shell Photo Service (9.4 fig 4); Steetley Quarry Products (8.5 fig 1); Teesside Development Corporation (11.5 fig 7b); West Air Photography (7.1 fig 2).

All other photographs were supplied by the authors.

We are grateful to the following for permission to reproduce copyright material:

Acid Rain Information Centre, Manchester Polytechnic, Chester Street, Manchester M1 5GD (3.5 Fig 3); Cartoon image of a North Easterner from *North East England*, Macdonald Colour Unit, 1974. Reproduced by permission of Simon & Schuster Young Books, Hemel Hempstead, U.K (11.5 fig 2); Extracts from *Digest of UK Energy Statistics 1991*, reproduced with the permission of the Controller of Her Majesty's Stationery Office (8.3 figs 2 & 3); Graves & White for map from *Geography of the British Isles* (7.3 fig 2); Carrsides Farm, County Durham (10.3 figs 2 & 3); Civil Aviation Authority (9.5 fig 1); Danmarks Statisik (10.5 figs 3 & 6); Deutschen Kommission zur Reinhaltung des Rheins from 'Rhein-Bericht 1985–87 mit Rheingutebericht 1986' (4.5 fig 1); Eurotunnel, Folkestone (9.3 fig 4); Forestry Commission (5.3 fig 1 and 5.4 fig 3); Gateshead Metropolitan Borough Council (7.4 fig 1); Department of the Environment *Environment in Trust* reproduced with the permission of the Controller of her Majesty's Stationery Office (5.4 fig 2); Heinemann Publishers (Oxford) Ltd and George Philip Ltd for extracts from *Geographical Digest* 1990 (6.2 fig 3, 10.1 fig 3, 10.2 fig 3); Herausgegeben vom Landesvermessungsamt, Baden-Wurttemberg for extract from Topographische Karte 1 : 50 000, Speyer L6716 (2.4 fig 2); Hodder & Stoughton Publishers for figure 2, 'The Site and Growth of London' from Young & Lowry *British Isles* (course in world geography series) published by Edward Arnold (7.3 fig 2); IDG Geografisch Instituut (6.1 fig 4, 9.4 figs 2, 3 & 6, 9.5 figs 2, 6 & 7); The *Independent* 8.6.91 (8.4 fig 9); Macmillan Education (5.2 fig 1) from L. Hobley *Mediterranean Europe and North Africa*; Thomas Nelson & Sons Ltd (5.1 fig 6, 6.4 fig 5) from Sue Warn *Fieldwork Investigations*; Ordnance Survey for extracts from 1 : 50 000 Malham, Yorks, 1 : 25 000 Swanage Bay, 1 : 50 000 Snowdon, 1 : 50 000 Trossachs Region, 1 : 50 000 Yorkshire Dales. Reproduced with the permission of the Controller of Her Majesty's Stationery Office © Crown copyright reserved (2.4 fig 4, 4.2 fig 8, 4.3 figs 7, 5.3 fig 6); OPCS (6.2 fig 7 & 8, 6.3 fig 2); George Philip, London and Hobsons Publishing plc (3.1 fig 8 and 10.2 fig 1);

We have, unfortunately, been unable to trace the copyright owner of the following and would appreciate any information which would enable us to do so: 3.2 fig 3

1 Sense of Place and Global Location

1.1 What is Europe?

What is Europe? What is a European? Both of these questions are difficult to answer as people have many different ideas. Read the list of statements in Figure 1 given by a group of 13 year olds. How many do you agree with?

The **continent** of Europe can be shown as a map. Look at Figure 2. It is bounded in the south by the Mediterranean Sea; in the west by the Atlantic Ocean; and in the east by the Ural mountains in the USSR. Notice how small Europe is compared with the other continents of the world.

Europe is a group of countries (Most have better weather than Britain)

Europe is a continent

Europe is all the countries as far as the USSR?

Europe is divided into Western Europe and Eastern Europe

The European countries are all grouped together with no sea between them – apart from the British Isles

A European is a person who is born or lives in Europe

Europe is the 6th largest continent

Most Europeans drive on the wrong side of the road and speak a foreign language

Some of the USSR is in Europe

Figure 1

ARCTIC OCEAN

NORTH AMERICA

PACIFIC OCEAN

ATLANTIC OCEAN

SOUTH AMERICA

USSR IN EUROPE

Ural mountains

EUROPE

ASIA

INDIAN OCEAN

AUSTRALIA

N

0   2000 kms

Figure 2 Continents of the world

ANTARCTICA

The influence of Europe has spread worldwide. In the past Spain and Portugal, for example, greatly influenced the development of South American countries such as Chile and Brazil. Britain influenced several countries such as India, Kenya, and Australia.

Europe can be divided by **political** boundaries into countries. After the Second World War several countries in the West and the East grouped together for military and economic reasons. They hoped that, with various agreements, disputes leading to war might not occur again. In 1989 changes began to take place in Eastern Europe. By October 1990, West and East Germany had united, to form one country and other East European countries began to seek closer relationships with those of the West.

Activities

1 Look at the word search in Figure 3. Find the names of 12 European countries. The remaining letters spell out a message. Write this out and list the countries you have found.

2 a On a copy of Figure 4 name the 12 countries you have listed in activity 1. See how many you know already and use an atlas to fill in the rest. (Do not colour the map in yet.)

  b The dots show where the capitals are; name these.

  c name the following on your map:
    i Sicily   ii Sardinia   iii Corsica
    iv Balearic Islands   v Crete

  d Add a title, scale and north arrow to your map. You now have an outline map of Europe which you will colour and complete after reading the next section – 1.2.

Figure 3

T	H	E	E	C	N	A	R	F	M	I
R	L	E	A	R	E	E	T	W	O	T
E	U	L	G	V	T	S	E	M	D	A
E	X	M	B	R	H	B	P	E	G	L
W	E	S	T	G	E	R	M	A	N	Y
R	M	S	I	L	R	E	N	T	I	H
E	B	E	G	U	L	R	C	O	K	N
P	O	I	K	R	A	M	N	E	D	E
A	U	N	C	O	N	M	M	U	E	N
M	R	I	T	E	D	Y	T	U	T	R
K	G	E	I	Y	S	W	O	U	I	L
P	O	R	T	U	G	A	L	D	N	L
I	E	K	E	T	O	J	O	I	U	N

Figure 4   Europe

1.2 The formation of the European Community

After the Second World War some European countries decided to form trade and industrial links. These can be summarised as follows:

- 1948 the Benelux countries (**Belgium**, **Netherlands** and **Luxembourg**) formed an agreement to trade with each other.
- 1952 **France** and ~~West~~ **Germany**, who had been at war several times, joined with **Italy** and the Benelux countries to form the ECSC (European Coal and Steel Community). This was to supervise the recovery of the coal and steel industries after suffering in the war.
- 1958 The EEC (European Economic Community) and Euratom (European Atomic Energy Community) were established. There were six member

countries. The aim of the communities was to encourage co-operation with trade, industry, agriculture and nuclear power development. The ECSC, EEC and Euratom together are now known as the EC (European Community).

- 1973 **United Kingdom**, **Denmark** and **Eire** joined the EC to make nine members.
- 1981 **Greece** joined to make 10 members.
- 1986 **Spain** and **Portugal** joined to make 12. ALSO Austria, Sweden, Finland.
- 1987 Turkey applied to join the EC although they have not yet been accepted, Austria and Malta also intend to apply.
- 1992 The Single European Market. From 1993 Europe should then work as one unit without barriers. Figure 1 summarises what this means for *you*.

Figure 1
1992: A single market
The United States of Europe

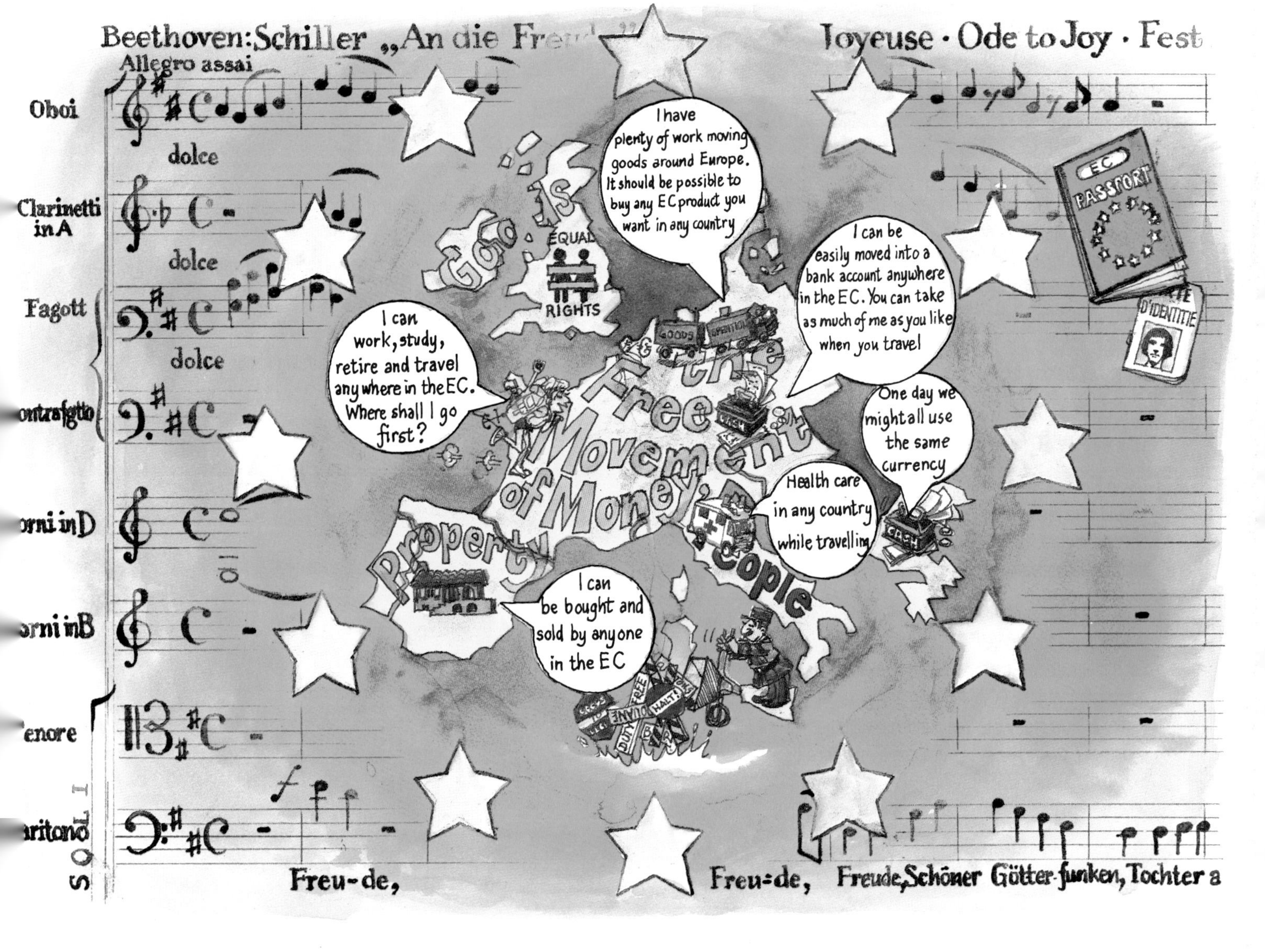

The Structure of the EC

Look at Figure 2 which shows you the different sections of the EC. There are three main sections which influence the lives of European people: The European Court of Justice in Luxembourg, the Council of Ministers in Brussels and the European Parliament in Strasbourg.

How is the EC financed?

Every country in the EC pays a contribution to a central account according to how much they can afford. Extra money comes through taxes. Each year this is divided up and allocated to different funds. Figure 3 shows the allocation of funds in 1989.

65%	Agricultural modernisation, fisheries, maintaining crop prices
11%	Regional development for areas with problems such as unemployment
8%	Social fund for encouraging training schemes where there is high unemployment
4%	Research, energy, industry, environment and transport
3%	Aid to the third World
5%	Administration costs for 20 000 officials in the EC
4%	Other

EUROPEAN PARLIAMENT

Strasbourg

518 elected members (MEPs) sit in one of ten party groups. e.g. Socialist People's Party, Democrats, Liberals.
Meet for one week per month.

COUNCIL OF MINISTERS

Government ministers e.g. Ministers of Agriculture or Foreign ministers meet to discuss policies. They make the decisions and meet 2 to 3 times a year.

COURT OF JUSTICE

13 judges look at disputes according to the law

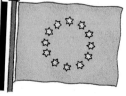

EUROPEAN COMMISSION

17 members check that decisions made are being followed. They manage the funds.

COURT OF AUDITORS

12 people look at finances

ECONOMIC AND SOCIAL COMMITTEE

189 members give opinions over proposals

EUROPEAN INVESTMENT BANK

Responsible for borrowing and lending money

Brussels

Figure 2   The EC machine

Figure 3   Allocation of EC funds

Activities

1 Read the text in this unit to discover when each member joined the European Community (EC). Use the outline map you produced for activity 4 in section 1.1. Use colours to shade in each country according to the dates of joining the EC. You should have about four colours or groups in total. Remember to colour in the islands depending on which country they belong to and add a key to the map.

2 a When was the EC formed?
b Why was the EC formed?

3 a Using Figure 1 to help you list five changes which should take place after 1992.
b For one of the changes mentioned in Figure 1 can you think of a disadvantage?

4 a Look at the design of the European flag in Figure 2. Is this design appropriate?
b Each member country has its own flag which flies outside the various EC buildings. These are all shown in Figure 4. How many can you match up with their countries? You may have to use some reference books to find the answers.

5 The main EC buildings are located in Strasbourg, Luxembourg and Brussels.
a Use an atlas to locate these places.
b Why do you think these locations were chosen for the main meeting places?

6 a Show the information in Figure 3 as a pie chart.
b What takes up the greatest proportion of the EC funds?
c What percentage is allocated for helping areas with high unemployment?

Figure 4

1.3   The EC and the world

Besides the EC countries, there are other groups of countries in Europe which encourage trade between themselves. Some belong to the **European Free Trade Association (EFTA)**. These countries are shown in Figure 1 and they have close links with the EC.

The countries of Eastern Europe formed part of a trade bloc with the Soviet Union, which was called **COMECON** – the Council of Mutual Economic Assistance. These are also shown in Figure 1. With the changes in Eastern Europe, some countries are hoping to transfer from COMECON to the EC.

The influence of the EC does not stop in Europe. Several links have been established with countries in other continents. Look at Figure 1: 66 African–Caribbean–Pacific countries signed an agreement at a meeting in Lomé, Togo. All these countries are in the developing world and the EC has agreed to lend money, give advice and buy products from them. **Aid** is also sent in times of particular need, like the Bangladesh Cyclone in 1991. There are similar agreements with the other countries shown on the map.

The EC benefits from these links just as the other countries do. All the countries depend on each other for products. This means they are **interdependent**.

Figure 1
The EC and the world

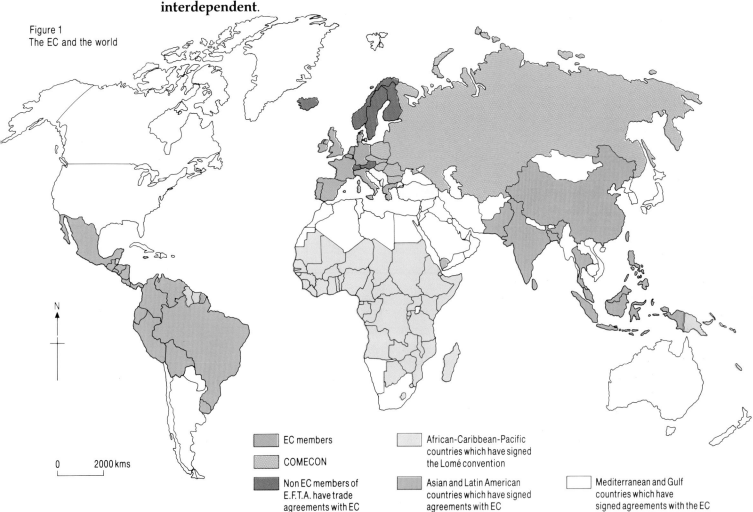

▦ EC members	▦ African-Caribbean-Pacific countries which have signed the Lomé convention
▦ COMECON	▦ Asian and Latin American countries which have signed agreements with EC
▦ Non EC members of E.F.T.A. have trade agreements with EC	☐ Mediterranean and Gulf countries which have signed agreements with the EC

0   2000 kms

Activities

1 Using an atlas and Figure 1, answer the following questions:
   a Give two examples of countries which belong to EFTA.
   b Give two examples of countries which belong to COMECON.
   c i Give three examples of countries in Europe which do not belong to either the EC, EFTA or COMECON
     ii Which of these three countries has links with the EC?
   d Write a sentence about trade links in Europe using your map to help.

2 a Look at Figure 1. Name the country which has been coloured green in Latin America.
   b Why has this country been coloured in green?
   c Name two examples of countries with EC links in each of the following areas:
     i Asia
     ii Africa
     iii Latin America

1.4   Variety in the EC

There is a great difference between the landscapes, climates and people of the EC countries. Many of these contrasts are covered in later chapters.

You will probably have some ideas of typical features you associate with a country. Some countries are associated with famous landmarks. Look at Figure 1. Perhaps you have read books or seen television programmes or films set elsewhere in Europe. You may have some ideas from your French, Spanish or German lessons. All these help to make up your perception of a country and its people. Figure 2 shows the result of a 'brainstorming' session on Italy – what would you add?

Figure 1

Figure 2
'Brainstorming' Italy

spaghetti   Opera singers   Venice
gondolas   St Marks square
beaches   Sinking city
Etna   Vesuvius   Pompeii
wine
Parmesan   Mad drivers
Ice cream
Earthquakes   Mountains
pizza   pope   Vatican city
mafia   St. Peters square
cornettos
World Cup 1990   Italian language

Activities

1 Look at the landscapes in Figure 1. Try to name the city and the country where they can be found.

2 a Try 'brainstorming'. In pairs, one of you choose a country in the EC. Write down any words which come into your head associated with that country. Time yourselves for two minutes. Compare your lists. Do you have the same perceptions as each other? Repeat the exercise with another country. If you do this exercise at the end of using this book, your perceptions may be different. It would also be interesting to 'brainstorm' the UK.

3 Working in small groups of two or three, choose one of the EC countries. As a class you should cover all 12 of the countries. Visit the library and local travel agent and produce a poster to show information about the country. Include the following:

● Is the country run by a king/queen or president?
● What variety of physical landscapes are there?
● Are there any famous landmarks?
● Are there any important festivals or customs?
● Are there any products which are typical of the country (e.g. Brie cheese)?
● Are there famous people associated with the country?

Try to put as many drawings or pictures as you can onto your poster.

Dictionary

aid   help given to another country in the form of food or money or technical advice

COMECON   a trade group consisting of Eastern European countries and the USSR

Europe   a continent including Western and Eastern European countries as well as the western part of the USSR

European Community   a group of 12 countries which joined together for economic reasons

interdependence   the reliance of countries on each other, i.e. the Third World relies on the developed world and vice versa

trade   buying and selling of goods and services

2.1   Recognising shapes

A map or plan shows things in plan view, from a **vertical viewpoint**.

Maps can be drawn of small areas such as the classroom, your bedroom or your house and garden. These maps are usually called **plans** and we use the word map for larger areas like a country or the world.

Sometimes, maps are not drawn as we would expect. Study Figure 1 which shows a **cartogram**. Each country in the EC has been drawn according to its population size and not its area. The countries are arranged in approximately the correct positions but their shape is very different from the usual map you would see in an atlas. In Figure 2, the UK has been drawn based on fastest journey times by public transport from London. Notice how distorted the country looks. These maps are called **topological** maps.

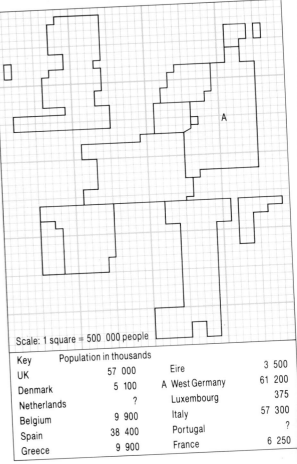

Scale: 1 square = 500 000 people

Key	Population in thousands		
UK	57 000	Eire	3 500
Denmark	5 100	A West Germany	61 200
Netherlands	?	Luxembourg	375
Belgium	9 900	Italy	57 300
Spain	38 400	Portugal	?
Greece	9 900	France	6 250

Figure 1
Topological map of the EC
showing population size

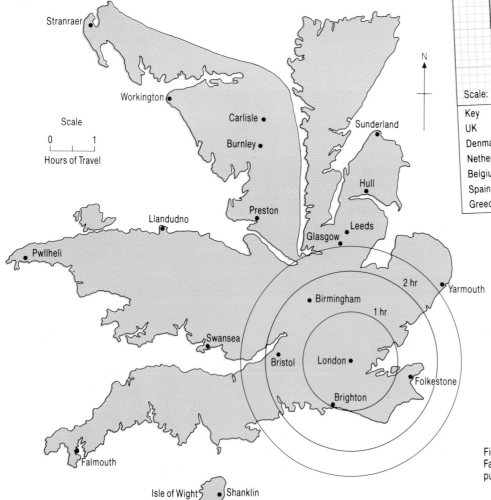

Scale
0   1
Hours of Travel

Figure 2
Fastest journey times by
public transport from London

Activities

1 Imagine you are up in a hot air balloon, hovering above your house. Sketch a plan view of what your house would look like.

2 Study Figure 1.

a The countries have not been named for you. Copy Figure 1 onto graph paper. Study the key and name each country correctly – give each country a letter or a number and write it alongside the country in the key. West Germany has been done for you.

Try not to use an atlas for this activity – but you can check your answers at the end.

b Notice that Eire has not been shown on the map. The population figure is given for you in the table. Using the scale, work out how large the area for Eire should be. Use an atlas to help you with the shape and position of the country. Finish the cartogram by adding Eire.

c In the key, the population totals for the Netherlands and Portugal are missing. Fill in the gaps by counting the squares for each country and using the scale to find each population.

Look at the table of population figures on page 52 to check how accurate your calculations are!

3 *a* In pairs, compare an atlas map of the UK with Figure 2. Discuss the main differences between the shapes of the outlines. Record your results.

b Using Figure 2 and an atlas map work out the fastest journey time and the distance between London and the following places. Copy and complete the table.

	Fastest Journey time	Distance
London – Glasgow		
London – Pwllheli		
London – Carlisle		
London – Shanklin		

c Explain why it takes so long to get to Shanklin. (Hint – the town is on the Isle of Wight!)

2.2   *Measuring area on a map*

The size of any feature shown on a map depends on the scale of the map being used. An area of land use such as a wood or lake would be larger on a 1:25 000 map than on a 1:50 000 map of the same area. But, each grid square on a 1:25 000 and a 1:50 000 map equals 1 square kilometre. This makes it an easy task to estimate or measure exactly the total area of a particular land use.

How to measure area on a map

1 Trace the area of the land use whose area you wish to discover.

2 Lay your tracing over a sheet of metric graph paper.

3 Count the number of squares completely enclosed by the outline. Use shortcuts like those shown in Figure 1 to count large blocks of 100, 50 or 25 squares.

4 Count up the part squares, using quarter, half or three-quarter measures.

5 Add up the total number of squares – check your work as it is easy to make a mistake. In the example (Figure 1), the total number of squares is 476.

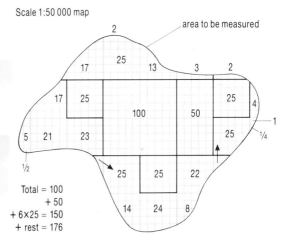

Figure 1   Total squares = 476

6 Now check the scale of your map and using Figure 2 work out the
   area in either hectares or square kilometres. (1 square kilometre =
   100 hectares)
   In the example (Figure 1), the scale of the map is 1:50 000.
   In hectares, the area = 476 × 1 = 476 hectares.
   In square kms, the area = 476 × 0.01 = 4.76 km².

map scale	If you want the answer in :-	
	hectares multiply the number of small squares by	square kilometres multiply the number of small squares by
1:50 000	1.0	0.01
1:25 000	0.25	0.0025
1:10 000	0.04	0.0004

Figure 2

2.3   Relief and cross-sections

A landscape has many ups and downs. This is the **relief** of the land
and an OS map tells us a lot about the relief of an area. Relief is
shown on a map in three ways and these are shown in Figure 1:

● Spot heights are black points on a map with the height in metres
  above sea-level printed next to them.
● Triangulation points have a blue triangle symbol on a map with
  the height written next to them. Triangulation pillars can be seen
  on the landscape often as concrete pillars and they are used to
  survey the land so they are often at a good vantage point.
  Figure 2 shows a triangulation or 'trig' point.
● Contour lines on maps are brown or orange lines joining places
  with the same height above sea-level. They are numbered with
  the height in metres. The contour interval is the difference in
  height between each contour, on the 1:50 000 map the interval is
  10 metres. The closer together the contour lines, the steeper the
  slope. The pattern contour lines make can also help us to
  recognise features of the landscape.

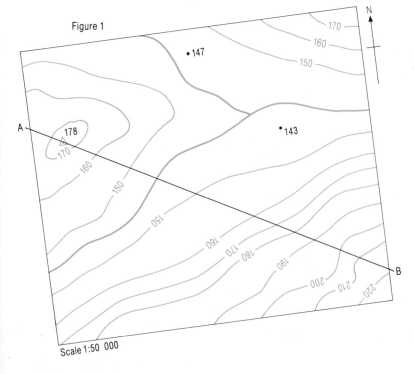

Figure 1

Scale 1:50 000

Figure 2
Triangulation pillar

Planning a walk in the countryside is one time when it is important to know the relief of the land. You need to know whether the land is flat, gently sloping or very steep! A cross-section allows you to see clearly what the relief is like.

Read through the 10 steps below using Figure 3 to help you.

How to draw a cross-section

1 Draw the line of section on your map (X-Y on Figure 3a).

2 Look carefully at the contours – is the land rising or falling? Do any contour lines cross the line more than once?

3 Place a straight edge of paper along the line of your section. On the paper mark the start and the finish (Figure 3b).

4 Carefully mark the points where all the contour lines cross the piece of paper. Note the height of each one (Figure 3b).

5 Mark any other important features such as rivers.

6 Place the paper along a piece of graph paper. Mark and draw a line from the start to the finish of your section (Figure 3c).

7 Work out a scale for the vertical axis. Experiment with this, you need to show enough detail of the landscape without it looking silly. A good guide is 1 cm to 20 metres on the 1:50 000 map and 1 cm to 100 metres on the 1:25 000 map.

8 Put small crosses on your graph at the correct heights and locations.

9 Join the crosses freehand, using curves at hilltops and valley bottoms (Figure 3d).

10 Add a title and labels.

If the contour lines are very close together it is acceptable to only mark every other one.

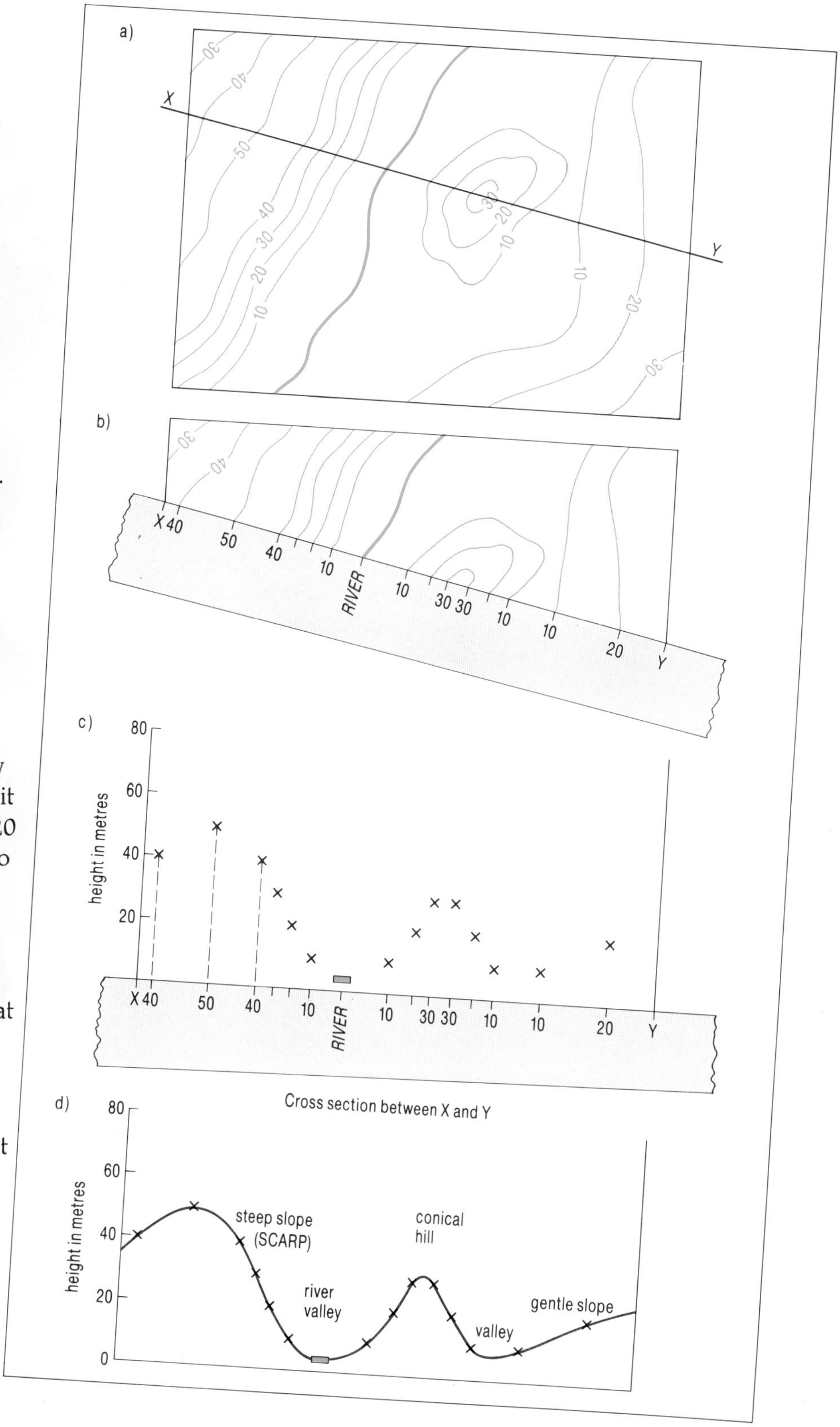

Figure 3

2.4   Sketch maps

Sometimes when we look at a map it seems very complicated. Being able to draw a **sketch map** can help simplify map reading for you.

Figure 1 shows a sketch map of the location of Speyer in West Germany. It is based upon the map shown in Figure 2. The sketch map has simplified the map for us. We can now use it to help us understand the landscape.

Where is most of the forest located? There is a large area of forest in the north-west corner of the map and also along the river banks. Why is Speyer the largest settlement on this map? Looking at the sketch map we can see that Speyer is on the banks of the river Rhine at a **bridging point**. All the main roads and the railway lead into the town so it is also a **route focus**. The land that the town is built on is some of the lowest on the map.

A sketch map can be drawn to the same scale or it can be reduced or enlarged. The grid lines on a map make it easy to draw accurate sketch maps. The lines act as a guide.

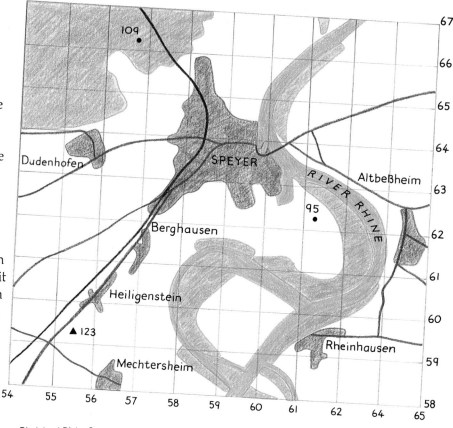

Figure 1   Speyer Rheinland-Pfalz, Germany

 Built up areas

 Forest

 Main roads

 Railway

How to draw a sketch map

1   Draw a grid frame which matches the area of the map to be sketched. If you are drawing the map to scale the grid squares will be the same as on the map. If you are reducing the scale the squares will be smaller and if you are enlarging the scale they will be larger. Draw the lines faintly so that they don't spoil your final sketch.

2   Mark on the grid numbers around the edges.

3   In pencil mark onto your sketch the features you are interested in. This might include roads, rivers, woodland and settlement. Use the grid lines to help you place the features accurately.

4   Complete your sketch by:
   ● adding colour, a key, a title, the scale and a north arrow.
   ● numbering the grid lines in ink.
   ● adding labels where necessary.

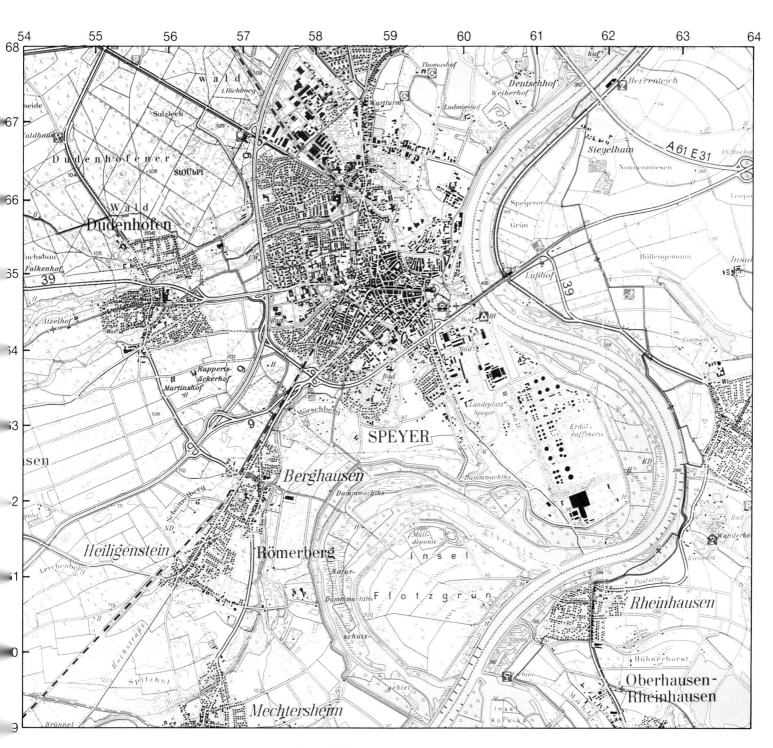

Figure 2   Speyer Rheinland-Pfalz, Germany, Topographische Karte 1:50 000

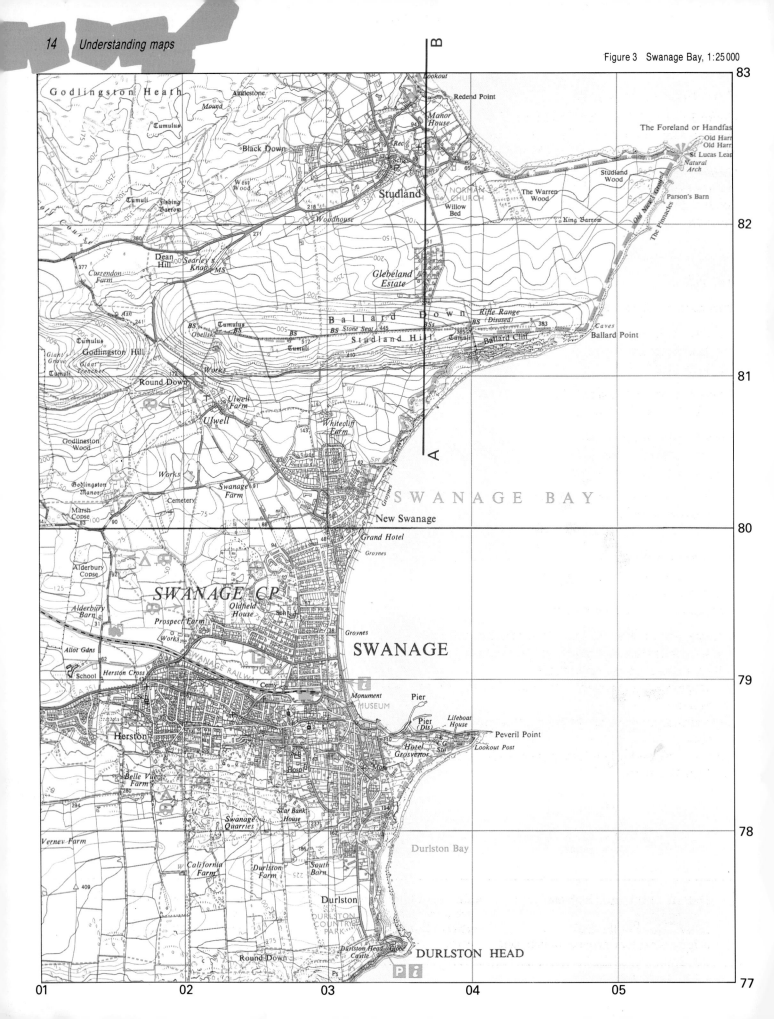

Figure 3   Swanage Bay, 1:25 000

Case study – Swanage Bay

Figure 3 is a 1:25 000 OS map extract of the Swanage area of the UK; find Swanage in your atlas. Figure 4 is a geology map of the same area. This map shows the rocks of the area and tells you how **resistant** they are. Resistance refers to how hard or soft the rocks are. Hard rocks stand out on the landscape as hills or ridges or cliffs. Softer rocks erode or wear away more easily and they tend to form valleys and other low areas.

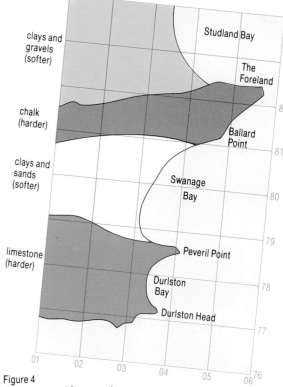

Figure 4
Geology map of Swanage Area

Activities

All the questions below are based on the OS map and the geology map in Figures 3 and 4.

1 Give the four-figure grid references for:
 a Glebeland Estate
 b Ulwell Village

2 Name the woodland found in each of the following squares:
 a 0482 *b* 0180 *c* 0282

3 Give the six-figure grid reference for:
 a The Youth Hostel at Swanage
 b The Norman Church at Studland

4 *a* Measure the distance from Ballard Point to the viewpoint at St. Lucas Leap. Give your answer in kilometres.
 b In what direction would you be walking if you started from Ballard Point?

5 Draw a cross-section from A to B along the line shown on the map.
 Use a vertical scale of 1 cm to 100 metres.
 Label your cross-section with the following:
 ridge, cliffs, steep slopes, gentle slopes, sea

6 You are going to draw a sketch map to show the location of Swanage.
 In pairs discuss what you are going to include on your sketch.
 There is no need to draw all of the map.
 a Compare your sketch map with another pair. Did you choose to mark the same features?
 b In which square do you think the 'old' part of Swanage is? Give reasons for your answer.
 c In which two directions has Swanage grown? Can you explain this? The geology map in Figure 4 may help you.

7 *a* Name one example of a headland and one example of a bay.
 b Which rocks make up the headlands? Why?

8 Imagine that you are working in Swanage at the Tourist Information Office. A young couple, Mr and Mrs Bowen, have written to the office to ask for some advice. They plan to visit Swanage for five days:
 a Where can they stay in Swanage?
 b They are keen walkers and want to walk from Durlston Head (0377) to St Lucas Leap (0582). They would like to know the coastal scenery they would see on their walk.
 c Where can they visit and what else can they do?

 Either write a letter to Mr and Mrs Bowen or design and produce a travel brochure setting out the information they want to know.

Dictionary

plateau flat topped high land with steep slopes	**scale** used to show how big things are or how far apart they are	**1:25 000**	means 4 cms equals 1 km
relief shape of the land	**vertical viewpoint** 'bird's eye' view	**1:50 000**	means 2 cms equals 1 km
ridge long, narrow piece of high land			

3 Weather and atmosphere

Here is a typical weather forecast you might hear on the radio: 'The weather outlook for today is warm and sunny with patchy cloud, light breezes and some showers later.'

This weather forecast looks at temperature, the clouds, the wind and the rainfall. These are all **elements** of the weather (see Figure 1). The **weather** is the state of the atmosphere at any one time.

Across Europe the weather is often very different at any one time. Look at Figure 2 which shows the weather at different places on one day in June. Notice that Oslo in Norway has a temperature of 15°C whereas Athens in Greece has a temperature of 28°C. This is largely the effect of **latitude** (see Figure 3). Oslo is much further from the Equator and so receives less concentrated energy from the sun.

Figure 1

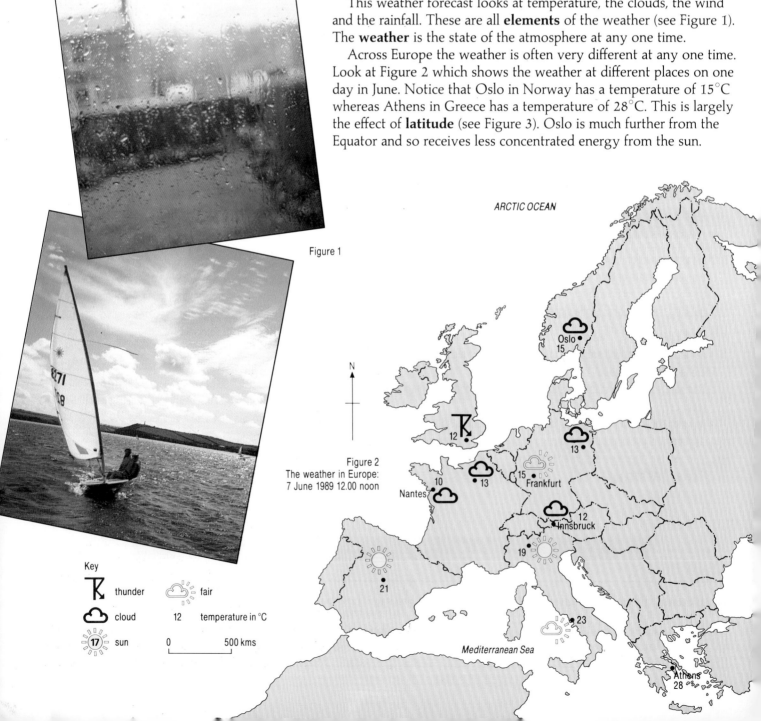

Figure 2
The weather in Europe:
7 June 1989 12.00 noon

ARCTIC OCEAN

Mediterranean Sea

Key

thunder   fair

cloud   12   temperature in °C

17 sun   0   500 kms

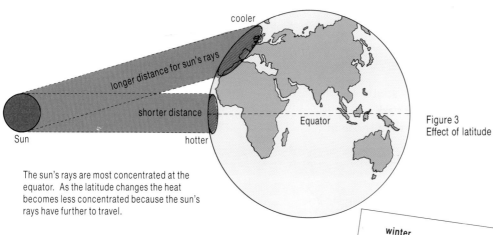

Figure 3
Effect of latitude

The sun's rays are most concentrated at the equator. As the latitude changes the heat becomes less concentrated because the sun's rays have further to travel.

The temperature in Nantes (France) is 10°C but in Frankfurt (Germany) it is 15°C. Notice that these two places are on the same line of latitude! This difference is due to the effect of **land and sea**. The sea takes longer to heat up and cool down than the land. In the summer, therefore, the seas tend to be colder than the land. Coastal areas, like Nantes, have lower temperatures because the cool sea breezes keep temperatures down. Frankfurt has an inland location, not affected by the sea, so temperatures are higher in the summer. In winter, the reverse happens. Nantes will be warmer than Frankfurt. In winter, the seas are warmer than the land and onshore breezes raise the temperatures of coastal areas. This effect of the sea is called the **Maritime Effect**. The diagram in Figure 4 shows this effect.

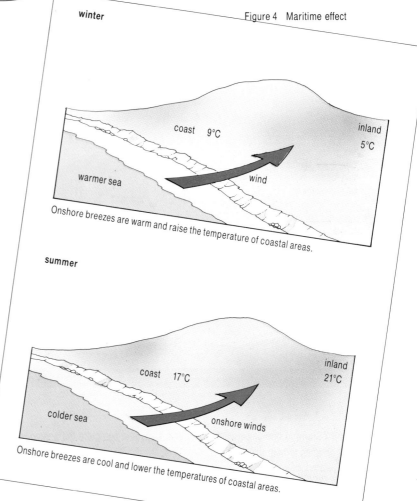

Figure 4 Maritime effect

Figure 5 Effect of altitude

Look again at Figure 2 and notice that Innsbruck (Austria) has a lower temperature than Frankfurt although they are quite close together. The difference this time is due to **altitude**, the height of the land (see Figure 5). The temperature falls as the altitude increases – usually about 1°C every 160 metres. If you climbed a mountain 1600 metres high the temperature would be 10°C colder!

The **climate** is the average weather of an area. To work out the climate, the average temperature and rainfall are taken over as many years as possible. There are several different climates in Europe and

these are shown on the map in Figure 6.
   Notice that:
● Climates in the north are colder than those in the south
● Climates in the west are wetter than those in the east
● Climates in upland areas e.g. the Alps are colder than those in lowland areas
● The climate around the Mediterranean in summer is hotter and drier than the rest of Europe.

Figure 6   Climatic regions

Key

West Coast Maritime
mild winters, cool summers, rain all year

Mediterranean
mild wet winters, hot dry summers

Alpine Mountain
cold winters with snow,
warm summers with showers

Continental
cold dry winters, hot damp summers

Tundra
cold all year, little rain

0   500 kms

Activities

1 Study Figure 2 showing one day's weather in June. Copy and complete the sentences below. Use an atlas to help you.

As you move north from the Mediterranean Sea to the A .... O ...., the temperatures become (warmer/cooler). In Athens, the temperature is .... C but in Oslo, the temperature is only .... C. This is because Oslo is (a long way from/closer to) the Equator. In the Alps, the temperatures are the (lowest/highest). The temperature at Innsbruck is .... C. This is because the Alps are in a (mountainous/lowland) area and temperatures decrease as the (altitude/latitude) increases.

2 The table in Figure 7 shows the weather information in December for the same places as shown on Figure 2. Using an atlas to help you, make a similar map for the December information. You will need to design your own symbols for some of the weather types. Don't forget to add a key to show what all the symbols mean and a title.
   a Why is there snow in Oslo but sunny warm weather in Milan?
   b Why is it 9°C in Nantes but only 6°C in Frankfurt?

Figure 7

London	Cloud	7°C
Oslo	Snow	−3°C
Athens	Fair	18°C
Innsbruck	Sleet	3°C
Naples	Sun	18°C
Madrid	Cloud	8°C
Paris	Rain	4°C
Frankfurt	Fair	6°C
Berlin	Sleet	2°C
Milan	Sun	13°C
Nantes	Rain	9°C

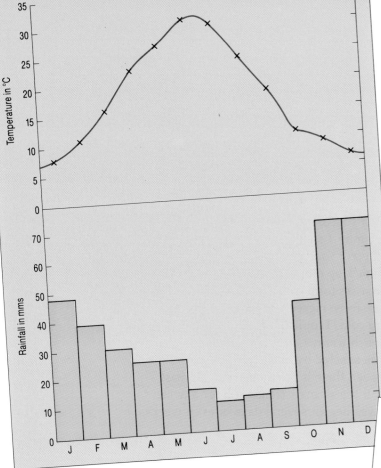

Figure 8   Climate graph for Athens, Greece

	J	F	M	A	M	J	J	A	S	O	N	D
Temp °C	8	11	16	23	27	31	30	24	17	11	9	7
Rainfall in mms	48	39	30	25	25	15	10	12	13	43	70	70

Figure 9a   Climate graph for London, UK

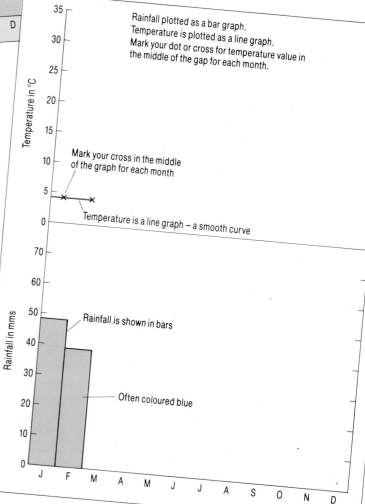

3 *a* Look at Figure 6. What type of climate does Athens have?

b Study Figure 8. It is a **climate graph** of Athens. Copy the sentences below choosing the correct word for the gaps to describe Athens climate.

In summer the climate in Athens is (hot/cold) and (dry/wet). In winter, the climate is (mild/cold) and (dry/wet).

4 Use the information in Figure 9 to draw a climate graph for London. The first two months have been done for you. Colour the rainfall bars in blue and use red for the temperature line.

5 Project idea.

Collect weather charts and reports – make sure you know the date of each one. Start a scrapbook or display them in your classroom. Notice how the weather changes from place to place and from time to time.

	J	F	M	A	M	J	J	A	S	O	N	D
Temperature in °C	4	4	7	9	13	16	17	17	15	12	7	5
Rainfall in mms	48	39	39	40	50	48	58	65	52	57	63	54

Figure 9b   Climate figures for London, UK

3.2   Air masses

Around the Earth, there is a blanket of air called the **atmosphere**. In the lower atmosphere there are large bodies of air which are called **air masses**. These air masses form over large areas of land or sea. The place where an air mass forms is called its **source region**. In its source region, the air mass stands still for a long time and picks up the temperature and moisture characteristics of that area.

Air masses are moved from their source region by **wind**. Europe is affected by *four* main air masses. Figure 1 shows their source regions.

Each air mass comes from a different source region. **Maritime** air masses form over oceans so they pick up moisture and often bring rain to Europe. **Continental** air masses form over land so they are drier because there is less moisture to be picked up. **Polar** air masses come from the north and they are cold. **Tropical** air masses come from the south and so they are much warmer.

At any one time, Europe will be affected by more than one air mass. In the UK, because it is smaller, there is often only one air mass which covers the whole country. If the air mass stands still for a while then the UK will have the same weather for several days or even weeks.

Figure 1

	Air Mass			
	Polar continental	Tropical continental	Tropical maritime	Polar maritime
Source region	Siberia (land)	North Africa (land)	The Azores (sea)	Arctic Ocean (sea)
Summer weather	warm, dry	hot, dry	warm/hot, wet	mild, wet
Winter weather	very cold, snow possible	mild, dry	mild, wet	cold, wet (sleet or snow)

Activities

1 a What is an air mass?
  b What is the source region of an air mass?
  c On a map of the world, mark and label the four source regions for each air mass.
    Plot the course taken by each of the air masses towards Europe. Draw arrows to show the movement starting each arrow in its **source region**. Label each arrow with the *name* of the air mass.
  d Which air mass will bring heavy snow in winter, and very cold weather to the UK?
  e Which air mass will bring the UK the 'heatwaves' in summer?

2 Figure 2 shows the weather at four different weather stations in Europe.
  a Copy each weather station report A–D.
  b Using the symbol key, describe the weather at each station.
  c Which air mass do you think brought the weather to each station?

Figure 2   Readings for weather stations in Europe in summer

Key

wind (knots)
◎ calm
1–2
3–7
8–12
13–17
for each additional half feather add 5 knots

48–52
NB The 'tail' always points in the direction from where the wind has come, eg the north-west in the examples above.

weather
= mist
≡ fog
, drizzle
• rain
✳ rain and snow
▽ rain shower
✳ snow shower
▽▲ hail
R thunderstorm

cloud (in oktas)
○ 0
◍ 1
◕ 2
◔ 3
◐ 4
◑ 5
● 6 →
● 8
⊗ sky obscured

○ → 7

3 Complete the table below using the information provided by the weather map in Figure 3:

Weather map: Date _____

	Scandinavia	Germany, Belgium and the Netherlands
Temperatures		
Wind direction		
Cloud cover		
Air mass		

4 The table in Figure 4 shows how often (the frequency) the four different air masses affect the UK. This information can be shown on a **rose diagram**. Copy and complete the rose diagram which has been started for you in Figure 5.

a Which air mass affects the UK for the most part of the year?

b From which direction does this air mass come?

c Use your answers to *a* and *b* to suggest the most common weather in winter and summer in the UK.

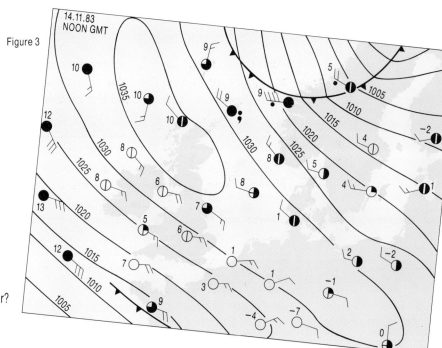

Figure 3

Air Mass	Frequency (%)
Polar maritime	
Polar continental	35
Tropical maritime	8
Tropical continental	10
	5

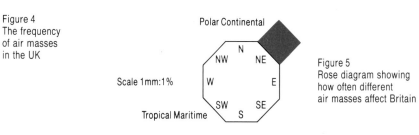

Figure 4
The frequency of air masses in the UK

Polar Continental

Scale 1mm:1%

Tropical Maritime

Figure 5
Rose diagram showing how often different air masses affect Britain

3.3   Depressions and anticyclones

Air pressure

Although you cannot feel it, the air pushes down on the Earth's surface. This is called **air pressure**.

Pressure is measured by an instrument called a **barometer**, in units called millibars. On a weather map, the pressure is shown by black lines called **isobars**. An isobar joins together places with the same pressure. They are like contour lines which join together places with the same height above sea level. Isobars are usually drawn at four millibar intervals. Figure 1 is a simple weather map showing isobars.

Figure 1

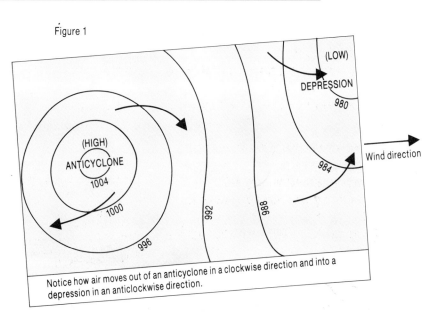

Notice how air moves out of an anticyclone in a clockwise direction and into a depression in an anticlockwise direction.

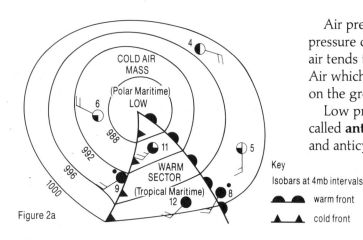

Figure 2a

Key

Isobars at 4mb intervals

warm front

cold front

Air pressure varies from place to place and from time to time. The pressure changes because the temperature of the air changes. Warm air tends to rise and this forms relatively **low** pressure on the ground. Air which is cold is heavier and sinks giving relatively **high** pressure on the ground.

Low pressure areas are called **depressions**. High pressure areas are called **anticyclones**. In the UK and the rest of Europe, depressions and anticyclones have a large effect on our weather.

Depressions

A depression is an area of low pressure. It often brings wet and cloudy weather to the UK and the rest of Europe. Depressions are formed over the Atlantic Ocean and are carried across Europe by the westerly winds.

Figure 2a shows what a depression looks like on a weather map. Notice that there are two **fronts**. You can see these on the satellite photo in Figure 3. A front is formed where two air masses meet. At the fronts, there is a lot of **turbulence** in the air. The warm air is forced to rise above the colder, heavier air. As the warm air rises, it cools and the water vapour in the air condenses. The water droplets form clouds and rain. So this explains why fronts tend to be associated with belts of cloud and rain. Between the two fronts there is a **warm sector** where there is less likely to be rain — the typical weather is 'sunshine and showers'.

As a depression with its fronts moves across Europe, a sequence of weather usually takes place. This sequence is shown on Figure 2b which is a cross-section through a depression.

A weather forecast looks forward and tells us what the weather will be like. The sequence of weather associated with a depression and its fronts is usually the same. So, if you are standing in one place for a period of time, you will see that sequence of weather go through.

Figure 2b   Cross section through a depression

Figure 3   Satellite view of a depression

Activities

1 Using Figure 2 and the text, copy and complete the sentences below:

A depression is an area of (high/low) pressure. The lowest pressure on the diagram is .... millibars. The winds are blowing in a (anticlockwise/clockwise) direction (towards/away from) the centre of the depression. The depression has two fronts, a .... front and a .... front.

2 Make a large copy of Figure 2b, the cross-section through the depression.

   a Add the following labels in the correct place:

       warm sector   cold air mass   tall rain clouds
       heavy rain for a short time (2–3 hours)
       light rain for a long time (4–6 hours)   high wispy clouds.

   b On Figure 2b, A is ahead of the warm front, B is in the warm sector and C is behind the cold front. Match the three places to the correct weather report.

Report 1 – the sky is dark and heavy rain is falling. The temperature has fallen a few degrees in the last hour.
Report 2 – The sky is covered in cloud and it has been raining steadily for the last few hours.
Report 3 – The temperature is warm and the sky is clear. The weather is dry.

3 Study the satellite photograph of the depression in Figure 3.
   a What are the white patches on the photograph?
   b Match the photograph with the weather map in Figure 2a. Where are the white patches thickest? Why?
   c Choose the correct statement from the list below to describe the location of X and Y.
     ● Ahead of the warm front.
     ● In the warm sector.
     ● Behind the cold front.

4 Look at Figure 3. Write an account of how the weather changes as you move along the line from Y to X.

Anticyclones

An anticyclone is an area of high pressure. It represents an area of sinking air and is usually associated with stable, dry weather (see Figure 4). In the summer a typical anticyclone brings hot, sunny weather. In winter, the weather will be cold and crisp. However, if the air is particularly moist in winter, cloud and fog give rise to gloomy conditions.

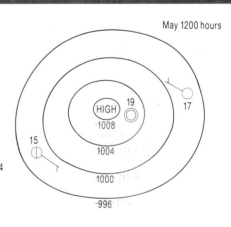

May 1200 hours

Figure 4

Activities

5 Look at Figure 4 which shows an anticyclone as it is drawn on a weather map. Copy the table on the right and complete it using the text to help you.

Typical weather in the UK associated with depressions and anticyclones

	Depression	Anticyclone
Pressure at the centre	Low	
Fronts	A cold front and a warm front	
Wind direction	Anticlockwise towards the centre	
Weather in summer	Cloud and rain	
Weather in winter	Cloud and rain	

3.4   Climatic hazards in Europe

Sometimes severe weather causes problems to the people living in the area. Avalanches, droughts, strong winds and floods are all **climatic hazards**. Figure 1 shows some newspaper reports of some recent climatic hazards in the UK.

Severe weather can cause loss of life, damage to property, and great anxiety and fear. If it is possible to predict the hazard then the people can try to protect themselves and their property.

In the south of France, the **Mistral wind** blows down the Rhône valley from the Alps. The wind is very cold and damages the young buds and blossom on the fruit trees. Farmers in the area protect their crops by building cypress hedges and fences which act as a windbreak. Figure 2 shows a typical farm landscape in the Rhône valley in France.

Figure 3 shows the range of climatic hazards in Italy. Avalanches are a particular problem. An avalanche is a mass of snow or ice that moves very rapidly down a mountainside. Many thousands of avalanches occur every year. Only a few cause any real damage or loss of life.

An avalanche is very sudden and can be very powerful. The snow and ice may move at speeds up to 300 kph, flattening trees, damaging property and killing people in its path.

COOL IT! Rain is on its way

by FIONA BARTON

But yesterday the sun shone relentlessly in southern England. Hosepipe bans are in force in Sussex, Kent, Oxfordshire, Buckinghamshire, Gloucestershire, Worcestershire, Devon, Cornwall, Herefordshire, Dorset, Somerset and Wales.

Ice cream giants Birds Eye Walls, of Gloucester, predict they will smash the record 71 million ice creams and lollies sold in one week in 1976. They have hired 200 temporary staff to cope.

Marion Nairn, who runs a hedgehog rescue service near Bristol, is urging people to leave out water because the animals are dying of dehydration.

The cost of potatoes could rise to 30p a lb as the lack of rain reduces the size of the crop.

Mail on Sunday 25.6.8

Figure 1

Floods as Britain battered by wind and heavy rain

by MICHAEL SHANAHAN and OONAGH BLACKMAN

SNOW closed roads, galeforce winds lashed coasts and torrential rain brought flooding to Britain yesterday.

The heaviest snow fell in Scotland, North Yorkshire and Cumbria and many trans-Pennine routes were impassable.

In the South, Cornwall was hardest hit with floods closing promenades at Penzance and Porthleven.

Waves up to 100 feet high smashed over the front at Mousehole, and flooding was also reported at Flushing and Falmouth.

Winds were reported gusting up to 90 mph in places, and coastguards were on alert for ships in trouble.

At Plymouth, Devon. the old Barbican area saw some of the worst flooding in years with shops and cars under nine inches of water.

And when winds prevented the city's Torpoint ferry from berthing at Devonport, workmen used a tractor to drive out and rescue a family who had an urgent connection to make.

Sunday Express 17.12.89

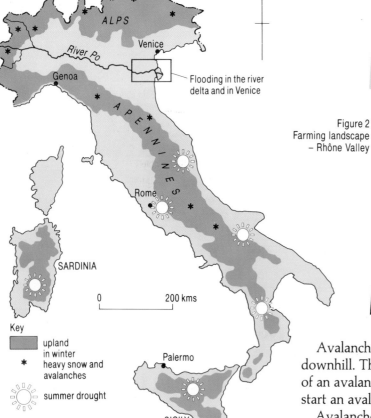

Figure 3
Climatic hazards in Italy

Key
- upland
- in winter
- * heavy snow and avalanches
- summer drought

Figure 2
Farming landscape
– Rhône Valley

Avalanches occur when a patch of snow breaks away and slides downhill. The photograph in Figure 4 shows an avalanche. The start of an avalanche may be triggered by a loud noise. Even a skier can start an avalanche.

Avalanches are most common in areas of heavy snowfall, where the snow has built up to a great depth. The weight of snow and the force of **gravity** cause the snow to slip.

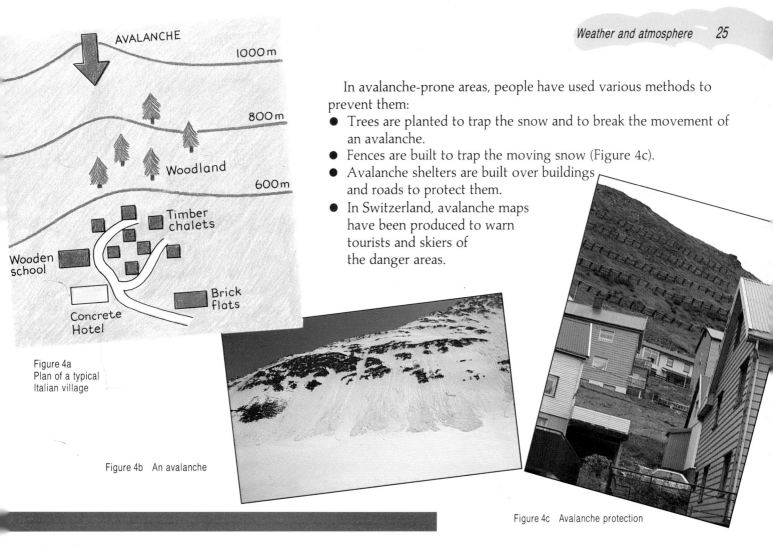

AVALANCHE
1000 m

800 m

Woodland

600 m

Timber
chalets

Wooden
school

Concrete
Hotel

Brick
flats

Figure 4a
Plan of a typical
Italian village

Figure 4b   An avalanche

In avalanche-prone areas, people have used various methods to prevent them:

- Trees are planted to trap the snow and to break the movement of an avalanche.
- Fences are built to trap the moving snow (Figure 4c).
- Avalanche shelters are built over buildings and roads to protect them.
- In Switzerland, avalanche maps have been produced to warn tourists and skiers of the danger areas.

Figure 4c   Avalanche protection

Activities

1 Read the newspaper reports in Figure 1. Write a short account with the title 'How the weather can affect us'. Illustrate your account with drawings and refer to any recent events.

2 Sketch the photograph in Figure 2.
   a Add the following labels:

   small fields   cypress hedges   windbreak trees   crops.

   b Explain why the farmers have small fields and rows of windbreak trees.

3 Figure 3 shows some of the climatic hazards of Italy.
   a Make a list of the hazards that Italy suffers and for each one give an example of a place or region which is affected.
   b Choose any two of the hazard areas in Italy and explain why the area is so prone to the hazard.
   c Figure 4a shows a plan of a typical village in the Italian Alps. Describe the likely effects of the avalanche as it moves down the hillside into the village.
   d Make a copy of the diagram and add two features which the villagers could build to stop an avalanche taking place.
   e Work in pairs to list other effects that snow can have on human activities.

4 In pairs or small groups take three of the following roles and prepare short statements to present to the rest of the class explaining why you like or dislike the hot, sunny, drought conditions in Southern Italy.
   Roles:
   - An ice-cream manufacturer
   - A local farmer growing tomatoes
   - A hotel owner
   - The chief fire officer

3.5   Acid rain in Europe

Rainwater is a 'cocktail of chemicals'. Rainwater reacts with gases in the atmosphere such as carbon dioxide and sulphur dioxide. These gases change into weak acids creating **acid rain**.

Acid rain is a great worry to many people around the world. The main cause of acid rain is **sulphur dioxide**.

The acid rain problem began with the growth of industry and the burning of fuels. Some countries like the UK are large producers of gases and they are called net **exporters** of acid rain. The acid rain is carried long distances by winds so that other countries are net **importers** of acid rain. This means that they receive more acid rain than they produce. These countries are concerned that countries like the UK have done little to reduce the pollution. Figure 1 shows the export and import of acid rain in Europe.

The main effects of acid rain are shown in Figure 2. Notice how it affects plants, water and even buildings.

To deal with the acid rain problem some international agreements have been reached. These limit the amount of sulphur dioxide a country can emit. Power stations can add equipment to remove the sulphur dioxide but this is expensive and could lead to higher electricity prices. Effects of the acid rain can be reduced. Lime can be added to lakes, rivers and soil to reduce the acidity. Special breeds of fish and plants can be bred to cope with the acidity. Buildings can be covered with protective sprays to stop the damage.

Key

■ export of sulphur

■ import of sulphur

Scale
1 cm represents
400 000 tonnes
of sulphur per
year

Figure 1

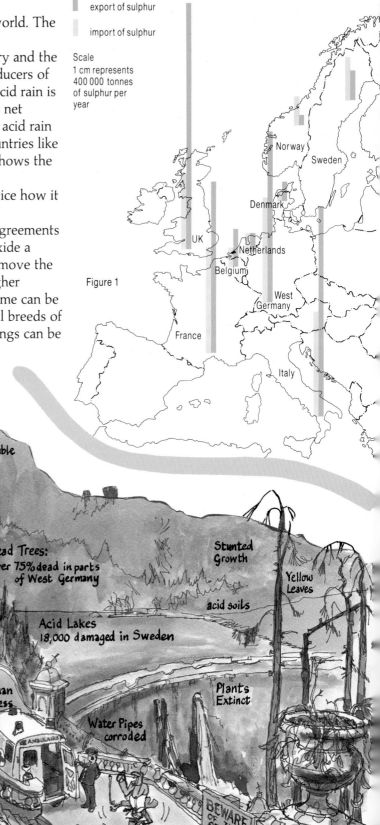

Figure 2
Rain – is it
only water?

Bird Life killed: e.g. dippers

Sandstone and Limestone crumble

Decaying statues

Dead Trees:
– over 75% dead in parts of West Germany

Stunted Growth

acid soils

Yellow Leaves

Acid Lakes
18,000 damaged in Sweden

Plants Extinct

Crumbling Buildings:
e.g. Taj Mahal, York Minster

Toxic Metals in Water Supplies:
e.g. aluminium

Human Illness

Water Pipes corroded

Dead Fish
(pH 4.5 kills trout, salmon)

BEWARE OF THE STEP

Activities

1 Why is the phrase 'cocktail of chemicals' a good way of describing our rainfall?

2 How much do you and your family contribute to the acid rain problem? Copy the list below and mark with a tick the items you have in your home or garden or garage:

- Car
- Television
- Incinerator
- Coal fire
- Electric lamps

a Choose one of the items that you ticked and explain how using it contributes to the acid rain problem.

b Your family has decided to reduce its contribution to the acid rain problem. Write down any alternatives you can think of to stop or reduce the use of the items you ticked in the list e.g. walking to school instead of using the car.

c Ask your parents if they would be prepared to pay more for electricity in order to reduce acid rain. Record the results of your interview.

3 Study Figure 1:

a Which countries are net importers of sulphur?

b Which countries are net exporters of sulphur?

c Why do you think the UK is sometimes called the 'dirty man of Europe'?

d In a small group discuss the following questions:

- Why does the UK export so much sulphur?
- Why does the UK import so little sulphur?
- Who should pay the costs of reducing sulphur pollution?
- Who should pay the costs of reducing the effect of the acid rain?
- Should we be concerned about acid rain?

Put your points forward in a class discussion on acid rain.

4 Using Figure 3 plot the **pH values** for Manchester on a line graph.

a Draw bars on your graph to show the **rainfall figures** for the same weeks. On your line graph draw a line at 5.6 to represent 'normal' rainfall. What does the graph tell you about Manchester's rainfall in January and February?

b In the week ending the 13th January 1987 there was heavy snowfall which came from the east. The winds were quite strong. How has this affected the acid rain reading in the following weeks? Can you explain this?

c What other reasons might there be for a change in the pH value from week to week?

5 a Look at the cartoon in Figure 4. What message is the cartoon putting across?

b Draw your own cartoon illustrating any of the effects of acid rain you choose.

Figure 3

pH and Rainfall Values for Manchester 1987		
Date (week ending)	pH Value	Rainfall in mms
6.1.87	4.18	62.9
13.1.87	4.85	– (no rain)
20.1.87	3.50	3.2
27.1.87	3.36	1.0
3.2.87	4.26	5.5
10.2.87	4.4	15.0
17.2.87	5.27	4.6

Figure 4

Dictionary

air mass   a large body of air

anticyclones   areas of high pressure

avalanche   a rapidly moving mass of snow and ice

depressions   areas of low pressure

front   the meeting place of two air masses

isobar   a line joining together places of equal pressure

latitude   the distance north or south of the Equator

wind   the movement of air

4 Landscape and Processes

4.1 The physical geography of Europe

Europe has a great variety of different landscapes ranging from dramatic mountains to flat plains. Some of these contrasts are shown in the map and photographs in Figure 1.

The contrasting scenery affects human activities. Agriculture, tourism and other economic activities all vary according to the physical geography of an area.

Figure 1

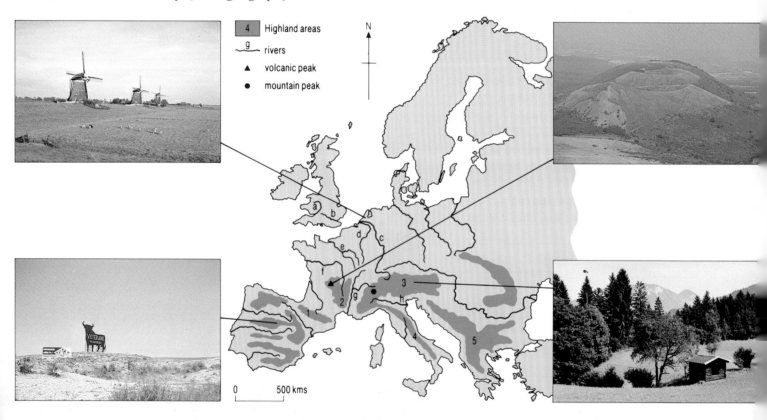

Activities

1 Find a map of the physical geography of Europe in your atlas. Make a copy of the map in Figure 1. Add labels to name the following features:
- the major mountainous areas labelled 1 to 5 on the map in Figure 1
- the rivers marked a to h
- the mountain peak and the volcanic peak marked.

2 Using your completed map and the photographs in Figure 1, choose two contrasting landscapes. For *each*:
- describe its location in Europe.
- describe the typical landscape.
- describe the human activity in the area. Suggest reasons for your answer.

4.2   Weathering and limestone scenery

Weathering is the slow breakdown of rocks into smaller particles. These can then be picked up by wind, water or ice and moved. This is known as **erosion** and is studied in the next units.

Weathering can be of three different types, but the end result is still the same. Look at the information in Figure 1.

In the highland areas of the EC (look at the map of the physical areas in the EC in section 4.1) **physical weathering** is common. **Biological weathering** is widespread over a variety of areas. **Chemical weathering** is common where there are limestone rocks because this rock type tends to dissolve (Figure 1b). This results in a characteristic type of scenery called **Karst scenery** named after an area in Yugoslavia which is famous for limestone features.

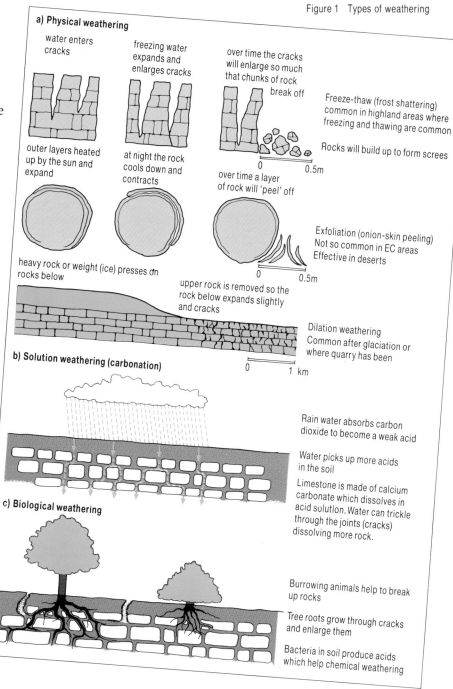

Figure 1   Types of weathering

a) Physical weathering

water enters cracks

freezing water expands and enlarges cracks

over time the cracks will enlarge so much that chunks of rock break off

Freeze-thaw (frost shattering) common in highland areas where freezing and thawing are common

Rocks will build up to form screes

outer layers heated up by the sun and expand

at night the rock cools down and contracts

over time a layer of rock will 'peel' off

Exfoliation (onion-skin peeling) Not so common in EC areas Effective in deserts

heavy rock or weight (ice) presses on rocks below

upper rock is removed so the rock below expands slightly and cracks

Dilation weathering Common after glaciation or where quarry has been

b) Solution weathering (carbonation)

Rain water absorbs carbon dioxide to become a weak acid

Water picks up more acids in the soil

Limestone is made of calcium carbonate which dissolves in acid solution. Water can trickle through the joints (cracks) dissolving more rock.

c) Biological weathering

Burrowing animals help to break up rocks

Tree roots grow through cracks and enlarge them

Bacteria in soil produce acids which help chemical weathering

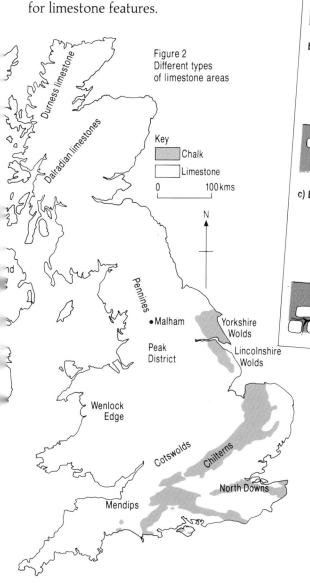

Figure 2 Different types of limestone areas

Key
Chalk
Limestone
0   100kms
N

Durness limestone
Dalradian limestones
Pennines
Malham
Yorkshire Wolds
Peak District
Lincolnshire Wolds
Wenlock Edge
Cotswolds
Chilterns
North Downs
Mendips

Karst landscapes

As you can see from Figure 2 there are large areas of limestone in the UK. One important area is the Malham area of the Yorkshire Dales National Park. Grass covering is sparse so sheep grazing is often the only method of farming possible. Limestone is a **permeable** rock which means it lets water pass through it. Therefore, rivers do not exist where limestone is at the surface. It is different from an **impermeable** rock such as shale which doesn't let water pass through.

Some features typical of limestone scenery

- **Limestone pavement**: this is a flat area of exposed limestone with huge cracks called **grykes**. The blocks in between are called **clints**. Look at the diagram and photograph in Figure 3 to see how these features were formed.

- **Swallow holes**: again these are formed from solution weathering (see Figure 1). Notice that a covering of soil helps to increase the acidity of the rain water. As this seeps through the joints in the limestone, they are slowly enlarged. Eventually a huge depression is formed. Sometimes rivers which have developed outside a limestone area and flow onto the limestone disappear down a swallow hole. Look at Figure 4 and the photograph of Gaping Gill in Figure 5. Caving and potholing are common activities associated with swallow holes provided they are large enough!

Exposed limestone has joints in it. Water can seep into them and solution weathering occurs.

Joints become enlarged.

clint

gryke

Figure 3
Formation of a limestone pavement

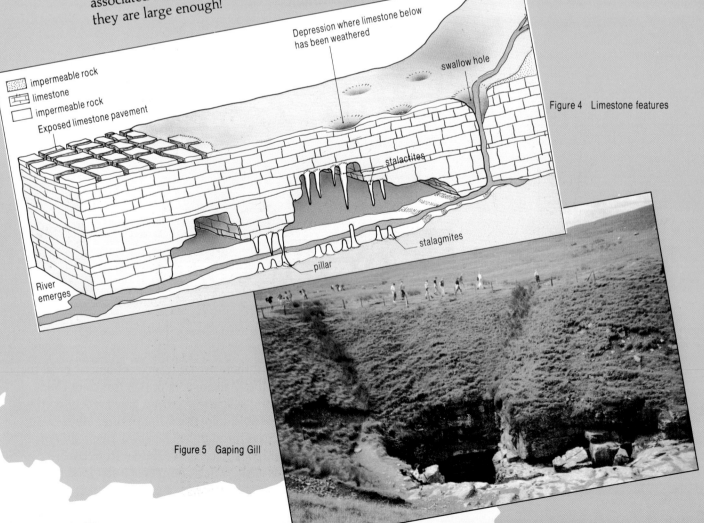

Depression where limestone below has been weathered

swallow hole

Figure 4   Limestone features

impermeable rock
limestone
impermeable rock

Exposed limestone pavement

stalactites

stalagmites

pillar

River emerges

Figure 5   Gaping Gill

● **Cave systems**: when water disappears underground it can help to form more features. This water has calcium carbonate dissolved in it. (This is what makes **hard water** and can 'fuzz' up the inside of a kettle if you live in an area receiving water from chalk or limestone.) As this water slowly trickles through the joints and over the rocks, some of it evaporates. This leaves behind a deposit of calcium carbonate which can build up over the years to form **stalagmites** and **stalactites**. Look again at Figure 4 and the photographs in Figure 6. The underground river may eventually re-emerge at the surface.

Some of the cave systems are so large that they must have been forming for hundreds of years. Eventually a cave roof may collapse forming a very steep sided valley called a **gorge**. Look at the photograph of Goredale Scar. In wet weather when there is a lot of water around, there are waterfalls in this gorge.

Figure 6b   Goredale Scar

Figure 6a   Stalagmites and stalactites

Human activity in limestone areas

Limestone areas such as the Yorkshire Dales are widely used in various ways. Despite the pressures, attempts are being made to keep the area free from too much change. Grants from the Ministry of Agriculture are available to help restore old barns and stone walls. Some paths are being toughened with matting and gravel where necessary to combat footpath erosion.

Activities

Look at the OS map extract Figure 7 and the satellite image of the area in Figure 8.

1 a i Name the feature found at T6 on the satellite image.
     ii Use the OS map to give a four figure grid reference of the feature.
   b What happens to the river on the satellite image in U5?
     Give a reason for your answer.
   c Give the satellite reference for Malham cove.
   d Give two other examples with grid references from the OS map of features which indicate that this is a limestone area.

Figure 7   Malham, UK, 1:50 000

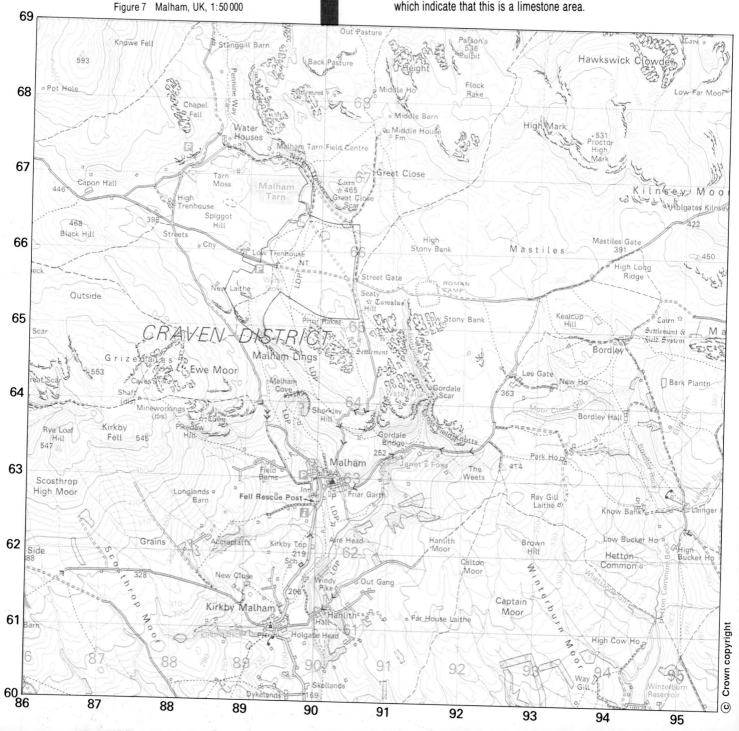

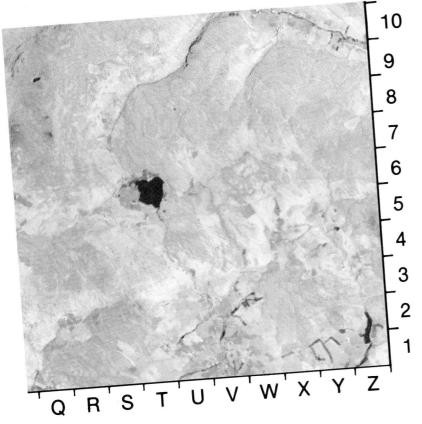

Figure 8   Satellite view of Malham
(Landsat 5 TM bands 453)

2 a What activity is found at Z8 on the satellite image?
  b Using the satellite evidence, what other activity is
     carried out in the area? Give a reason for your answer.
     Why is the map not as good as the satellite image in
     helping you answer this question?

3 Draw diagrams to explain how a swallow hole is formed.

4 Draw a sketch of Goredale Scar from the photograph in
   Figure 6. Label it carefully to show the steep sides.
   Suggest how it may have been formed.

5 Using the information in this section, suggest reasons why
   the Yorkshire Dales National Park is an important area for
   tourists.

Key for the satellite image
Orange – hay meadows
Yellow – pasture
Green-blue – rough grazing
Bright turquoise – limestone pavements
Black – water
White – quarries

4.3   Glaciated landscapes

In the past, Europe has experienced different
climates. In the last Ice Age (2 million–10 000
years ago), large parts of the continent were
covered by ice as you can see in Figure 1. Ice
forms after snow builds up several layers in
highland areas. Eventually the lower layers
are compressed so much that they form solid
ice. If there is enough ice it will cover whole
landscapes as huge **ice sheets**. Often, the ice
will only fill a valley and it is known as a
glacier.

Figure 1

MORAINES
zones of glacial debris
often in the form of
hillocks

boulder clay
strewn

melt waters sand and gravels

LÖESS a mantle of
fine-grained soil due
partly to wind
action

centres of ice accumulation
main directions of ice flows
terminal moraine
maximum limit of ice

0   500 kms

Erosion by ice

Ice is an extremely powerful agent of erosion. Look at the photograph in Figure 2 and the diagram in Figure 3. As ice moves slowly from highland to lowland areas it shapes the landscape as it moves. Notice that the **snout** (the front) of the glacier changes its position in summer and winter depending on how much melting is taking place. The ice will only remain whilst it is cold enough. There are still areas where glaciers remain in the Alps today and glacial processes are still taking place here. In these areas the bare rock surfaces are severely affected by frost weathering.

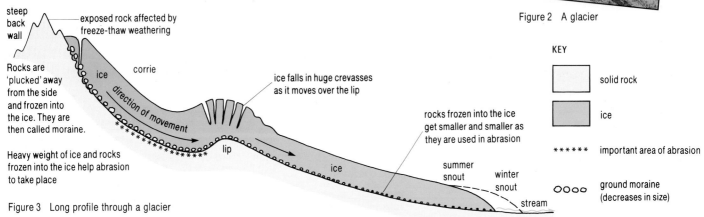

Figure 2   A glacier

Figure 3   Long profile through a glacier

steep back wall

exposed rock affected by freeze-thaw weathering

Rocks are 'plucked' away from the side and frozen into the ice. They are then called moraine.

Heavy weight of ice and rocks frozen into the ice help abrasion to take place

ice

corrie

direction of movement

ice falls in huge crevasses as it moves over the lip

lip

rocks frozen into the ice get smaller and smaller as they are used in abrasion

ice

summer snout

winter snout

stream

KEY

solid rock

ice

✱✱✱✱✱✱ important area of abrasion

OOoo ground moraine (decreases in size)

Ice carries out erosion in two main ways:
● **plucking** where chunks of rock are frozen into the ice as it moves past. They are 'plucked' away from the valley side.
● **abrasion** where the rocks frozen into the ice help to grind away the valley floor and sides. They produce large grooves or scratches on the rocks called **striations**.

Where the ice forms in the highland areas several features are produced. The ice builds up in hollows and these are gradually enlarged as the ice moves away. A steep sided, armchair-shaped hollow is produced called a **corrie**, **cwm** or **cirque** (see Figure 4). Where two corries develop side by side, a ridge known as an **arête** is formed. These can be very jagged if frost weathering attacks them further. Where several corries form back to back, a steep **pyramidal peak** is formed. In the UK there are examples of these features in the Snowdon area. After the ice disappears a lake or **tarn** may be formed in the corrie. Screes also form where frost weathering is common.

If the ice moves out from the corrie, it can carve out and enlarge valleys. Normal **V-shaped** river valleys become steep sided, flat floored **U-shaped** valleys (Figure 5). Where the ice has eroded an area of softer rock a depression may form. Once the ice disappears, this depression may become filled with water to form a **ribbon lake**.

Hanging valleys are produced where a small tributary glacier leads into the main glacier, but is not so big and erosive. Therefore, when the ice melts, a smaller valley is left hanging above the main valley. If a river forms in the valley after the ice has disappeared, it will form a waterfall into the main valley.

arête

steep back wall

tarn

Figure 4
A corrie

Figure 5

Deposition by ice

When the ice begins to melt as the climate gets warmer it starts to deposit the material it is carrying. This material is called **moraine**. It consists of a mixture of rocks, boulders and finer ground-up rock — clay and sand. Some of the material is dropped by the ice and some is carried further by the meltwater. Look at Figure 6.

The ice deposited material is called **boulder clay** and it is smeared and moulded over the landscape. It may be formed into hills called **drumlins**. Boulder clay makes good farming land.

Large amounts of meltwater are also produced and they pick up finer materials and transport them great distances. These **outwash deposits** cover large flat areas and eventually may be used for farmland, but they are not as fertile as boulder clay areas.

However, some of the finest particles are blown great distances by the wind where they build up to form **loess** deposits. These make very fertile soils and are some of the best farming areas in Europe. Look again at Figure 1.

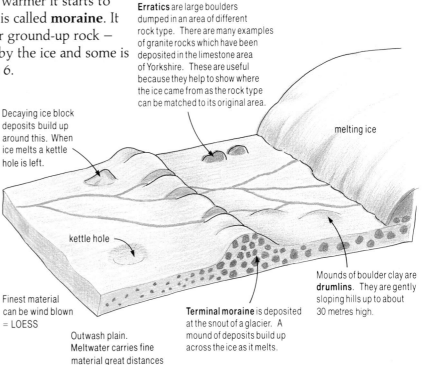

Erratics are large boulders dumped in an area of different rock type. There are many examples of granite rocks which have been deposited in the limestone area of Yorkshire. These are useful because they help to show where the ice came from as the rock type can be matched to its original area.

melting ice

Decaying ice block deposits build up around this. When ice melts a kettle hole is left.

kettle hole

Finest material can be wind blown = LOESS

Outwash plain. Meltwater carries fine material great distances

Terminal moraine is deposited at the snout of a glacier. A mound of deposits build up across the ice as it melts.

Mounds of boulder clay are **drumlins**. They are gently sloping hills up to about 30 metres high.

Figure 6   Features of deposition

Activities

1 a Look back to Figure 1. On an outline map of Europe use a colour to shade in the areas once covered by ice. Use a different colour to shade in the areas covered with meltwater sands and gravels and wind blown loess.

  b On the map, name the countries which you have partly or completely shaded in. These have experienced some degree of glacial activity.

  c On the map name the highland areas which were centres of ice flow.

  d Suggest a reason why the ice flowed from these areas.

Questions 2–3 refer to the map extract in Figure 7.

2 a Give the six figure grid reference of the highest point on the map. This is the summit of Snowdon.

  b In this area, draw or describe two ways in which steep slopes are shown on the map.

  c Snowdon is an example of a pyramidal peak. Give the name of: one of the corries with a lake in it surrounding the peak. (NB in Welsh – 'llyn' = 'lake' and 'cwm' = corrie.) another corrie without a lake. an arête (ridge between two corries). As these are high ridges they are used for district boundaries which are marked as —•— —•— on the map.

  d Look closely at the contour pattern of a corrie. Why is a corrie described as an armchair shaped hollow?

  e Look at square 6053. What map symbol indicates that the slopes have scree?

  f What type of station is found at the summit of Snowdon?

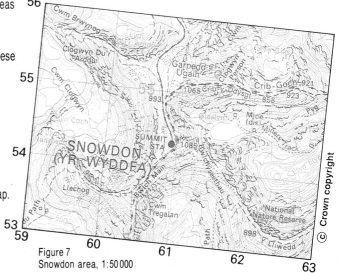

Figure 7
Snowdon area, 1:50 000

© Crown copyright

3 From map evidence only, suggest human uses made of the area (past and present).

4 Draw a sketch of the photograph of the U-shaped valley in Figure 5. Put the following labels in the appropriate places on the sketch.
   ● U-shaped valley
   ● truncated spurs (steep sides)
   ● scree (blocks of rock formed by physical weathering after the ice disappeared)
   ● settlement on flat ground
   ● bare rock
   ● waterfall
   Suggest a use for the huts/chalets in the foreground of the photograph.

5 Look at the map of Denmark in Section 10.5 (Figure 4).
   a Which direction did the ice come from? Why?
   b What type of farming is carried out on:
      ● boulder clay soils   ● outwash soils?

6 a Look at the diagram in Figure 6. What is the difference between the shapes and sizes of particles in the boulder clay and the outwash deposits?
   b which of these is deposited by the ice and which by meltwater?

4.4   River processes and landforms

Rivers flow from highland to lowland areas. The **source** or start of the river is usually a small stream flowing high up on a hillside. The river flows along a narrow **V-shaped valley**. Notice the features of a river in a highland area shown in Figure 1. The river is narrow, clear and fast flowing over a rocky bed. The water is turbulent and there are **rapids** and **waterfalls**.

By the time the river has reached its **mouth** at the sea or in a lake, the water is flowing in a deeper and wider **channel**. Often the river has large bends called **meanders** and it is cloudy because of the sand and silt being carried. The river also flows on a gently sloping but wide valley floor known as the **floodplain**. This is the area which could flood if the river overflows its banks. Sometimes the river changes its course over the floodplain and leaves **ox-bow lakes**. Look at Figure 1 and notice the old course of the river.

As a river flows downstream, it becomes wider and deeper as the volume of water it carries increases. The main reason for these changes is the number of **tributaries** (smaller rivers) which join the main river. The river and its tributaries drain an area called the **drainage basin** or **catchment area**.

Figure 1

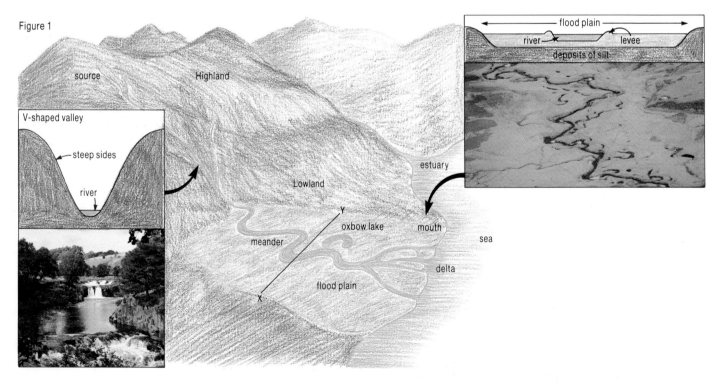

River processes

Flowing water is able to do a lot of work. It can **erode** (wear away) the bed and banks of the river. Sometimes river banks have to be strengthened to reduce erosion. Types of erosion include:

1 The force of the water hitting the bed and banks. This is called **hydraulic action**.

2 Pebbles being carried by the water can grind away the bed and banks. This is called **abrasion** or **corrasion**.
Sometimes pebbles swirl around in small holes making them larger. These are called **potholes**. Look at the photograph in Figure 2.

3 Sometimes the river flows over rocks which contain soluble minerals, the water can help to dissolve minerals such as limestone or salt. This process is known as **solution**.

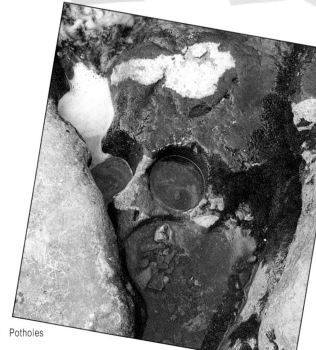

Figure 2   Potholes

Figure 3
River boulders

Once eroded, the rocks in the river gradually get worn down by rubbing against each other. This is called **attrition** and it causes particles to become rounded and smaller in size.

A river also **transports** material. The flow of the river picks up smaller particles or rolls larger material along its bed. The material carried by a river is called the **load** and it is composed of pebbles, sand and silt sized particles. If the river is flowing very quickly or has a lot of water in it after a storm, very large rocks and boulders can be carried. Look at the photograph in Figure 3. The river is only shallow yet in storm conditions it was able to transport the huge boulders seen in the photograph.

Eventually, when the river is nearing its mouth, much of the load will be **deposited**. The river creates its floodplain by depositing silt in times of flood. It may also build up **levées** which are high banks of silt at the side of the river.

At the river mouth, a **delta** may develop (see Figure 4). Here the sea is unable to remove the deposits as quickly as they are laid down. This happens where the seas do not have large waves and strong currents. In Europe there are many rivers with deltas leading into the Mediterranean Sea, for example the river Rhône in France and the river Po in Italy. A delta is a large expanse of flat land extending out into the sea. It is divided up by channels called **distributaries** and there are marshes, lagoons and sand spits.

The UK is surrounded by seas which are more powerful so deltas do not develop. Rivers enter the seas via **estuaries** which are enlarged river mouths. An estuary is **tidal** and the water level rises and falls with the tides. At low tide when the water level in the river is low, mud banks are uncovered. The Thames and Severn both have important estuaries which are useful harbours for shipping. Parts of these have to be **dredged** (deepened by removing material from the river bed). This maintains a deep water channel for ships.

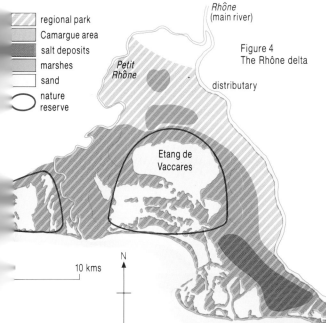

regional park
Camargue area
salt deposits
marshes
sand
nature reserve

Rhône
(main river)

Figure 4
The Rhône delta

Petit
Rhône

distributary

Etang de
Vaccares

10 kms

N

Activities

1 *a* Sketch the photograph in Figure 1 showing the features of a river and valley in a highland area. Add the following labels where appropriate:

   steep   narrow V-shaped valley   clear water
   fast flowing river   rocky bed   rapids; waterfall.

   b Suggest reasons why the river is small and flowing in a V-shaped valley.

2 In pairs, compare the photograph and diagram in Figure 5 which show the features of the waterfall at High Force in Teesdale and discuss the following questions:

   a Which rock forms the **cap rock** and is the most resistant (hardest)?

   b Why do you think the valley above the waterfall is shallow?

   c Use the information on river processes to explain how a **plunge pool** will be formed.

   d Which rock types will make up the boulders found in and around the plunge pool? Suggest where these might be from.

3 The diagrams in Figure 6 show the formation of an ox-bow lake. Copy the diagrams and label them using the sentences provided.

4 Look at Figure 4.

   a Describe the **natural** features of a delta. Include a simple labelled diagram in your answer.

   b What uses can be made of deltas?

   c Describe one of the problems which affect delta areas. Suggest how this problem can be solved.

   d Look up the delta of the river Nile in your atlas. How does it compare to the delta in Figure 4? Use a sketch to show the differences.

5 Tops and tails. Copy the list of words and select the correct definition from the list and write it alongside.

   1 Tributary   a A flat piece of land built out to sea
   2 Floodplain   b A smaller river flowing into a larger river
   3 Meander   c A small river formed by a river splitting up, e.g. in a delta
   4 Ox-bow lake   d A bend in a river
   5 Delta   e A lake, formerly part of a meander sealed by deposition
   6 Distributary   f A flat expanse of silt either side of a river near its mouth

Whinstone (very resistant igneous rock). As it is a harder rock protecting weaker rock below, it is called a cap rock.

shallow valley

waterfall

plunge pool

slates   also
shales   relatively
limestone   weak

Figure 5
High force, UK

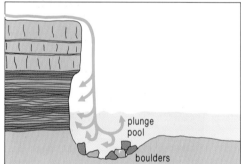

plunge pool

boulders

a A narrow neck between two meanders is formed, called a swan's neck.
b The old meander loop is sealed off by deposition to form an ox-bow lake.
c The river cuts a straight path through the meander neck.
d The river meanders and erosion is concentrated on the outside bend of a meander.

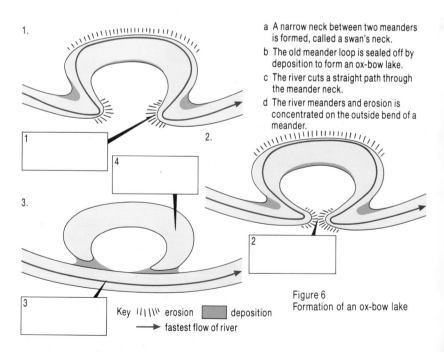

Key //|\\\\ erosion   ▨ deposition
→ fastest flow of river

Figure 6
Formation of an ox-bow lake

Flooding

The flow of rivers varies daily and seasonally. For example, a heavy rainstorm may cause the level of the river to rise rapidly. Rain falling in a river basin may travel over the surface as **overland flow** and reach the river very quickly. Most of the rain, however, will sink into the soil and gradually seep down towards the river as **throughflow**.

If the flow of a river is measured during and after a rainstorm, a graph can be drawn like that in Figure 1. It is called a **hydrograph**. It is very useful to know how a river is going to respond to rainfall in case there is a danger of flooding. The information in Figure 2 shows various causes of flooding.

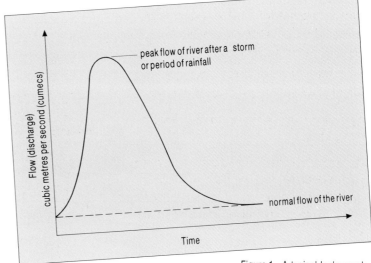

Figure 1   A typical hydrograph

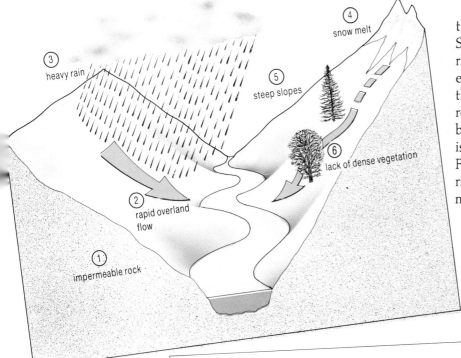

Figure 2   Some causes of flooding

A study has been carried out to compare the catchment areas of the rivers Wye and Severn in western Britain. (Find these two rivers in an atlas.) The two basins are next to each other and, therefore, receive more or less the same amount of rainfall. However, they respond in different ways to a rainstorm because one basin is forested while the other is not. Study the hydrographs drawn in Figure 3 which show the flow in each of the rivers after a rainstorm. Note which river is most likely to flood.

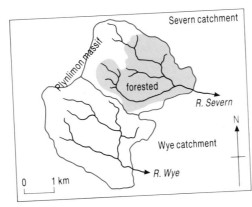

Figure 3
Hydrographs for the
rivers Wye and Severn

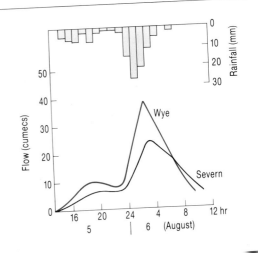

The flow of a river can also vary seasonally. The river Rhine, for example, has its source in the Alps where melting snow provides water and may cause flooding. In the spring, snow melt is rapid and the river carries a large volume of water. Look at Figure 4 which shows details of the variations of flow over the year along the river Rhine. Many rivers and basins have been altered by people to try to reduce the effects and problems of flooding. Look at the information in Figure 5.

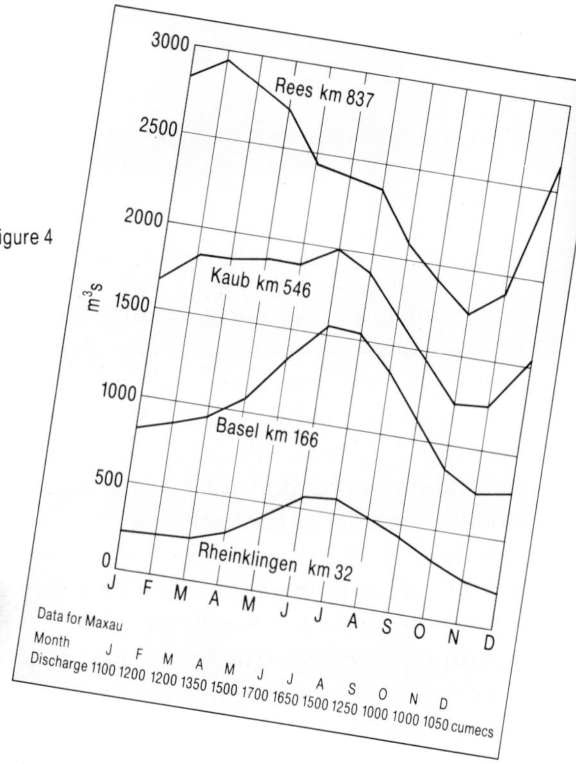

Figure 4

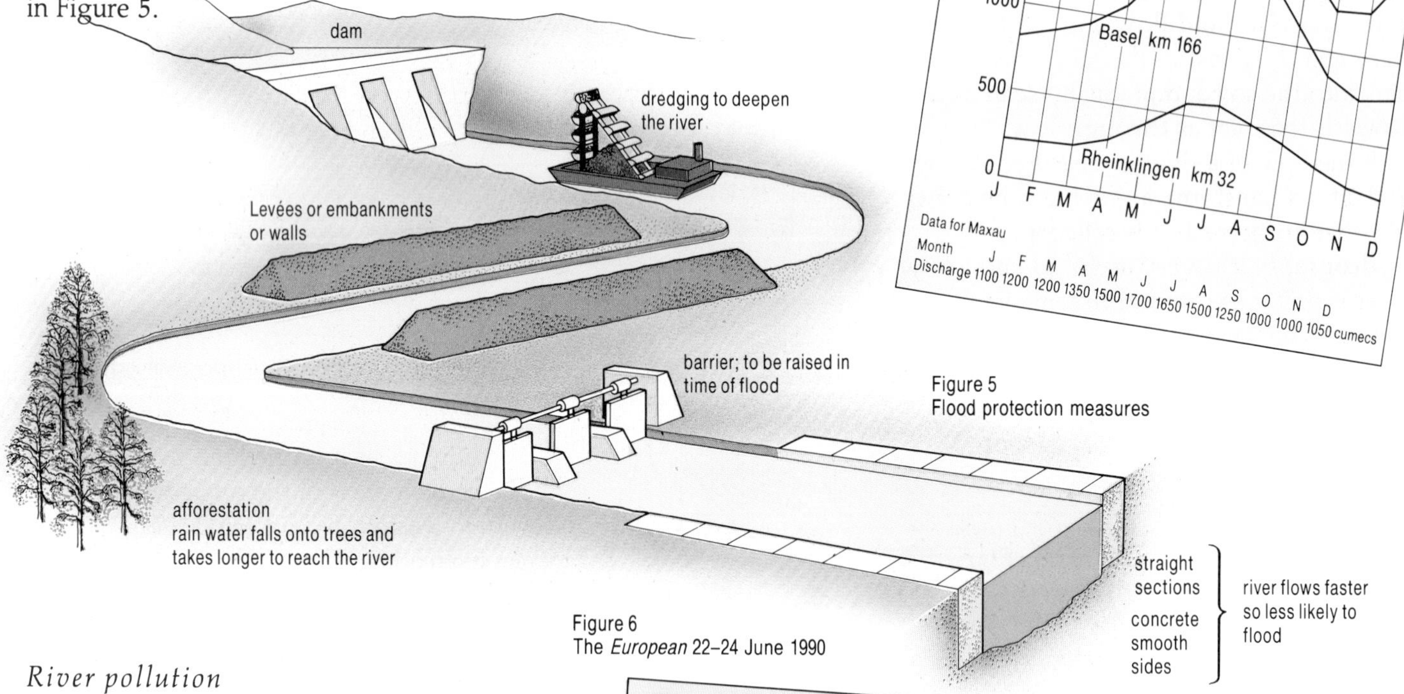

Data for Maxau

Month	J	F	M	A	M	J	J	A	S	O	N	D
Discharge	1100	1200	1200	1350	1500	1700	1650	1500	1250	1000	1000	1050 cumecs

dam

dredging to deepen the river

Levées or embankments or walls

barrier; to be raised in time of flood

afforestation
rain water falls onto trees and takes longer to reach the river

Figure 5
Flood protection measures

straight sections
concrete smooth sides
} river flows faster so less likely to flood

Figure 6
The *European* 22–24 June 1990

River pollution

Human activity results in river **pollution** which at its most serious kills fish and makes the water unsafe for human use. Rivers are frequently used for the discharge of waste products. Although the waste is usually treated to some extent before being put into the rivers it is not always harmless. Accidents like oil spills and chemical leaks also have harmful effects.

The river Rhine, for example, flows through several countries and one of the most important industrial regions of Europe (see Chapter 9). In November 1986 there was a major public outcry when toxic chemicals were discovered to have been released into the river after a fire at a chemical plant. Study the newspaper article in Figure 6. The effects of pollution are felt along the length of the river. Scientists have estimated that it will take the river many years to recover.

The countries of the EC have agreed to try to reduce the pollution in the river by 50% by the year 1995.

Dutch tackle pollution head-on

The victim of neighbouring polluters, densely populated Holland has given itself 25 years to tackle the problem of its environment ● **Rommert Kruithof** in The Hague

THREE of Europe's largest rivers meet the heavily-navigated North Sea on the Netherlands coast. Thanks to this geography, the country has served as a waste dumping ground for the industrialised nations of its vast European hinterland.

The Netherlands' location has meant that the Rhine, Maas and Waal rivers carry vast quantities of heavy metals, organic compounds, nitrates and phosphates from Switzerland, Germany, France and Belgium through the Dutch countryside, contaminating water supplies and soil which are vital for factory farming. The Netherlands is also especially vulnerable to global warming, as any rise in sea level could swamp half of the low-lying country.

Domestic pollution presents a serious problem. Holland is one of the most densely populated countries in the world,; more than 14 million people share 40 000 square kilometres with more than 12 million pigs, five million cattle and millions of chickens. While livestock produce the milk, meat and eggs on which much of the country's agricultural prosperity is based, the animals are also responsible for generating more than 100 million cubic metres of manure a year, the disposal of which has yet to be satisfactorily tackled.

Five million Dutch motor vehicles on only 2,000 kilometres of motorway cause a twice-daily traffic jam along the Randstad – the Amsterdam-Hague-Rotterdam conurbation – and, even more seriously, contribute to a threatening smog.

The Christian Democrat-Socialist coalition elected last autumn agreed a comprehensive National Environmental Policy Plan (NMP), published this month. It aims to bring the country's environmental problems under control within 25 years, at an estimated cost of F150 billion ($26.5 billion).

One important element of the plan is tighter management of the entire waste-processing cycle, from raw materials to the removal of waste matter. Another is a reduction in the use of fossil fuels through improved energy conservation and increased use of renewable energy sources, such as sun, wind and water.

High-tech, three-blade windmills seem likely to become as familiar a feature of the Dutch landscape as their wooden predecessors. Finally, the plan emphasises "quality enhancement": if consumer durables are made to last longer, there should be less waste and fewer environmental problems.

To prevent further ozone deterioration, the government hopes to ban the use of CFC-based propellents by 1995, ahead of the scheduled Europe-wide ban by 2000.

The NMP is based on the internationally accepted principle that the polluter pays. A good example of this is soil sanitation, which is often a matter of cleaning up damage that has been done in the past while trying to get the original perpetrator to pay for it. The government is presently involved in more than 100 court cases of this kind.

Activities

1 a Using the data for Maxau shown on Figure 4, draw a hydrograph for the location. Use the same scale as those already drawn in Figure 4.

b What is the discharge (flow) of water in Basle in October?

c When is the peak flow in the Rhine at Basle? Why?

2 Find a map of France in your atlas. Locate the rivers Rhône and Saône.

a Where are the source regions of the two rivers?

b Use your atlas to look up the climate for these two areas. Record any differences you discover.

c What is the name of the large city at the **confluence** of the two rivers (i.e. where the two rivers meet)?

d Plot the figures below of river discharge in the two rivers on two separate line graphs. (Make sure you use the same scale so you can compare the two graphs.) The graphs show the **river regime** for each river.

Volume of water in the Saône: cubic metres

J	F	M	A	M	J	J	A	S	O	N	D
660	630	600	500	350	250	190	160	200	350	480	560

Volume of water in the Rhône: cubic metres

520	520	620	700	740	780	820	720	620	600	600	570

e State the season in which each river is likely to flood.

f Using your answers to *a* and *b*, try to explain the differences between the two rivers.

3 Study Figure 2. For each of the statements numbered 1–6 suggest a reason why flooding may be caused.

4 Study Figure 7 showing a river liable to flood. Make a large copy of the diagram and design your own flood protection scheme. Figure 2 should help.

Figure 7   An area prone to flooding

5 Study the information in Figure 6. Imagine you are a newspaper reporter and design your own newspaper front page about the pollution. Think of your own headline and include pictures and a map if you want to. If possible produce your final front page using computer software.

Dictionary

deposit   put or lay down material
discharge   the flow of the river measured in cumecs, i.e. it is the amount of water which goes past a certain point over a set time

erosion   removal of weathered material
glacier   a mass of ice confined to a valley
hydrograph   a graph to show river flow

ice sheet   a mass of ice spread out over the landscape. It covers most of the land
transport   carry material e.g. **load** in a river or **moraine** in ice
weathering   breakdown of rocks

5 Ecosystems

Biomes

You should remember from Chapter 3 that there are different climate zones in Europe. For example the **Mediterranean** climate of Spain and Greece and the **maritime** climate of the UK. Glance back at the map on page 18 if you need to refresh your memory. These zones are part of a global pattern of climate.

The climate zones also correspond to soil and vegetation zones. These vegetation/soil/climate zones are called **biomes**. The map in Figure 1 shows the biomes of Europe. Each biome has a particular type of vegetation e.g. deciduous woodland in the UK, forest and tundra vegetation in the Alps.

The biomes are the **natural vegetation** that would be found in an area. But there are variations in the pattern of vegetation because of the effects of mountains and local climates. The greatest effect on vegetation has been caused by **human activity**. In most of Europe the natural vegetation has been destroyed through people's use of the land. In the UK there is very little deciduous woodland left; over the centuries the land has been cleared for farming, housing, roads and other uses.

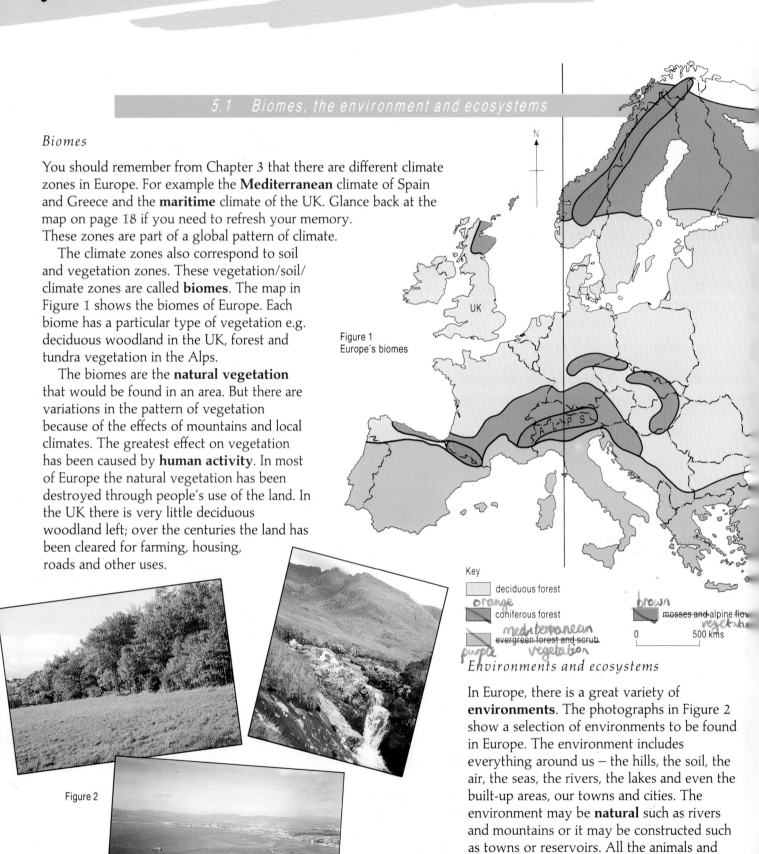

Figure 1
Europe's biomes

Key

- deciduous forest
- coniferous forest   *orange*
- evergreen forest and scrub   *mediterranean*   *purple*   *vegetation*
- mosses and alpine flowers   *brown*   *vegetation*

0   500 kms

Figure 2

Environments and ecosystems

In Europe, there is a great variety of **environments**. The photographs in Figure 2 show a selection of environments to be found in Europe. The environment includes everything around us — the hills, the soil, the air, the seas, the rivers, the lakes and even the built-up areas, our towns and cities. The environment may be **natural** such as rivers and mountains or it may be constructed such as towns or reservoirs. All the animals and

Figure 3

Figure 4   A natural ecosystem

plants, the soil, the water and the air are linked together in this enormous **global ecosystem**.

A simple way to study our environment is by looking at smaller **ecosystems**. An ecosystem can be just a part of our environment e.g. a wood, a hedgerow or a pond (Figure 3).

Look at Figure 4 which is a diagram of an ecosystem. Notice that the air, the soil, the plants, the animals and the climate are all linked together. Within the ecosystem, energy, water and nutrients are **cycled**. If anything happens to upset this cycling then the whole ecosystem would be disrupted perhaps even destroyed! For example, when a river valley is flooded to make a reservoir the ecosystem which existed is totally destroyed.

For centuries people have interfered with the ecosystems in the world often without realising the damage they are causing. Today, we are beginning to see that some of these environments need special protection otherwise they will decay and disappear forever.

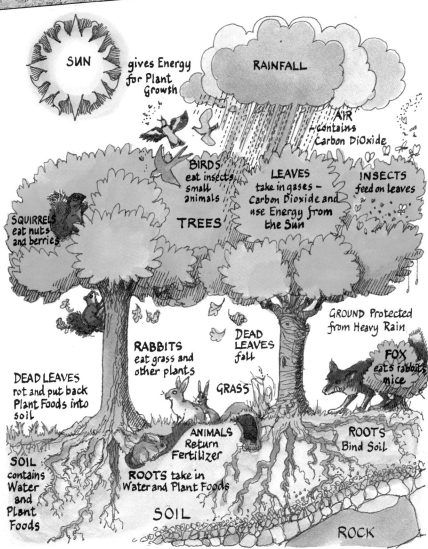

Activities

1 Write a definition for each of the following terms and include an example for each one:
   biome   ecosystem   environment.

2 Study the map in Figure 1. Follow the line from north to south which passes through Europe.
   a Draw a table with three columns. Label the columns:
      biome   climate   country.
   b In the first column, list the biomes that the line passes through.
   c In the second column, beside each biome, write down the type of climate(s). (Use the map on page 18 to help.)
   d In the third column, write an example of a country or area in the EC which falls into the zone.

3 Which biome;
  a is a **hostile environment** which will not attract many people?
  b do you think will be the easiest to live in?
  Give reasons for your answers.

4 Study the photographs in Figure 2. They show different environments. The environment can be divided into **habitats**. A habitat has the same appearance, range of plants and animals and soils.
  a Which photographs have examples of the following habitats?

  mountains fields hedgerows streams woodland ponds
  urban area

  b Draw a sketch from *one* of the photographs. Label all the different habitats you can recognise. In a suitable place on your sketch draw and label five animals you would expect to live there. Use reference books to help you if you don't know.
  c Use the photographs to write two lists, one of examples of living (organic) things and one of examples of non-living (inorganic) things.

5 a Make a large copy of the diagram in Figure 5. Use the information in Figure 4 to help you to complete the diagram.
  What would be the effect on the ecosystem if:
  b The trees were removed?
  c The fox population increased?

6 Which of the environments shown in the photographs in Figure 2 do you like the best? This is your **perception** of the landscapes. Is your choice the same as your neighbour's?

It is possible to assess the quality of a landscape by filling in an **evaluation sheet** (see Figure 6). It uses a points system to discover the quality of a landscape.

- In pairs or small groups, choose *one* of the photographs and complete the evaluation sheet individually.
- Compare your results with others in the group. Did you all give the photo the same score? Why are your scores not the same?

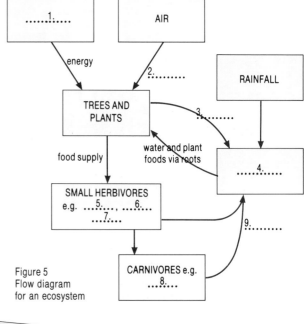

Figure 5
Flow diagram for an ecosystem

Landscape Evaluation Sheet

Location
Your Name

Items	Score
1. How much of the area is open space? Score 1 point for 10% 2 points for 20% up to 10 points for 100%	
2. What variety of natural features is there?:- Score 1 point for each of the following:- cliff, valley, marsh, waterfall, cave, moorland, hills, lake, river, wood, hedge, beach, sea, grassland.	
3. What plants and animals are there? Count the varieties of plants, trees and animals you identify. Give a mark out of 10 for your count.	
4. How do you feel about the area? Is it pretty boring? exciting? ugly? Do you like it? Appealing 3 2 1 0 Unappealing Beautiful 3 2 1 0 Ugly Interesting 3 2 1 0 Boring Spectacular 3 2 1 0 Dull Varied 3 2 1 0 All the same Inviting 3 2 1 0 Hostile (Points) Choose between the opposites, if you think an area is quite dull give it 1 mark, if you think an area is very varied give it 3 marks.	
5. Manmade features usually spoil a landscape. Look at the features and see how each one scores on this scale:- Blends in with environment – no points deducted Only a little impact – 1 point deducted Strong impact – 2 points deducted Pollutes the environment – 3 points deducted	Total Score = Deduct points for item 5 = Final Score

Figure 6

5.2 The Mediterranean biome

You have already studied the Mediterranean climate in Chapter 3. You should remember that the climate has hot, dry summers and mild, wet winters. In the summer it is so dry that often there are a few months' total **drought**. But there are differences across the whole area. The season of drought is longer in the east than in the west. The summer temperatures are also higher in the east while winter temperatures are lower. The maps in Figure 1 show how the climate varies in the Mediterranean lands of Europe.

WINTER November 1 to April 30

Rainfall
Key

▨	over 750 mm
▨	500–750mm
▨	250–500mm
☐	under 250mm

0   1000 kms

Figure 1

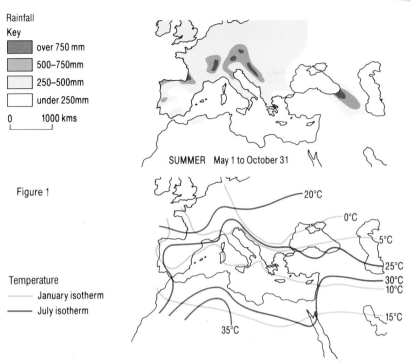

SUMMER May 1 to October 31

Temperature
— January isotherm
— July isotherm

The Mediterranean area has many extremes and there are also climatic hazards. Cold winds like the **Mistral** and **Borah** blow from the north while the hot, parching **Sirocco** wind blows from the south. Heavy rain in autumn after the dry summer easily washes away the soil from the steeper land.

The vegetation in the Mediterranean areas is mainly evergreen forest and **scrub** (Figures 2 and 3). Scrub is mainly bushes which are drought resistant such as the olive and gorse. Heather and grasses also grow.

The woodlands are evergreen e.g. the cork oak and the maritime pine. Any vegetation growing in these areas must be well **adapted** to the drought otherwise the plants would **dehydrate** and die. The diagram in Figure 4 shows the adaptations of vegetation growing in Mediterranean areas. The deep roots reach down to tap the water stored deep in the ground. The thick bark and tough leaves help to reduce water loss. The leaves are also small to cut down water loss.

As in other parts of Europe much of the Mediterranean vegetation has been cleared. It is not too hot that people cannot live and work and it is not too dry to grow crops. Also, many of the trees and plants which grow in these areas are useful to people. So, for hundreds of years people have lived in the Mediterranean areas growing wheat and barley, cultivating trees especially the olive and citrus fruits and raising sheep and goats on the pasture land.

Figure 2 Mediterranean scrub

Figure 3 Mediterranean vegetation

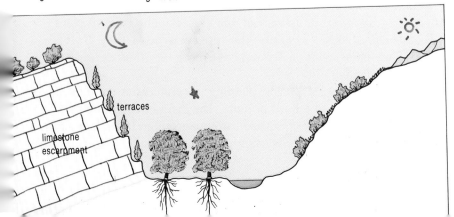

terraces

limestone escarpment

Figure 4 Adaptations to drought

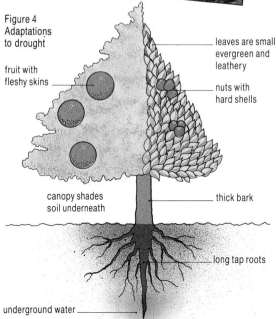

fruit with fleshy skins

canopy shades soil underneath

leaves are small evergreen and leathery

nuts with hard shells

thick bark

long tap roots

underground water

Activities

1 Using the information on climate (Figure 1) and an atlas:

a Copy the following table and complete it with the correct figures and words.

	Gibraltar	Aleppo (Syria)
Latitude		
Longitude		
West or east in the Mediterranean		
Winter rainfall		
Summer rainfall		
January temperature		
July temperature		
Annual range of temperature		

b Copy the paragraph, choosing the correct word from inside each of the brackets.

The Mediterranean regions lie just (north/south) of latitude 30°N but a little (north/south) of latitude 40°N. They are (nearer/further from) the Equator than the UK so they are (hotter/cooler). They receive most of their rain in (winter/summer). The east of the Mediterranean has (hotter/colder) summers than the west although winters are (colder/warmer).

2 Make a copy of the diagram in Figure 3 and add the following labels in the best place:

cork oak woodland   scrub   bare rock
deep tap roots   heather   gorse   vines

3 Study Figure 4 and answer the following:

a In what ways do Mediterranean trees reduce water loss?

b How do the trees obtain water during the drought?

5.3   Trees and forests

Forestry in the UK

Look out of your classroom window. Can you see a **wood** or a **forest**? If you can you are very lucky because today only 10% of the UK is covered in trees! Figure 1 shows the extent of woodland in all of the EC countries.

A few thousand years ago most of the UK was covered in **deciduous trees**, e.g. beech, oak and elm. Gradually, people cleared the woods and forests for farming, fuel, building land, industry and other uses. Figure 2 describes how tree removal happened.

In the UK today, only 27% of the woodlands and forests are deciduous trees. Most of these are in the **Ancient Woodlands**. The woodlands have names like wood, coppice, copse or dingle. They have an irregular boundary and are often in uplands, along narrow river valleys or on steep slopes. They usually contain very old trees with carpets of woodland flowers such as bluebells, wild daffodils and wood anemones. They are rich in wildlife.

The replanting of woodlands is called **afforestation**. In the UK afforestation began in 1919, shortly after the First World War. During the war the demand for wood for the 'war effort' was enormous and the UK was unable to obtain supplies from abroad.

The Government decided to replant large areas to improve the UK's timber supply so that there would be sufficient timber should another war occur. Since then most of the planting has been of **coniferous trees**. The **plantations** are easy to recognise. They are large areas with straight boundaries and forest tracks cutting across them. Conifers have been the most popular trees to plant because they are **softwoods**, they grow faster and have more uses than deciduous trees.

The planting of conifers has not always been popular. The diagram in Figure 3 compares the coniferous and deciduous forest ecosystems. Study it carefully. Which of the ecosystems do you prefer?

Forested Areas in the EC 1988 (% of total land area)	
United Kingdom	10%
Belgium/Luxembourg	21%
Greece	20%
Denmark	12%
France	27%
West Germany	30%
Eire	5%
Italy	23%
Netherlands	9%
Spain	31%
Portugal	40%

Figure 1

Large new forests have been planned e.g. the Midlands New Forest. One of the reasons behind the scheme is to help farmers **diversify**. By the year 2000, 2 million hectares of farmland will no longer be needed for food production and forestry could bring the farmers some extra income. In the Midlands there are areas of derelict land and infertile soil yet there are millions of people close by who would welcome the forest for recreation. It is hoped that the forest will create jobs and increase timber production as well as improving the landscape and attracting wildlife.

More **native** deciduous trees are being planted. These take longer to mature but they are the 'natural vegetation' of the UK and they create a better environment. They harbour more species of plants and animals and create a high-quality soil.

More 'community forests' are to be planted around cities such as London and Newcastle-upon-Tyne (Figure 4). Modern society is demanding a better environment with more 'green' space, particularly close to the urban areas with their large populations.

Within these forested areas, more recreation facilities are being provided such as nature trails, log cabins and picnic areas. This reflects the growing trend for leisure activities in the UK (see unit 12.1).

Community forests

These are a new idea in the UK but not in the rest of Europe. The Netherlands' Bos Park and Germany's Bremen Stadtwald are fine examples.

The Bos Park (see Figure 5) is on the outskirts of Amsterdam. Forty years ago several million trees were planted on polder land separated by canals and lakes. An artificial hill was built with a restaurant carefully sited on the top. In winter the slopes are used for sledging and skiing. In other areas, there are swimming pools, tennis courts, an open-air theatre and nature reserves. There are paths, cycle tracks, bridleways and nature trails.

It is a favourite spot for the Amsterdammers as well as an important tourist attraction.

Figure 2 Tree removal in the UK

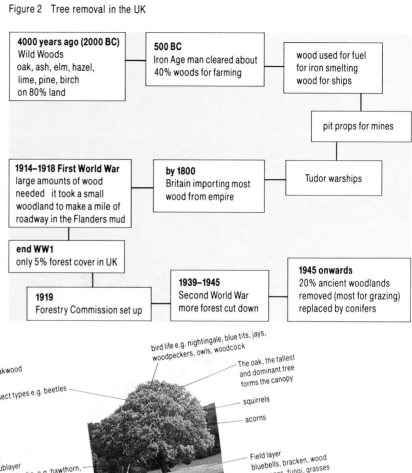

Figure 3 Forest ecosystems

Figure 4

The 12 planned community forests

South Tyne and Wear
Cleveland
West Manchester
Sheffield
East Liverpool
North Nottingham
South Staffordshire
Cardiff
Swansea
Neath/Port Talbot
North Bristol
East London

Figure 5 Bos Park, Amsterdam

Activities

1 On an outline map of Europe plot the percentage of woodland for each country. Use a symbol, perhaps of a tree, to represent 1% of forested land. Work out how many symbols each country will need e.g. the UK will need ten symbols. Complete your map. Think carefully about how large to draw your symbol – make sure you can fit all the symbols needed into each country. Finish your map by adding a title and a key.

  a How many countries have less than 10% of their land forested?

  b Which two countries have the greatest percentage of forested land?

2 Study the OS map extract of part of the Trossachs in Scotland in Figure 6.

  a Draw a sketch of the map. Label the following:
  - Endrick Water.
  - The land over 100 metres.
  - The areas of woodland.
  - Coniferous plantations.
  - Ancient Woodlands.
  - Shelter belt or windbreak trees.

  b Measure the area of the largest plantation. Give your answer in hectares. (See page 9 for 'How to measure area on a map'.)

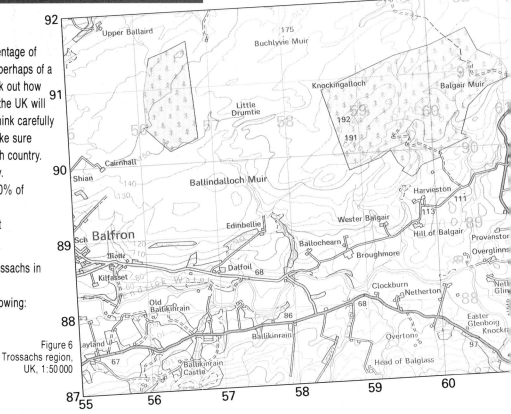

Figure 6
Trossachs region,
UK, 1:50 000

3 A forestry group wishes to create a new area of coniferous forest near where you live. You would prefer a deciduous forest. Write a letter to the Editor of your local newspaper outlining the reasons why you are against the coniferous plantation.

5.4   Conservation and environmental protection

There is great pressure on our environment – more land is needed for housing, industry and roads and there is a need for more timber and open space. This causes **conflicts** of land use. There are environmental problems such as acid rain, water and air pollution, derelict land and buildings. The information in Figure 1 shows some of the problems affecting our environment.

Today the need for **conservation** is great. Careful management and plenty of money are needed to allow people to enjoy the environment while at the same time preventing it from being damaged.

The need for conservation and management is not new and over the years the Government has set up groups to look after the natural environment e.g. the Council for the Preservation of Rural England, the National Trust and the Countryside Commission.

The map in Figure 2 shows the protected areas in the UK. The Government protects wildlife habitats through 5,000 **Sites of Special Scientific Interest** and 279 **National Nature Reserves**. Landscapes

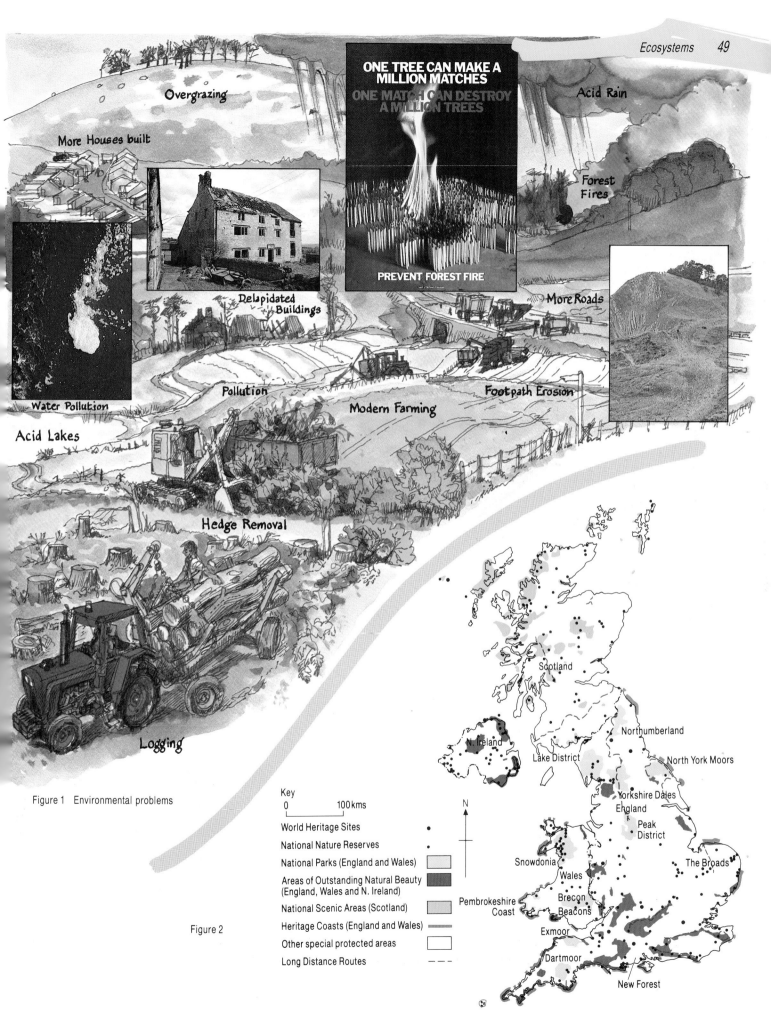

ONE TREE CAN MAKE A MILLION MATCHES
ONE MATCH CAN DESTROY A MILLION TREES

PREVENT FOREST FIRE

Overgrazing

More Houses built

Acid Rain

Forest Fires

Delapidated Buildings

Water Pollution

Acid Lakes

Pollution

Modern Farming

More Roads

Footpath Erosion

Hedge Removal

Logging

Figure 1 Environmental problems

Key

0   100kms

World Heritage Sites   •

National Nature Reserves   .

National Parks (England and Wales)

Areas of Outstanding Natural Beauty
(England, Wales and N. Ireland)

National Scenic Areas (Scotland)

Heritage Coasts (England and Wales)

Other special protected areas

Long Distance Routes   - - -

Figure 2

Scotland

N. Ireland

Northumberland

Lake District

North York Moors

Yorkshire Dales
England

Peak District

Snowdonia

The Broads

Wales

Pembrokeshire Coast

Brecon Beacons

Exmoor

Dartmoor

New Forest

are protected through the 10 **National Parks**, **The New Forest** and the **Norfolk Broads**. There are also 46 **Areas of Outstanding Natural Beauty** (AONB) and 39 **Heritage Coasts**. AONBs are used to protect areas too small to be designated as National Parks. In Scotland there are 40 **Natural Scenic Areas** and 80% of the mainland coast is protected.

Moorland is one area needing conservation. The pressure of farming, recreation and forestry is threatening to destroy the moorlands:

- Bracken is increasing. In the North Yorkshire Moors 35 000 acres of the 125 000 acres are now covered in bracken. Many people think it is the UK's fastest growing weed.
- The soils are becoming more acid, altering the plant life. This is caused by **acid rain** pollution.
- Modern farming has caused the removal of heather e.g. 75% of heather in Cumbria has been lost. It does not recolonise easily. The land is also being planted with conifer plantations.
- Poorly planned drainage schemes have caused flooding and soil erosion.
- The increased use of moorlands by people is disturbing the birdlife and eroding the footpaths; carelessness has caused more forest fires especially during the dry years of 1989 and 1990.

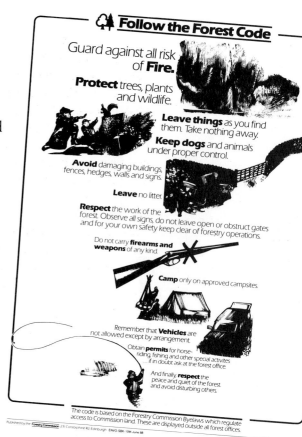

Figure 3

Figure 4   Conservation of the environment in the North East

One attempt at conservation has been the introduction of the Forest Code for visitors to follow. The code is shown in Figure 3.

Conservation and preservation are not only needed in the natural environment; 80% of people in the UK live in the towns and cities and so it is important that the **urban environment** is conserved and improved. There are many reminders of our **heritage** in our urban areas e.g. old buildings such as churches, houses of architectural interest and parks. The cities also need to be improved by reducing pollution and making them more *green*. Planting trees, planning parks and green belts are all important. Conservation Trusts, the National Trust and local councils are some of the organisations involved in looking after our heritage in urban areas of the UK. Figure 4 shows some of the ways the environment in the North-East is being conserved and improved.

Activities

1 What is the meaning of conservation?

2 Study Figure 1. The information shows some examples of problems in the environment. With a friend or in small groups make a list of the problems.

Select *one* problem from your list. Decide how the problem has been caused – do some research on your own if you are not sure.

On a large sheet of paper make an interesting and colourful poster to inform the public of the problem and the ways it is being caused. Be prepared to talk about your poster to the rest of the class.

3 Look at the map in Figure 2 and answer the following questions. Put the title 'Conserving the Natural Environment'.

a List the National Parks in England and Wales.

b Northern Ireland has no National Parks. What *does* it have? Can you think why? (Hint: look at the size.)

c Choose one of the Long Distance footpaths marked on the map. Use an atlas to help you decide where the walk starts and ends. Describe the route the walk takes – through which protected areas does it pass? How long is the route?

d Are the long distance routes in 'good' locations? Why? Can you think of any disadvantages of having these long distance routes?

e Choose the county in which you live or one that is close by. Name the county you have chosen and list all the protected areas within it.

4 Figure 4 describes some of the ways conservation of the environment is succeeding in the North-East. Study the information and give examples for each of the following (one example has been done for you):

- Conserving old buildings e.g. the restoration of Holmside Hall.
- Conservation groups.
- Improving the landscape.
- New buildings.

5 Study your local area – collect and display information about problems and conservation measures.

Dictionary

biomes   zones having the same climate, soil and vegetation

coniferous trees   trees which have cones, they are mostly evergreen

conservation   preserving the environment

cycling   movement of water and nutrients in a system

deciduous trees   trees which lose their leaves in winter

diversification   changing to another activity

'green'   environmentally aware

heritage   buildings, monuments etc. of historical interest

6 Population

Population is distributed very unevenly in the EC. (See Figure 1.) There are areas of low, medium and high population **density**. Density is the number of people living in an area. It is calculated using a simple formula:

$$\frac{\text{Number of people in an area}}{\text{Size of the area in km}^2} = \text{people per km}^2$$

Look at Figure 2 which shows some simple calculations. The densities in diagrams (b) and (c) are the same but the people are distributed differently within each area. The densities in (a) and (d) are the same although (d) involves a larger area. Densities are useful measures to compare population characteristics in countries. Look at the table in Figure 3, which shows some of the densities for the countries of the EC.

High densities of population are often found in areas which favour settlement. Such areas tend to have flat, fertile land; a reliable water supply; nearby raw materials and a reasonable climate. Sometimes nearness to the coast is an added advantage especially for trade with other countries.

Figure 1 shows you the population distribution in Europe. The central densely

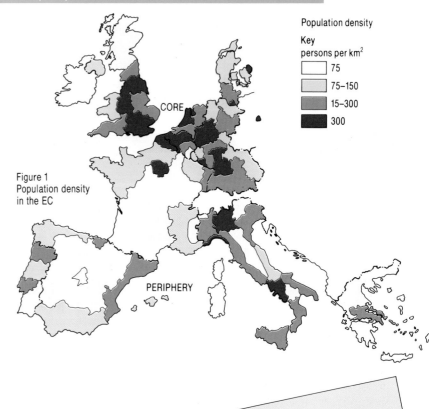

Population density

Key
persons per km²

☐	75
▨	75–150
▨	15–300
■	300

Figure 1
Population density
in the EC

CORE

PERIPHERY

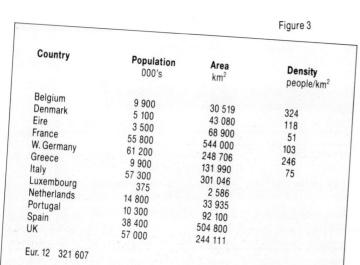

Figure 2

Each area is 1km²

a
$\dfrac{1 \text{ person}}{1 \text{km}^2} = 1 \text{ per /km}^2$

b
$\dfrac{4 \text{ people}}{1 \text{km}^2} = 4/\text{km}^2$

area 4km²

c
$\dfrac{4 \text{ people}}{1 \text{ km}^2} = 4/\text{km}^2$

d
$\dfrac{4 \text{ people}}{4 \text{km}^2} = 1 \text{ per/km}^2$

Figure 3

Country	Population 000's	Area km²	Density people/km²
Belgium	9 900	30 519	324
Denmark	5 100	43 080	118
Eire	3 500	68 900	51
France	55 800	544 000	103
W. Germany	61 200	248 706	246
Greece	9 900	131 990	75
Italy	57 300	301 046	
Luxembourg	375	2 586	
Netherlands	14 800	33 935	
Portugal	10 300	92 100	
Spain	38 400	504 800	
UK	57 000	244 111	

Eur. 12   321 607

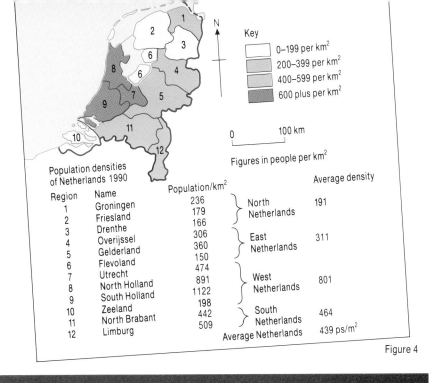

Region	Name	Population/km²		Average density
1	Groningen	236	North Netherlands	191
2	Friesland	179		
3	Drenthe	166		
4	Overijssel	306	East Netherlands	311
5	Gelderland	360		
6	Flevoland	150		
7	Utrecht	474	West Netherlands	801
8	North Holland	891		
9	South Holland	1122		
10	Zeeland	198	South Netherlands	464
11	North Brabant	442		
12	Limburg	509		
		Average Netherlands		439 ps/m²

Population densities of Netherlands 1990

Figures in people per km²

Key
☐ 0–199 per km²
☐ 200–399 per km²
☐ 400–599 per km²
☐ 600 plus per km²

0   100 km

Figure 4

populated region is called the **core** region and it includes areas such as the Netherlands and south-east UK. Areas which do not favour settlement and have a low population density are called the **peripheral** regions. Examples include southern France, Spain, Italy and Greece.

Population densities can also vary within countries. Cities usually have very high densities compared with rural areas. Some of the high densities in the Netherlands are shown in Figure 4. Look in an atlas to find the locations of the major cities in south Holland.

Activities

1 a Figure 3 contains data for the EC countries. Some of the densities have been worked out for you. Make a copy of the table and complete the figures. (Round the results up to the nearest whole number.)

 b On a copy of an outline map of Europe produce a **choropleth map** to show population density using your table completed in a. You will need five colours ranging from light to dark. The lightest colour is for the lowest density population and the darkest colour is for the highest density population. Suggested categories are:
 Less than 100 people per km²; 101–200; 201–300; 301–400; over 400 people per km².

 c Compare your map with Figure 1.
 i Do the core and periphery areas show up clearly on your map?
 ii If you wanted to know details about the population distribution in one country, why is your map not as good as the map in Figure 1?

 d Why are population density figures for whole countries often misleading?

2 Make a copy of Figure 5. Using the labels provided annotate the diagram to show physical factors influencing population density.

3 a In pairs or small groups complete the following:
 On a large sheet of paper draw an imaginary island. On your island there are:
 ● high mountains
 ● two rivers and a lake
 ● flat land and fertile soil
 ● marsh land
 ● one small village and a port
 ● isolated farms
 ● 100 people
 Decide where you are going to locate all the features and complete your island. Add a key and title.

 b Write a short paragraph to explain why you located the population in your chosen area(s).

Figure 5

1 Farming is difficult in drier Mediterranean areas even if the area is flat.
2 Highland has a cooler climate.
3 Water for drinking, crops, industry and washing.
4 Tractors are difficult to use on steep land.
5 Farming is easy on flat land.
6 Soils are rocky and shallow.

6.2   Population change

Populations are constantly changing. They usually increase over a period of time because the number of babies born is greater than the number of people dying. The number of births per year is known as the **birth rate**. It is measured as births per 1000 people per year. **Death rates** are deaths per 1000 per year. The rate at which the population is growing can be calculated by subtracting the number of deaths per year from the number of births. This is called the **natural increase**.

Figure 1
Factors causing population change

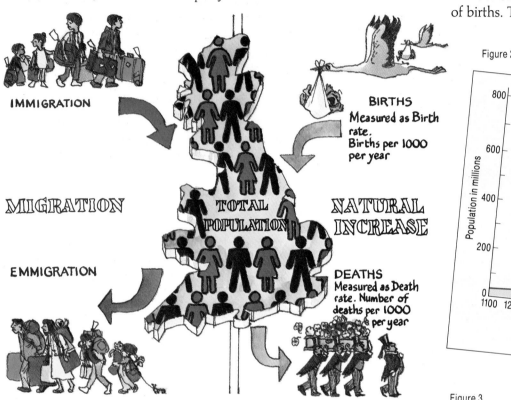

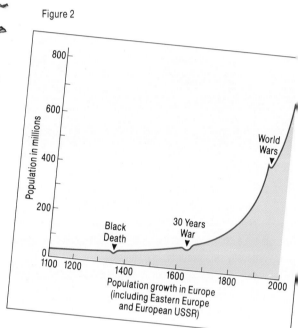

Figure 2

Population growth in Europe (including Eastern Europe and European USSR)

Population totals can also change if people move into or out of a country. This is called **migration**. (See section 6.3.) Figure 1 summarises the factors affecting population change. Notice that both natural increase and migration need to be considered when working out total population change.

Figure 2 shows a population growth graph for the continent of Europe. Notice how steeply the line rises in the 1900s when the population was increasing very rapidly. Birth rates were very high and families included large numbers of children.

Although the world population seems to be growing very rapidly, there are great differences between individual countries. (See Figure 3.) The population of Europe is now growing much more slowly than the developing world areas of Asia and Africa as shown in Figure 4.

Figure 3

	1950	1960	1970	1980	1988	estimated 2000
Belgium	8.6	9.1	9.6	9.8	9.9	10.0
Denmark	4.3	4.6	4.9	5.1	5.1	5.0
France	41.7	45.7	50.7	53.8	55.9	57.2
W. Germany	50.0	55.4	60.7	61.7	61.2	59.5
Greece	7.6	8.3	8.8	9.6	10.0	10.4
Ireland	3.0	2.8	3.0	3.4	3.5	4.3
Italy	46.8	50.2	53.6	56.1	57.4	58.6
Luxembourg	0.3	0.3	0.3	0.4	0.4	0.4
Netherlands	10.1	11.5	13.0	14.2	14.8	15.1
Portugal	8.4	8.5	8.6	9.7	10.4	11.2
Spain	27.9	30.3	33.8	37.5	39.0	42.2
UK	50.8	52.7	55.7	55.9	57.1	56.4

Population change in the EC.   Populations in millions.

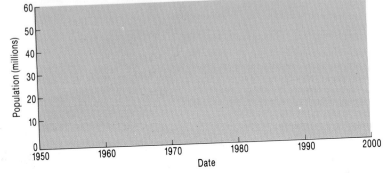

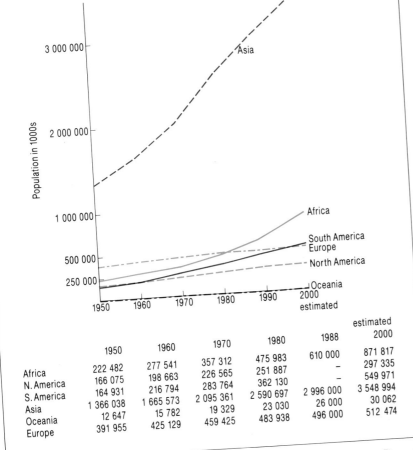

Figure 4

	1950	1960	1970	1980	1988	estimated 2000
Africa	222 482	277 541	357 312	475 983	610 000	871 817
N. America	166 075	198 663	226 565	251 887	–	297 335
S. America	164 931	216 794	283 764	362 130	–	549 971
Asia	1 366 038	1 665 573	2 095 361	2 590 697	2 996 000	3 548 994
Oceania	12 647	15 782	19 329	23 030	26 000	30 062
Europe	391 955	425 129	459 425	483 938	496 000	512 474

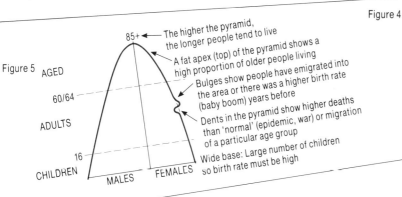

Figure 5

Population pyramids

Information about the population of a country or a town can be divided into age groups and into male and female. A **population pyramid** shows the age/sex characteristics for a country at a particular time. Figure 5 shows you the features to look out for when interpreting such a diagram. Some of the pyramids for EC countries have been drawn in Figure 6. Notice that the percentages of males and females do vary. More boys than girls tend to be born, but more boys die in their first year of life. The numbers, therefore, even out in the younger age groups. In the elderly age group, there are differences again. Females tend to have a longer **life expectancy** than males. Differences elsewhere will be due to wars, epidemics, migration and changes in birth rates.

Planners are interested in numbers of people in different age groups; they have to plan for housing and schools. Children under 16/18 and adults over 60/65 are known as **dependants** because they rely on the working population to look after them.

Figure 6   Population pyramid

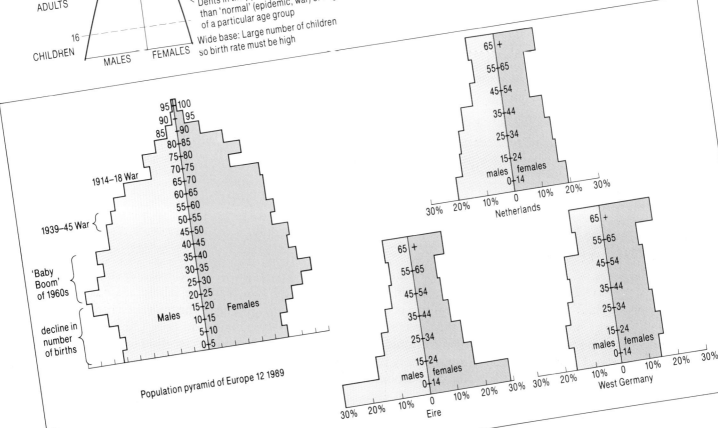

Activities

1 Using the data given in Figure 7 work out the natural increase rates for the EC countries. (This is calculated by birth rate − death rate and is converted to a percentage. Some examples have been worked out for you.)

   a Which country in the EC has the highest rate of natural increase?

   b Which country in the EC has the lowest rate of natural increase? What is unusual about the figures for this country compared with the rest of the table?
Suggest a problem which might occur if the trend in either of these countries continues.

   c Which country's natural increase is expected to remain the same in the future?

   d Which country in the EC has the highest birth rate? Suggest a reason for your answer.

   e Which countries in the EC have the highest death rates? Suggest a reason why these are higher than other areas in the EC.

   f If Turkey joins the EC, what do you think will happen to the average natural increase rate of the EC?

2 Draw three lines on the same graph Figure 3) for the data for West Germany, Spain and the Netherlands. Use different colours for each country.

   a Which of these countries has shown the fastest rate of growth of the population? (Look for the steepest line.)

   b Which country shows an estimated decrease in population?

3 *a* Use the information given in Figure 8 to draw a population pyramid for the UK.

   b Write one sentence about each of the following groups:
(Remember to compare males with females.)

    i The children under 15.

    ii The adults between 16 and 59.

    iii The elderly over 60.

   c For one of the three age groups try to explain your answer in *b*. (Consider the number of births, deaths, life expectancy and migration as some of the reasons for your answers. Refer to Figure 5.)

4 Make copies of the Eire and West German pyramids in Figure 6b and add labels to describe the main features. Use the information given in this unit to suggest reasons for the characteristics you have identified.

Country	Birth rates /1000 yr.	Death rates /1000 yr.	Natural increase /1000 yr.	%
UK	13	12	1	0.1
Eire	15	9		
Denmark	11	12		
W. Germany	11	12		
Netherlands	13	8		
Belgium	12	11		
Luxembourg	12	12		
Italy	10	9		
France	14	10		
Spain	15	9		
Portugal	17	9		
Greece	14	9	5	0.5
EC 12	12	10		
USA	16	9	7	0.7
Japan	13	6		
USSR	20	10	10	1
Turkey	33	9	24	2.4

Figure 7

Figure 8
Census data (1981)

U.K. 1981
% of male/female population

Age group	Male	Female
75+	4	7
70–74	4	5
65–69	5	5
60–64	5	5
55–59	6	6
45–54	11	11
35–44	12	12
25–34	15	14
16–24	14	14
5–15	17	13
0–4	7	16

1981 Census data

6.3   Migration

Populations can change quite dramatically as a result of people moving in (**immigration**) and out (**emigration**) of a country or an area. In the EC 40% of the present population growth is due to **migration**.

People move for a variety of reasons. These include political, economic (e.g. jobs), physical (e.g. climate, environment) and social (e.g. marriage, family) reasons. (See Figure 1.)

Some of the migrations are temporary and are for a short time. Others are permanent. Migrations can also be international (from one country to another) or internal (within one country).

Figure 1   Some reasons for migration

Migration in the UK

Look at Figure 2 which shows international migration into and out of the UK. Notice the importance of certain countries. These are the ones with strong links with the UK.

On a smaller scale, regional migration within a country is important. Look at Figure 3. Some areas are gaining population, whilst others are losing. In the UK many of the **rural** (countryside) areas in Scotland are losing people. This is known as **rural depopulation**. People have tended to drift into the towns and cities looking for work.

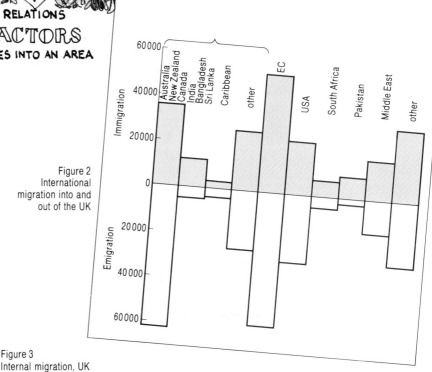

Figure 2 International migration into and out of the UK

Figure 3 Internal migration, UK

The Government now offers help to industries setting up in the areas where there is high unemployment and outmigration. Many of the major cities, like London, are also losing population. This is because people are moving out from inner city areas to live in the countryside on the outskirts of the city. **Commuting** to work is quite common and people prefer to live in a pleasant environment. This has resulted in the increase in numbers of large settlements near cities and is creating pressure on **green belt** areas.

Migration in West Germany before unification

In the EC there are large numbers of migrants who have moved to find jobs in other countries. Look at the data in Figure 4. Notice that certain countries provide more migrants than others. Also, certain countries like West Germany, favour migrants.

After the Second World War, West Germany had a lack of manual workers and so immigration was encouraged. In the 1960s and 1970s many migrants moved from the poorer regions in Europe to take advantage of the better jobs and higher salaries on offer in West Germany.

Many came from Turkey where the migrants tended to be young, single males. If married, their families may also have migrated too. Alternatively, they remained in their original country and the husband sent money home.

Education, housing and jobs have to be provided by a host country. Language is often a problem. In the 1980s some of the Turkish migrants were without jobs, yet in many ways they were settled in West Germany. The Government offered money for their train fares and pensions hoping that many would return home. Most of those that did were the 40–50-year-olds. Others felt they were better off staying in West Germany. Money from state benefits was higher than earnings they could have made from jobs in Turkey.

In 1989 large numbers of migrants arrived from East Germany. There were no language problems, but housing and jobs were needed. The effects of the migration were felt in both East and West Germany. Following unification in 1990, migration has continued from east to west.

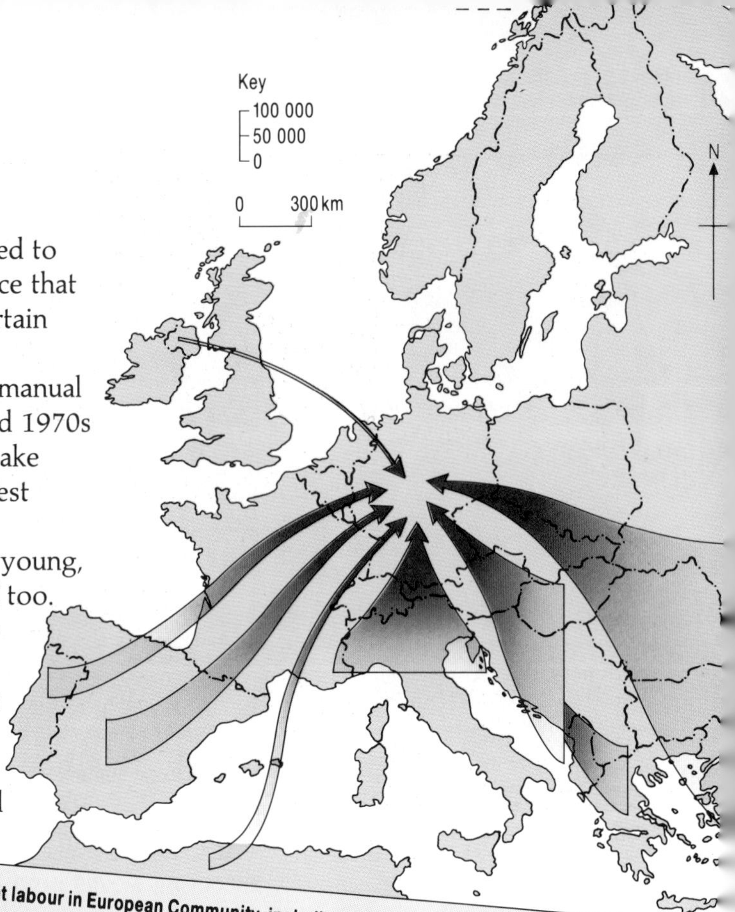

Figure 4   Flow map for West Germany

Migrant labour in European Community, including Greece, 1980 (000)

Country of origin	Benelux	France	W. Germany	UK	Community
Community	274	246	587	642	1 766
of which: Greece	12	4	133	10	159
Ireland	3	1	2	452	458
Italy	114	176	309	72	672
Portugal	24	385	59	10	478
Spain	45	185	87	37	672
Turkey	76	36	591	3	354
Yugoslavia	10	43	357	4	714
Maghreb[1]	80	616	28	3	421
Others	70	132	364	966	729[1]
Total	579	1 643	2 072	1 665	1 544
					6 016

Source: Commission of the European Communities.
[1] Algeria 367; Morocco 272; Tunisia 90.

Activities

1 a Look at Figure 2. Write a sentence to describe the migration pattern between the UK and each of the following countries:
  i Australia   ii India   iii Rest of the EC.
 b For one of the above statements try to give reasons for your answer.

2 a Describe the pattern of migration shown in the UK in Figure 3. Which regions have gained population and which have lost population?
 b On the map, find the region you live in. Has this region gained or lost population? Suggest some reasons for your answer.
 c Choose a contrasting region where migration has been different from your home region. Name the region. Explain why the pattern is different.

3 Look at the details of the two new students in a West German school in Figure 5.
 a Why did Fuat's grandparents originally come to Germany?
 b What problems did they have when they first arrived?
 c Use your atlas to work out how far Fuat's grandparents had to move from Izmir in Turkey to Hamburg in Germany and then to Munich.
 d Why do you think Fuat's family wanted to live close to Turkish people?
 e In what ways do you think Fuat's way of life in Germany is different from that of his grandparents?
 f Imagine you are Bettina. Relate your family story to Fuat. Explain why your family decided to migrate and how you are finding life in West Germany. (Either write it or present it as a cartoon.)

Figure 5

4 *a* As a result of migration over generations, we live in a **multicultural society** (mixed races, religion and cultures). Give reasons to show how this can be an advantage. (Think about your local area.)

b Complete the word search and table in Figure 6.

5 *a* How do minority groups, (i.e. those with a different language, culture or religion), keep their identities? (Again think about your local area – shops, religious buildings, clothes, festivals, language etc.)

b Discuss the following question in pairs and then with the rest of the class. 'Should migrants keep their own identities or adopt the traditions of the country they move to?' Make a few notes about your discussion giving some reasons for the conclusions you draw.

c Make a wall display of the way in which your town is a multicultural society. Include maps, sketches, photographs and newspaper articles.

6 Try to interview somebody who has migrated to the UK. Find out why they migrated and discover what, if any, problems they have faced in the UK.

Find as many different groups of people who have come to Britain in the word search below (there are 12.)

A	Y	J	B	A	H	G	R	O	M	A	N
I	R	B	F	E	E	G	C	F	S	L	P
H	Z	I	H	S	C	D	E	K	Q	T	N
S	Q	R	I	E	F	D	D	C	O	I	M
I	J	I	G	N	H	K	R	U	T	U	A
W	E	S	T	I	N	D	I	A	N	M	R
E	P	H	E	H	P	B	L	Q	E	V	R
J	K	L	N	C	O	I	D	R	W	I	S
G	E	A	Y	O	A	F	I	I	J	N	G
M	R	N	H	N	R	C	V	T	X	D	T
O	L	E	W	X	A	M	U	K	Y	I	S
Z	A	N	E	N	B	J	A	I	Z	A	K
M	X	B	C	K	W	M	V	N	U	N	L

Many of these people have brought new traditions or foods or building design into Britain. Using the word search to help you, complete the following table.

Group of people.	Evidence in the UK
1.	A ceilidh (gaelic dance).
2.	Sinagogues
3.	Churches constructed after conquest in 1066
4.	Chop suey from a Soho restaurant
5.	Steel band playing at the Nottinghill Carnival
6.	Doner kebabs
7.	The old names: Londinium, Watling Street.
8.	Sikh temples
9.	Muslim mosques
10.	McDonalds
11.	Spaghetti
12.	Taramasalata

Figure 6

6.4   The quality of life

Even in the EC there are great differences in the quality of life between countries. These are the result of the individual histories of the areas. Many factors are useful when comparing countries (see Figure 1).

The **GDP** (Gross Domestic Product) is an indication of the wealth of a country. When divided by the number of people it gives the average wealth per person. Other characteristics in the table also give information about the wealth of individual countries.

Figure 1

	Major Religions	Official Languages (underlined languages are the 9 EC official languages)	(1984) Calories per person per day	(1984) Population per doctor	(1988) Infant mortality (deaths per 1000 babies born)	(1988) Life Expectancy	GDP US$ per person (1987)	(1984) Televisions per 1000	(1984) Telephones per 1000	(1984) Cars per 1000
Belgium	RC	Dutch, French German	3850	330	11	74	14 348	303	417	335
Denmark	Evangelical-Lutheran	Danish	3512	400	8	75	16 673	369	718	282
W. Germany	Protestant, RC	German	3476	380	9	75	18 723	335	570	412
Greece	Greek Orthodox	Greek	3688	350	14	75	4 093	257	338	116
Spain	RC	Spanish	3365	320	11	75	7 416	258	352	229
France	RC	French	3273	320	8	75	15 699	375	544	340
Eire	RC	Gaelic, English	3692	680	10	74	6 184	206	236	208
Italy	RC	Italian	3494	230	11	75	13 052	243	406	366
Luxembourg	RC	French, German	3850	735	12	72	16 951	94	587	400
Netherlands	RC, Protestant	Dutch	3258	450	8	76	14 625	310	382	335
Portugal	RC	Portuguese	3134	410	17	73	3 250	151	169	N/A
U.K.	Protestant, RC	English, Welsh Gaelic	3218	680 (1981)	10	75	10 120	328	521	304
USA	–	–	3642	470	11	75	18 448	790	N/A	540
JAPAN	–	–	2858	660	6	77	19 464	556	517	226
USSR	–	–	3394	270	29	72	N/A	308	N/A	N/A
TURKEY	–	–	3146	1380	110	64	1 184	118	58	N/A

	Size of households %					
	1	2	3	4	5 or more	
Belgium	23	30	20	16	11	(81)
Denmark	30	31	16	16	7	(81)
W. Germany	31	29	18	14	8	(82)
Greece	15	25	20	24	16	(81)
Spain	–	–	–	–	–	–
France	24	29	19	16	12	(82)
Eire	17	20	15	16↑	32	(82)
Italy	18↓	24↓	22	21↓	15	(81)
Luxembourg	21↓	28	21	18↓	12	(81)
Netherlands	22	30	15↓	21↓	12	(81)
Portugal	13	23	23	20	21	(81)
U.K.	22↓	32↓	17	18	11	(81)
Turkey	4	9	11	16	60	(75)
USSR(¹)	N/A	25	26	24	25	(70)
USA	23	31	17	16	13	(88)

(¹) 2 or more persons

European lifestyles

If you have travelled to other countries in Europe or if you have a penfriend in another European country you will be fully aware of the different lifestyles which exist. Lifestyles depend on several factors. For example, the nature of jobs which people do, the environment and climate they live in, their religion, history and culture. Even in the UK we have experience of many of the lifestyles through the food and drink which we can now buy. Many countries have their own national dishes like paella in Spain and pasta in Italy. Countries also have their own national dress, traditions and festivals (see Figure 2). Many of these can be experienced in the UK. There are festivals (Cannes Film Festival), sporting competitions (Europa Cup) and contests (Eurovision Song Contest) which help to bring countries together.

Figure 2   Customs and traditions

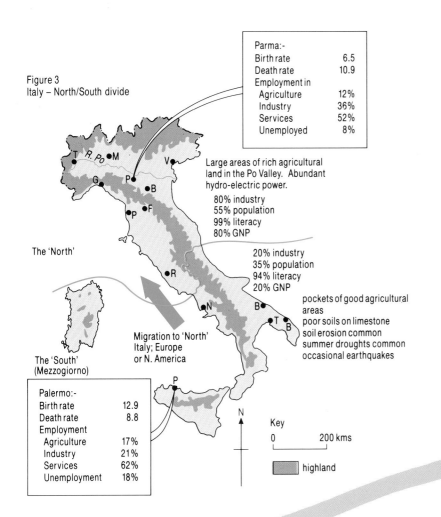

Figure 3
Italy – North/South divide

Parma:-
Birth rate   6.5
Death rate   10.9
Employment in
  Agriculture   12%
  Industry   36%
  Services   52%
  Unemployed   8%

Large areas of rich agricultural
land in the Po Valley. Abundant
hydro-electric power.

80% industry
55% population
99% literacy
80% GNP

The 'North'

20% industry
35% population
94% literacy
20% GNP

pockets of good agricultural
areas
poor soils on limestone
soil erosion common
summer droughts common
occasional earthquakes

Migration to 'North'
Italy; Europe
or N. America

The 'South'
(Mezzogiorno)

Palermo:-
Birth rate   12.9
Death rate   8.8
Employment
  Agriculture   17%
  Industry   21%
  Services   62%
  Unemployment   18%

Key
0   200 kms

highland

Case study – Italy

One country where there are great contrasts in the quality of life is Italy. Look at the information in Figure 3 to see the contrasts between the north and south (Mezzogiorno) of Italy.

The Mezzogiorno of Italy

One area which has been receiving large amounts of aid from the EC is the 'Mezzogiorno' (Southern Italy). Read the account of this area written just before the Second World War in Figure 4. In 1950 the 'Cassa per il Mezzogiorno' (Southern Fund) was set up by the Italian Government. Various plans have been adopted to help the area. Money was received from the Government and the EC and allocated to various reforms according to the needs at the time. These are shown in Figure 5. Over the

Figure 4

'The village itself was merely a group of scattered white houses at the summit of the hill. It is like being on a sea of chalk, monotonous and without trees. The square was no more than a widening of the single street, and it contained a fountain which was always surrounded by women, old and young, each with small wooden baskets balanced on their heads.
The houses were nearly all of one room, with no windows, drawing their light from the door. The one room served as kitchen, bedroom, and usually as quarters for the barnyard animals. On one side was the stove; sticks brought in every day from the fields served as fuel. The walls and ceilings were blackened with smoke. The room was almost entirely filled with an enormous bed; in it slept the whole family, father, mother and children. The smaller children slept in reed cradles hung from the ceiling above the bed, while under the bed slept the animals.'
'The second aspect of the trouble is economic, the dilemma of poverty. The land has been gradually impoverished; the forests have been cut down, the rivers have been reduced to mountain streams that often run dry, and livestock has become scarce. Instead of cultivating trees and pasture lands there has been an unfortunate attempt to raise wheat in soil that does not favour it. There is no capital, no industry, no savings, no schools; emigration is no longer possible, taxes are unduly heavy, and malaria is everywhere. All this is in large part due to the ill-advised intentions and efforts of the State, a State in which the peasants cannot feel they have a share, and which has brought them only poverty and deserts.
Finally, there is the social side of the problem. It is generally held that the big landed estates and their owners are at fault. The absentee owner, who lives in Naples, or Rome, or Palermo, is at least, far away and does not interfere with their daily life.'
(Carlo Levi, *Christ stopped at Eboli*)

Money spent by Cassa Per Il Mezzogiorno		
	1955	1980
Improving farming	68%	21%
Improving Communications	14%	8%
Improving water supply	10%	12%
Developing industry	4%	43%
Developing tourism	3%	6%
Others:-	1%	10%

Figure 5   Allocation of Southern Fund

Figure 6   Changes in the Mezzogiorno since 1950

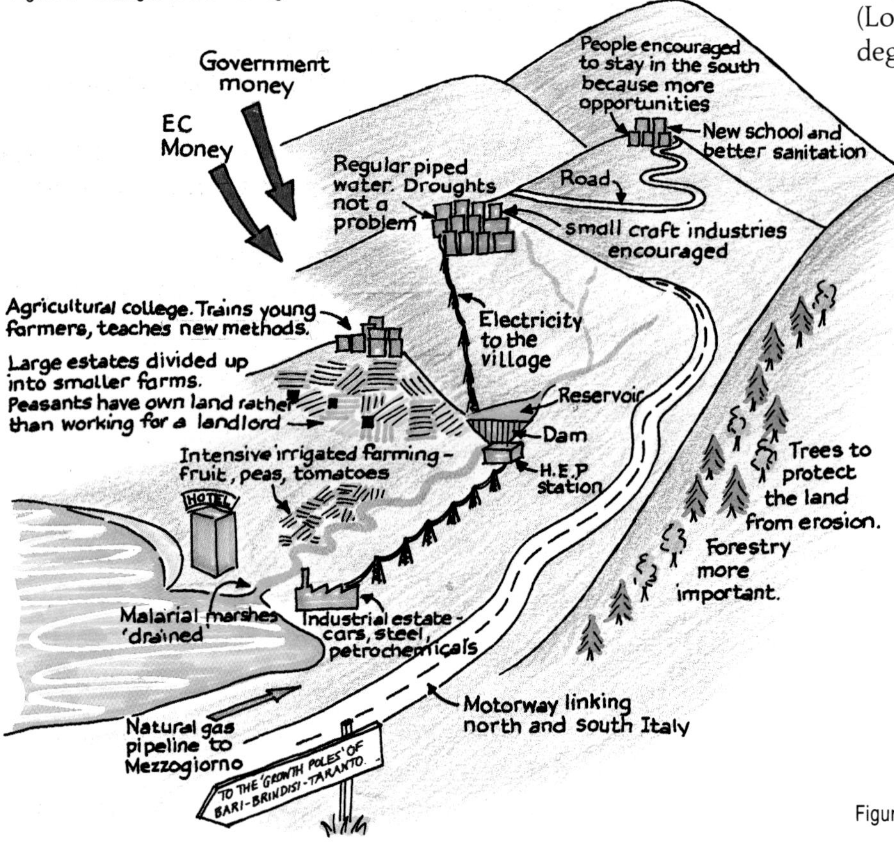

30 years several changes have taken place. (Look at Figure 6.) There have been varying degrees of success as you can see in Figure 7.

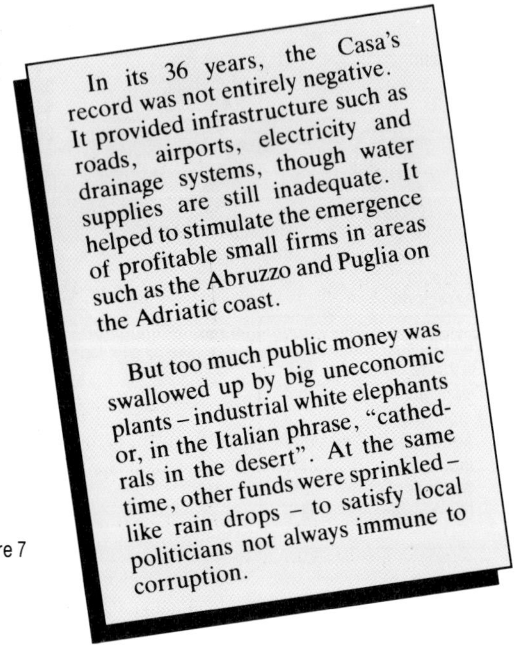

In its 36 years, the Casa's record was not entirely negative. It provided infrastructure such as roads, airports, electricity and drainage systems, though water supplies are still inadequate. It helped to stimulate the emergence of profitable small firms in areas such as the Abruzzo and Puglia on the Adriatic coast.

But too much public money was swallowed up by big uneconomic plants – industrial white elephants or, in the Italian phrase, "cathedrals in the desert". At the same time, other funds were sprinkled – like rain drops – to satisfy local politicians not always immune to corruption.

Figure 7

Activities

1 a Look at Figure 8 which shows some information about Paolo – a 13 year old boy living in southern Italy. Draw a similar diagram to show what you do in a typical day.
   b Paolo considered friends and family as being important to his quality of life. In two minutes write down 10 factors which *you* think are necessary for a good quality of life or standard of living. Rank these from 1–10 (1 being the most important).
   c Do you think this list would vary amongst children living in other EC countries? Give reasons for your answer.

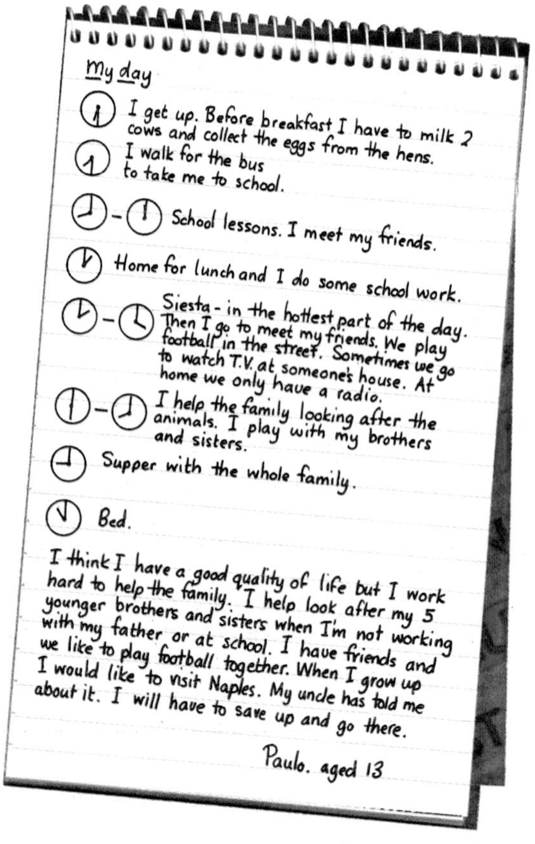

Figure 8

My day

① I get up. Before breakfast I have to milk 2 cows and collect the eggs from the hens.

① I walk for the bus to take me to school.

①–① School lessons. I meet my friends.

① Home for lunch and I do some school work.

①–① Siesta – in the hottest part of the day. Then I go to meet my friends. We play football in the street. Sometimes we go to watch T.V. at someone's house. At home we only have a radio.

①–① I help the family looking after the animals. I play with my brothers and sisters.

① Supper with the whole family.

① Bed.

I think I have a good quality of life but I work hard to help the family. I help look after my 5 younger brothers and sisters when I'm not working with my father or at school. I have friends and we like to play football together. When I grow up I would like to visit Naples. My uncle has told me about it. I will have to save up and go there.

Paulo. aged 13

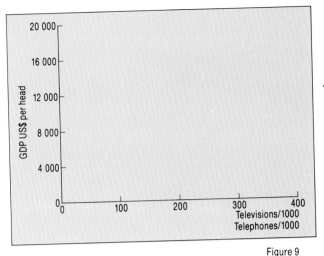

Figure 9

2 Using the data in Figure 1 answer the following questions:
 a Which is the richest country in the EC according to GDP per head?
 b Which is the poorest country in the EC according to GDP per head?
 c Compare the two countries mentioned in *a* and *b*. Consider those factors which show the greatest contrast between the countries.
 d i Make a copy of the graph axes in Figure 9. Plot the points comparing 'GDP per head' with *either* 'televisions' *or* 'telephones per 1000'. This is a **scattergraph**, so do not join the points.
  ii Using the instructions in Figure 10, draw on the **best fit line**.
  iii Describe the relationship you have produced. Are there any residuals? Label them on the graph.

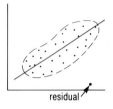

a positive relationship   a negative relationship   no relationship   residual

The best fit line joins as many dots as possible. It is a straight line and shows the general trend of the information. It is easier to draw if you lightly draw round the outline of all your dots. Then draw a straight line to cut the shape produced in half. A residual is a dot which is an 'odd one out' and does not agree with the rest of the information.

Figure 10   Drawing scattergraphs

3 Make a careful copy of the map of Italy in Figure 3. Name the following:
 ● The Alps and Appennines   ● Sardinia, Sicily
 ● The cities marked   ● The Mezzogiorno

4 In your own words write a few sentences about the differences in the quality of life in northern and southern Italy.

5 Look at Figure 5. What was the most important use for the money in
 a 1955?
 b 1980?
 c Figure 6 shows some of the changes which have taken place in the Mezzogiorno. Choose five changes and for each suggest the reasons why it was introduced.
 d Bari, Brindisi and Taranto are mentioned as **growth poles**. These are areas where development of industry is encouraged. Why do you think these areas are called growth poles?

e In Figure 7, the industrial developments were referred to as 'cathedrals in the desert'. Discuss with your neighbour what you think this means and why they are called this.

f How will the development of tourism help the area and the people?

g Write a summary paragraph giving your views on whether the quality of life has been improved.

Dictionary

core   a dynamic area with high population densities and immigration, most industry and investment etc.

GDP   (Gross Domestic Product) per head – the total value of the goods and services produced in the country divided by the population. It is a good indicator of the wealth of the country.

green belt   an area of protected land around a settlement where building and development are strictly controlled

migration   movement of people from place to place including **emigration** and **immigration**

multicultural society   a society with people of different races, colours, religions and cultures

periphery   the area on the outskirts where emigration and low industrial development are typical problems

population density   number of people per km²

rural depopulation   the decrease in population in countryside areas due to emigration

7 Settlement

Settlement site

Many settlements began their life hundreds of years ago. Most began as very small places, perhaps just a collection of a few dwellings. The first settlements were built with very different needs from today. People needed to farm so soils and climate were important. There were no mains water pipes, gas or electricity so a good supply of water and fuel was important. Often the people had to defend themselves from attack by invaders and so a good defensive site was important. This may be a hilltop (Figure 1), the inside of a river bend or near a castle (Figure 2). All these reasons why settlements were built are called **siting factors**. The site of a settlement is the point on the ground where it is built.

People began to trade and paths were worn from one village to another. The villages which were easier to reach grew as a market developed. These villages were often where several routes met (**route centres**), such as a gap between hills or at a bridging point of a river. As trade grew shops, churches and inns were built and gradually the village grew into a small town.

During the Industrial Revolution, roads and railways were built and industry developed. Towns grew quickly on coalfields as the mines and other industries attracted people to the area. Many people left the rural areas to come and work in the towns and cities. This process of **urbanisation** has continued today.

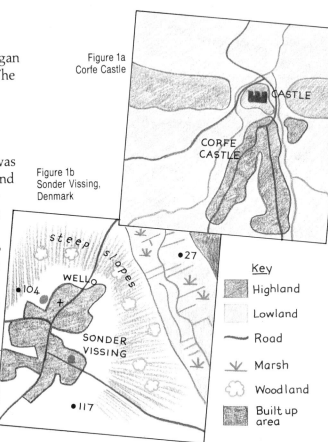

Figure 1a
Corfe Castle

Figure 1b
Sonder Vissing, Denmark

Key
- Highland
- Lowland
- Road
- Marsh
- Woodland
- Built up area

Settlement types

There are many different sized settlements. These can be arranged in order of size to give a **hierarchy** of settlements. The settlements also do a wide variety of 'jobs'. These are the **functions** of a settlement. The larger the town, the greater the number of functions it tends to offer.

Patterning settlement in the EC

In the European Community today there are three main characteristics of settlement:
- most people live in the urban areas (towns and cities), over 65% in most EC countries
- there are 'empty' areas where few people live, mostly in the remote rural areas
- many of the largest urban areas or **conurbations** are capital cities or on the coalfields of Europe.

Figure 2   Caernarvon

Activities

1 In small groups study the maps and photograph in Figures 1 and 2. Discuss the reasons why each one was a good site for an early settlement. Record your results and present your findings to the rest of the class.

2 The table in Figure 3 shows the percentage of people living in urban areas in the European Community. The countries are written in rank order, with the smallest percentage first.
On an outline map of Europe, label the EC countries. Shade each country according to which group it falls into. Use the following colour scheme:

Yellow 0–20%
Orange 21–40%
Red 41–60%
Brown 61–80%
Black 81–100%
Add the key to your map.

Figure 3

EC Country	%
Portugal	30
Eire	58
Greece	65
Luxembourg	68
Italy	69
Spain	74
U.K.	76
France	78
Denmark	84
Netherlands	88
West Germany	92
Belgium	95

3 a Mr and Mrs Oxley and their three children left their farm called Hare Hills in Yorkshire to go on holiday in Scotland. On the journey they stayed overnight in Newcastle-upon-Tyne, part of the Tyneside conurbation. The next day they motored north and stopped for lunch in the market town of Alnwick. They used the side roads to go further north passing through many small hamlets such as Newham. They arrived at their holiday village of Ford near the Scottish border at six o'clock. During their holiday, they are going to visit Scotland's capital city, Edinburgh and the town of Berwick-upon-Tweed which is also a port.

The table shows a settlement hierarchy. Copy the table and complete column 3.

1 Settlement	2 Population size	3 Example from paragraph above	4 Example from your own local area
Isolated farm	1–10		
Hamlet	11–100		
Village	101–2000		
Market town	2001–15 000		
Town	15 001–100 000		
City	100 001–1 000 000		
Capital city	Over 1 000 001		
Conurbation			

b Now complete column 4 by giving an example of each settlement from your own area.
c Which settlements in the hierarchy are
  i rural?
  ii urban?
d What is a **conurbation**? Where are they usually located?

7.2 Shops and services

In the last unit you saw how settlements can be put into a hierarchy or placed in order according to their size of population. Settlements can also be put into an **order** based on the shops and services they offer.

Large cities and conurbations tend to have more shops and services than smaller settlements. A village may have a church, post office, public house and general foodstore. The city centre or **Central Business District** in a large city has many shops and offices and large department stores.

In a town or city a shopping hierarchy can be identified as follows:
- Many small corner shops
- A few small shopping parades either alongside main roads or in housing estates
- Two or three larger shopping areas
- The Central Business District (CBD) which is the main central shopping area
- Modern out of town shopping centres and **hypermarkets** built on the edges of cities.

Figure 1   A hypermarket near Bordeaux

A CITY UNDER ONE ROOF

The North East weather is often unpredictable – but the weekly shopping always goes on. That's why the MetroCentre have ensured that comfort and necessity come hand in hand – regardless of the weather.

Pop into our 600 seating capacity Clockworks Food Court for example – there you'll find beautiful surrounds and the biggest range of appetising food in the North East, that will cater for all your family's tastes.

The Garden Court
Garden enthusiasts can take a leisurely stroll through the colourful garden court.

When the shopping is done there's always the AMC's superb 10 screen cinema to visit. Showing all the latest films all day and every day. Keep an eye on your local press for details.

From 27th November the kids can enjoy a special Christmas treat and meet the MetroCentre's Santa. This looks set to be an even bigger success than last year, only this year we're going to make it absolutely free! So no matter what you decide to do, you'll find the MetroCentre really has all your needs covered.

The first hypermarket was opened in France in 1960. It was a single store similar to the one shown in Figure 1. Today's hypermarkets are large shopping centres often with a large supermarket and other smaller shops. Figure 2 describes the MetroCentre Hypermarket at Gateshead.

Hypermarkets are built in *out of town* locations. The rates and rents are lower and this allows the buildings to be larger and prices to be cheaper. There is more space for the large single storey stores, for the free car parks and for future expansion. The hypermarkets are close to urban areas for customers and often beside a motorway. The motorway gives access for shoppers from an even wider area and for the delivery of goods.

Small shopping areas tend to provide 'everyday' or **low-order** goods. The larger shopping areas provide both low-order goods and luxury items called **high-order** goods. These high-order goods like carpets, furniture and televisions are bought less often by people. High-order goods are only found in large shopping areas because the shops need a large **catchment area** to support them. This catchment area is called the **sphere of influence**.

Figure 2

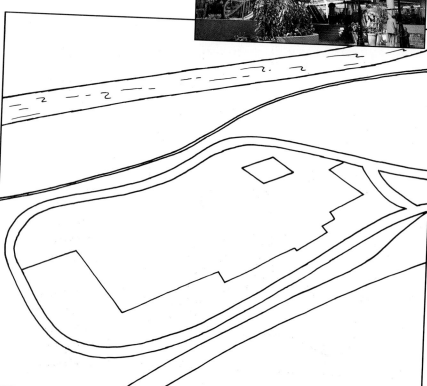

Activities

1 a Copy the checklist in Figure 3. Tick the boxes if you think each shop or service will be found in that settlement. Base your answers on settlements near where you live. The village has been done for you. Add up the total number of shops in each settlement.

b Copy the graph axes from Figure 4 and complete a **scattergraph** using the total figures from your table. Mark each settlement with a small cross on your graph. Add the following towns to your graph:

	Population	Number of shops
Settlement A	10 000	10
B	35 000	14
C	60 000	16
D	2 000	3
E	52 000	45
F	80 000	62
G	29 000	26
H	5 000	14
I	150 000	86
J	82 000	56
K	260 000	96

Draw a **best fit line** on your graph.

c What does your graph tell you about the size of a settlement and the number of shops it has? Explain your findings.

2 a Using the information in Figure 5, count the number of each type of shopping area. Put the result on a copy of the table shown below.

Shopping hierarchy	Number of each type of shop in a city
Hypermarket	
CBD	
Large shopping area	
Shopping parade	
Corner shop	

b Write down what the table tells you about the numbers of each type of shopping area in a town.

c What does CBD stand for?

d Copy the sentences below choosing the correct word(s).
The CBD is (in the centre/on the outskirts) of a settlement.
The corner shops are (scattered/clustered) in the housing areas.
Most corner shops are (close to/away from) the city centre.
The hypermarket is (on the edge/in the centre) of the city, near the (river/motorway).
Shopping parades are found along the (motorway/main roads) leading to the city centre.

Figure 3

Shops and Services	Village	Small Town	City
population	(2000)	(15 000)	(100 000)
Large chain store eg Marks & Spencer	✗		
Post Office	✓		
Newspaper Printers	✗		
Deparment Store	✗		
Bus Station	✗		
Factory	✓		
Primary School	✗		
New Housing Estate	✗		
Cinema	✗		
High Rise Flats	✓		
Pub	✗		
Library	✗		
Hospital	✗		
Railway Station	✗		
Electrical Shop	✗		
University	✗		
Supermarket	✗		
Government Offices	✓		
Church	✗		
Comprehensive School			
Total	4		

Figure 4

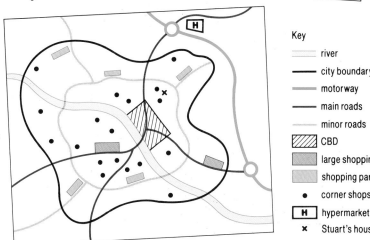

Figure 5

3 Figure 2 gives information about the MetroCentre Hypermarket in Gateshead, Tyne and Wear. It is the largest shopping and leisure complex in the EC. It is a modern out of town shopping centre.

a In small groups study the information and record your group's views on the following:
- Is the MetroCentre in a good location and why? Think about space, access, cost of land, nearby population centres.
- What effect is the Metro Centre likely to have on:
  – the CBD in Newcastle?
  – the edge of the urban area where it is built? Think about what the land may have been used for and what the centre looks like.
- What are the advantages for shoppers in hypermarkets?
- Are there any disadvantages of using hypermarkets?

b Study the aerial photograph of the MetroCentre in Figure 2c. Copy Figure 2d and complete the sketch map to show all the features of the hypermarket.

c Using a map of your local area, decide as a group where the best place would be to locate a new hypermarket or out-of-town shopping centre. On a large piece of paper, draw a sketch map to show its location. Write down the reasons why you chose the site and any disadvantages you can see. Present your idea to the rest of the class. Have a vote at the end of all the presentations – Where would your class build the next hypermarket in your local area?

7.3   Case study – conurbations

London

The table in Figure 1 shows that London is Europe's third largest conurbation, beaten only by Paris in France and the Rhine–Ruhr region in Germany. London is also the capital city of the UK and its largest urban area. The city has a great number of functions because of its national importance.

The city began as a small settlement on the banks of the River Thames. The early site of London is shown on the map in Figure 2. The first settlement was built by the Romans and called Londinium. It had a defensive wall and a small port for fishing and trade. This old part of the city covered the same area as the City of London today.

Since then the city has grown and its **form** or shape has changed. Notice in Figure 2 how the city has grown outwards in rings so that the newest buildings are on the edge. There are, however, some new buildings in the centre – these have been built to replace those bombed during the Second World War or to replace derelict buildings. Such building is called **infilling** and one example is the London Docklands scheme which aims to improve an inner city area.

London is such a large city that it can be divided up into areas or **zones** of different ages and zones of different **land uses**, such as housing, industry, offices, shops and recreation areas.

Conurbation	Population in millions
Paris	8.7
Rhine-Ruhr	7.8
London	7.7
Madrid	4.1
Rome	3.1
Athens	3.0
Milan	2.8
Barcelona	2.7
Naples	2.6
West Midlands	2.4
Manchester	2.3
West Berlin	1.9

Figure 1

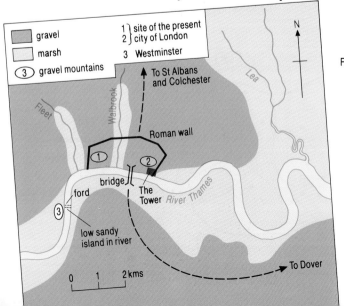

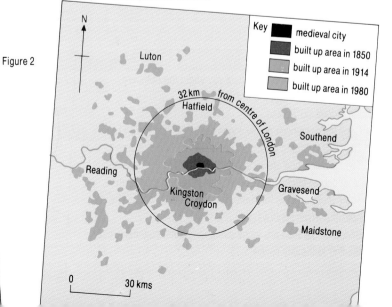

Figure 2

In London, the main CBD in the City is very specialised so there are many other smaller CBDs which cater for the needs of the local people. Figure 3 has a land use map of a part of London.

London also has its fair share of problems. In London there is great traffic congestion caused by over 1 million commuters trying to get to work each day; there are housing and employment shortages; decline in the inner city areas and the high cost of housing to name but a few. Large amounts of money are being spent in London to try to solve the problems and to give the 7.7 million people a better quality of life

Figure 3
Land use in
Central London

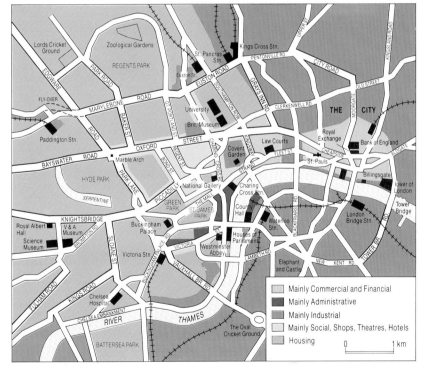

Legend:
- Mainly Commercial and Financial
- Mainly Administrative
- Mainly Industrial
- Mainly Social, Shops, Theatres, Hotels
- Housing

0   1 km

Activities

1 Study the table in Figure 1. On an outline map of Europe, mark and label the location of the 12 places in the table. Either plot bars at each location to show the population of the conurbation or use a symbol to represent 1 million people and build up a map using the **pictograms**. Your pictogram may be a stick figure like this ☆. Each one could represent 1 million people and so Paris would need 8.7 stick figures placed on the map. For the 0.7 you could draw a portion of your stick figure, say, missing off the arms or legs!
Add a key and a suitable title.

a Which of these 12 largest conurbations are capital cities?

b Which of these 12 are located on coalfields? (The map on page 128 (Figure 2) shows the EC coalfields.)

c Those which are left are either ports, important industrial areas or past capital cities. Which are which?

2 Study the maps showing the site and growth of London (Figure 2). In pairs discuss reasons for the early site of London and describe the way it has grown. Write a paragraph about the site and growth of London. Include how the form or shape of the city has changed over the centuries.

3 Figure 4 shows some silhouettes of landscapes you might see in London.

a Copy and complete the table. Choose a zone from the following list for column 2 and use the map in Figure 2 to give an actual London example of each zone.

    industrial zone   housing zone   CBD
    recreation/open space   Government offices

b Can you name the place or places in London famous for:

    tennis championships   cricket test matches   the FA Cup Final?

c Where would foreign visitors arrive by air into London?

d Where would you go shopping in London?

e What would you expect to see if you visited:

    Harley Street   Kings Cross   Billingsgate   Regents Park?

silhouette	zone	London example

Figure 4

Figure 5

Spain's "Top 7" Cities 1989

Rank	City	Population
1	Madrid	3 108 463
2	Barcelona	1 712 350
3	Valencia	749 574
4	Seville	669 976
5	Zaragosa	586 574
6	Malaga	555 518
7	Bilbao	384 129

Case study – Madrid and Barcelona

Study Figure 5 which shows the top seven cities in Spain in rank order. Find a map of Spain in your atlas and locate each city.

Madrid is the capital city and the largest city of Spain. It is Europe's highest capital at over 600 metres above sea level. It is located in the heart of the country on a large plateau called the Spanish Meseta. The countryside around Madrid is barren grassland and scrub (see page 45), it is unproductive farmland and the population is sparse.

Madrid began with the building of a castle by the Moors. In 1561 it was made the seat of Government. Since then the city has expanded although it had to be rebuilt after the devastation caused during the Spanish Civil War.

The city of Madrid has distinct zones. Industry is in the south-east near the Barcelona–Madrid railway terminal. Vehicles, electrical equipment, aircraft, textiles and food processing are important industries of the city. Service industries also employ many people with the Government and administration, transport and tourism. In the old centre of Madrid there are many fine buildings e.g. the Royal Palace and the Prado Museum (Figure 6) along with cafés, restaurants, theatres and nightclubs. The shops of Madrid are among the finest in Europe. The city centre is surrounded by modern suburbs.

Madrid is the centre of rail, road and air transport and has its own underground railway system. An aqueduct brings water to the city to supply the industry and domestic needs.

Barcelona is the second city of Spain with the main port (Figure 7) and the largest manufacturing sector. The port is man-made and it imports the raw materials and exports the finished goods for the industries in the local area e.g. textiles, diesel engines, cars, ships, foodstuffs. It is also important for commerce, finance and tourism. Barcelona airport receives most of the holidaymakers heading for the Costa Brava.

Figure 6a   Royal Palace, Madrid

Figure 6b   The Prado Museum, Madrid

Figure 7   Port of Barcelona

Activities

1 Draw an outline map of Spain and label the cities named in Figure 5. On your map locate and name the upland areas and the main rivers with the help of an atlas.
  a Describe the location of these 'top' cities in Spain.
  b Do you notice anything unusual about the location of Madrid?

2 Draw a line graph to show the figures in Figure 5. Plot the population on the y axis and the rank of the city along the x axis.
  a About how many times larger is Madrid than Barcelona?
  b Why are Madrid and Barcelona the largest cities in Spain?

3 a Madrid has a central location in Spain. Study an atlas map of Europe and write a list of the other European capitals which have a central location. Write a second list of those countries whose capital city is not in the centre of the country.
  b With your neighbour discuss the advantages of the capital city being in the centre of a country. Are there any disadvantages? Record your results and contribute to a class discussion about the location of Madrid and other capital cities.

7.4 Planning in urban areas

Many of the urban areas in the European Community have problems – housing shortages, traffic jams, overcrowding, decaying inner cities, and unemployment. Most EC Governments are planning to improve life in the urban areas and are providing money to carry out schemes. We shall study one way the planners are trying to **redevelop** or solve the problems of urban areas – Garden Festivals.

Garden Festivals in the UK

Garden Festivals (see Figure 1) are schemes aimed at revitalising old industrial areas. In these old industrial areas, much of the heavy industry has now closed down. The landscape is neglected with empty warehouses and derelict land.

In Liverpool in 1984, the scheme transformed rubbish heaps, silted docks and abandoned buildings into a place of beauty with thousands of trees, roses and other plants. It is hoped that each Festival will act as a **catalyst**, restoring confidence in an area and attracting investment.

For several years before the Festival takes place an area is cleared and the site is decorated with magnificent garden displays. National advertising attracts visitors from a wide area including overseas. Only one Festival is held every two years and they are gaining a reputation similar to the Olympic Games or World Cup. In Liverpool, the Queen opened the Festival and over 3 million people visited the site between its opening in May and its closing in October.

The 1990 Garden Festival at Gateshead was the 4th Festival in the UK, (see Figure 1). It was the launch of a large scheme which has reclaimed 81 hectares on the banks of the River Tyne. In the past the site had railway sidings, a cokeworks and gasworks. In four years the area was changed into parkland and space for recreation and housing.

The Garden Festival ran from May to October. About 4 million people visited the Garden Festival, boosting tourism in the area. After the festival new housing was built and a leisure park. The 2 000 000 trees and shrubs planted for the Festival all help to improve the area (see Figure 2).

Key

Garden Festival Sites

other assisted areas where government help is available in the form of grants and other incentives

Dundee

Glasgow 1988
Edinburgh

Newcastle
1990 Sunderland
Gateshead
Middlesbrough

Hull

1984 Liverpool
Manchester

Figure 1

Stoke 1986 Nottingham
East Anglia
Birmingham

1992 Ebbw Vale
Milford Haven
Swansea
London

Plymouth

0   100 kms

Figure 2a

Figure 2b

● The derelict soapworks next to the festival site.

Old factory may be given disguise

By MICK WARWICKER

A DERELICT factory towering above the National Garden Festival site may be disguised by an enormous work of art to give visitors a better impression of the North-East.

The former Co-op soapworks at Dunston, Gateshead, is an "eyesore" on the edge of the festival site which could not be demolished or altered because it is a listed building.

Festival organisers are seeking permission to cover the building with a huge floodlit painting of the George and Dragon statue in Old Eldon Square, Newcastle.

It was feared that the sight of the decaying complex could otherwise project an image of the region that the festival, due to open in May, is designed to overcome.

Gateshead planners are being asked to give special consent to cover the building with 30 billboards, to be painted by New York artist Mr. Tom Lawson.

The painting, covering 80pc of the stone walls facing the festival, will be part of the international contemporary art exhibition which will involve displays all over Tyneside.

The soapworks is listed by the Department of the Environment for its architectural interest, and is still owned by the Co-operative Wholesale Society, which has agreed to the painting project.

The Journal 31.3.90

Figure 2c

Aims of the Garden Festival

1. Reclaim derelict and polluted land
2. Improve an inner city area
3. Provide employment for 1400 people before and during the Festival
4. Long term employment
5. Attract investment
6. Change the image of the region
7. To provide enjoyment for people
8. Build housing, sport and leisure facilities

Figure 2d

Figure 2e

DIGGING FOR SUCCESS

The countdown to 1990 and Gateshead's National Garden Festival – the biggest ever seen in Britain – is already well under way.

The 180-acre site will be home for a six-month bonanza of flowers and fun which is expected to attract more than three million visitors to the Borough.

For Gateshead the Festival, which will cost around £30 million to mount, means a vital boost to the local economy with more jobs and a lasting legacy of new parkland stretching through the heart of the Borough making it a better place to live and work. Other parts of the site will be used for housing or leisure activities once the Festival closes.

Work on reclaiming 150 acres of derelict land has already started. The job at the Redheugh Gas Works is almost completed and work will start later this year on Norwood Sidings and Cokeworks.

To make it easy for visitors to tour the site, a new bridge has been built across the A692 Consett Route and surveys are now being done to see how Dunston Staiths can be repaired and used as a feature.

By the end of the year, a quarter of a million trees and shrubs will have been planted and already work has started on the enormous task of producing the millions of plants needed for the Festival. These will be propagated at the Council's Central Nursery in Lobley Hill.

The words National Garden Festival conjure up a picture of acres of flowers of every kind imaginable, but that's not the complete story. By 1990 the Gateshead site will have been turned into a feast of fun with something for everyone – from toddlers to grannies, from the serious student of gardening to the family who just want a good day out.

Festival Site

Checking timber from Dunston coal staiths.

Land reclamation at Redheugh.

Tree planting at Eslington Park.

Plants galore at the Central Nursery.

Bridges across the A692 Consett Route.

Activities

1 Study the map in Figure 1:

 a Name the five Garden Festival sites shown.

 b Choose five of the following statements which best describe the urban areas receiving help from the Government in England and Wales and give examples.

   on the coalfields   in East Anglia   in the conurbations
   along the south coast   at large ports   in the capital city
   mostly in the south and east   mostly in the north and west

 c What are the reasons why these areas need help?

 d Study the lists below. Copy down the statements from *both* lists which you think apply to the region in which you live.
   Features often found in:

Assisted Areas	Areas with no assistance
Industry closed down	In the south-east (not London)
In a coalfield area	Fertile farmland
In Cornwall	Industry is growing
A lot of derelict land, pitheaps etc.	A ferry port
Shipyards	Not a conurbation
Remote from London	Small towns and villages
Conurbation	A popular tourist resort
Hill sheep farming	A landscape with no pitheaps or quarries
Industrial estates	
Mining and quarrying	

Would you expect the area in which you live to be an Assisted Area?

2 Study the information on the Gateshead Garden Festival in Figure 2.

 a In small groups select one of the following roles and write a statement to present to the rest of the class saying why you think the Garden Festival and reclamation is a good or bad idea.
  ● A local resident of Dunston
  ● A hotel owner in the city of Newcastle
  ● The owner of a sports complex in Gateshead
  ● An unemployed person from Gateshead
  ● A bank manager and his family moving into the area
  ● A group of American tourists
  ● The Durham Gardeners' Club

 b Look again at the newspaper article – what would you do with the old Co-op Soapworks? Is the painting a good idea?

 c Draw a larger version of the Festival site. Design your own use of the land following the Festival. Include your ideas for the Dunston Staiths. You may like to do this in pairs or small groups.

7.5   Settlements in remote parts of the EC

There are many areas in the European Community which do not have large towns and cities (see Figure 1). Some of these areas are largely empty of people while others have some small settlements.

The settlements found in these rural areas are isolated farms, hamlets, villages and the occasional market town.

Just as our towns and cities have changed over the years, so have the rural settlements. Some farms and villages have been abandoned like the one shown in Figure 1. Others have expanded and changed their **function**. In some areas there have been few changes and the way of life has not altered very much in hundreds of years.

Figure 1

Case Study – Rural Greece

Greece is a small country in south-east Europe. It is a peninsula with an archipelago of islands. The islands such as Crete and the Cyclades make up 20% of the total land area. Large areas of the country are mountainous with dry, limestone scenery (see page 30). Find a map of Greece in your atlas and study the physical geography of the country. Notice how few large cities the country has.

Greece is one of the poorest members of the EC and much of its population of 9.8 million people live in small village communities. The most popular areas for settlement are the little plains near the sea because inland the mountains are steep, dry and have thin scrubby vegetation. The mountains can only be used for the grazing of sheep and goats so the carrying capacity of the land is low.

There are many small ports along the coast. The tiny harbours are surrounded by a cluster of small stone houses. At the base of the hills there are more small villages or even a town with its market square, white church and stone houses (Figure 2). The villages are surrounded by small fields of wheat, vines, olives and orchards. The life is very hard; the people work in the fields; they spin and weave their own clothes and the food is simple: bread, sheep-milk cheese, fish and fruit. In the mountains there are shepherds who look after the sheep and goats.

Figure 2

Figure 3

Figure 4

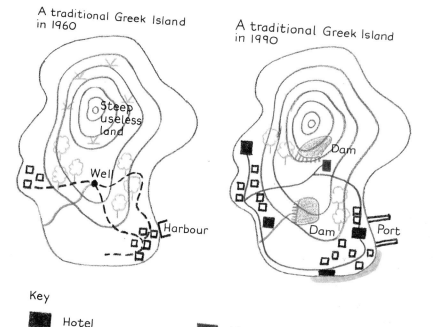

A traditional Greek Island in 1960

A traditional Greek Island in 1990

Steep useless land

Well

Harbour

Dam

Dam

Port

Key

■ Hotel

- - - Track

Orchards/vines

Houses

Mountain Barbeque Taverna

Grazing

Road

Beach

In the mountains there are some hilltop settlements (Figure 3). Greece has a long history of invasions and the frightened Greeks were often driven away from their coastal villages and forced to settle in the mountains. They chose a hilltop which provided them with a good defensive site and some of the villages have a hilltop fort. Around the village they cultivated small patches of land and grazed their animals.

In recent years, some of the hilltop settlements have become 'ghost towns'. Many of the villagers, especially the young people, have migrated to the cities in search of better jobs and living conditions. Only the old people are left behind and so the village and the fields decay. In other areas, there have been changes for the better. On the islands and in some inland villages tourism has helped to improve the services and the economy of the local people. Study Figure 4 which shows some of these changes.

Activities

Figure 5

1 In pairs, study the photographs in Figure 1. Explain why each one shows an area where few people will live. What types of work might be available in the places shown on the photographs?

2 Some of these low density areas are actually losing people. Farms and villages are being deserted as people **migrate** away to the towns and cities. Figure 1 shows a deserted farm in the Yorkshire Dales.

Why do you think people are leaving the rural areas? The cartoon in Figure 5 may give you some ideas.

3 Study the map in Figure 6 showing part of the Yorkshire Dales.

a On the map, isolated farms, hamlets and villages are shown. Count up the number of each type of settlement. Choose a symbol for each type of settlement (or you can use the ones shown) and finish the pyramid diagram shown in Figure 7. Don't forget a title and key.

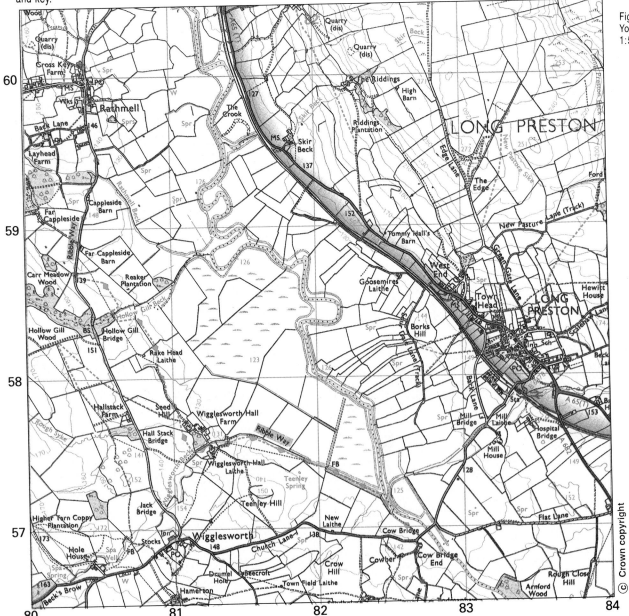

Figure 6
Yorkshire Dales,
1:50 000

© Crown copyright

b Describe what your diagram shows.

c Draw a sketch map of the area shown on the map. Mark and shade the land over 150 metres, the main rivers, the roads and the settlement. Use colour and add a key and title. (Look back to page 12 if you have forgotten how to draw a sketch map.) Add these labels: steepest slopes; flat land; flood prone land.

d Choose the correct sentences from the following list to describe the pattern of settlement:

The settlement is mostly along the roads
The farms are close together or **nucleated**
The settlements are mostly in the upland areas
The farms are far apart or **dispersed**
The villages are near a water supply
The settlements are mostly on the lower land
The people in this area are mostly farmers
The settlements avoid the land next to the river

4 Study an atlas map of Greece:

a What is the latitude of the most northerly and southerly points on the Greek mainland?.

b Crete is the largest Greek Island, what is its length?

c What countries border upon Greece?

d On an outline map of Greece, mark and label the main islands, mountains, rivers, seas and towns.

e What is the highest mountain of Greece?

5 Most people in Greece live around the coast. Why do you think this is? Write down as many reasons as you can. Write another list of the reasons why there are so few people living in the interior of Greece.

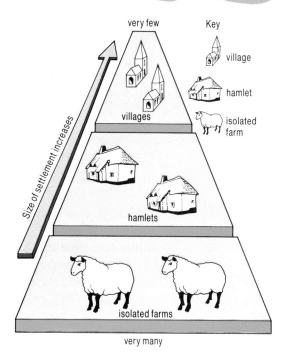

Figure 7

6 Study Figure 4 showing the changes on a Greek island. Imagine you have lived on the island during the changes. Write to your penpal describing the changes which have taken place and your feelings about them.

Dictionary

Central Business District the city centre with shops and offices
functions services and goods provided by a settlement
hierarchy a list in order of size or importance

high-order goods goods high in value, bought less often e.g. furniture
hypermarket a large out of town shopping centre on the edge of a city

low-order goods goods low in value, often bought frequently e.g. sweets
sphere of influence the area a settlement serves
urbanisation the concentration of people into towns and cities

8 Resources and energy

Europe is particularly rich in a variety of **resources**. Land is used for housing, farming, and forestry. Water supplies are used for fishing, drinking, watering crops, industry and power. From beneath the land surface, minerals and fuels are mined. Figure 1 shows how the Earth's resources are used.

Minerals, timber, energy supplies and water are all very important.

In the past people used the resources of the Earth without thinking much about it. If coal was needed mines were sunk. If timber was needed, trees were cut down. This still happens to some extent, although today more people are concerned that if resources continue

Figure 1
How the Earth's
resources are used

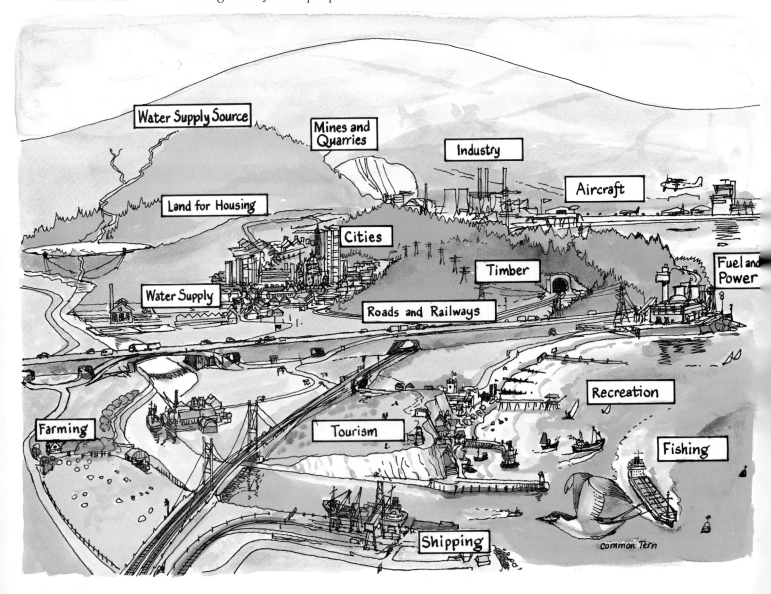

to be used at their present rate, some will become **exhausted**. Oil, for example, is only likely to last until 2020. Figure 2 shows the **depletion dates** for other minerals. Many resources are likely to be used up at an even faster rate. A growing population and a steady rise in living standards means more resources are needed.

As the population continues to increase the use of resources also increases so more waste is produced. This waste must be disposed of. As you have seen in Chapter 3 the atmosphere is polluted, causing acid rain. Other parts of the environment are also damaged by the **misuse** of resources. The North Sea, for example, is badly polluted and other environments are spoiled by mining and building. Figure 3 shows how human activity can harm our environment.

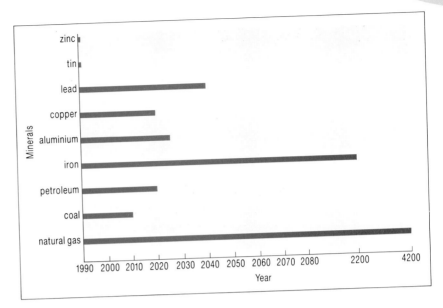

Figure 2   The life span of some minerals

Figure 3   How the Earth's resources are misused

Activities

1 Think about the following questions and write down any ideas you have.

What are the Earth's resources?

How do people use these resources?

How do people misuse these resources?

In small groups discuss your ideas and add any extra ideas to your own. Hold a class discussion about the resources of the Earth, their use and misuse.

After the discussion use the text and the Figures 1 and 3 to complete the table below to show how people use and misuse the resources of the Earth. Try to add some ideas of your own or from the discussions.

Resource	Uses	Misuse
Land		
Water		
Air		
Minerals		
Forest		
Energy supplies		

2 Human skills are used to turn natural resources into **manufactured** resources. Study the pictures in Figure 4 which show some natural resources, some human skills and some manufactured resources. Write each resource in the correct place in the table on right. One has been done to help you.

Figure 4   Resources and skills

Natural resources	Human resources	Manufactured resource
1 Stone	Sculptor	Statue
2		
3		
4		
5		
6		

8.2   Energy – keeping Europe going

Energy sources are among the most important resources. The types of energy used have changed over time. At first, people only had manpower and later came animal and wind power. Discoveries of coal, oil, gas and nuclear power have since taken place. In the future, **alternative** sources of energy such as solar, wind, wave and tidal power may be used. The photographs in Figures 2–5 show some examples of fuel and power.

People have learned to use new and different types of energy. This has allowed other developments to take place. For example, think of all the items you have in your home and school that use **electricity**.

The countries of the EC are some of the highest energy users in the world. Energy is vital for industry, transport, farming and in the

Figure 1

Energy sources of electricity in selected EC countries % (1989)			
	Fossil Fuels (Oil, Gas and Coal)	Hydroelectric Power	Nuclear Power
Belgium	39	1	60
Denmark	100	0	0
France	34	9	57
West Germany	86	2	12
Greece	98	2	0
Eire	97	3	0
Italy	86	13	0
Netherlands	99	0	1
U.K.	96	0	3
Spain	68	1	24
Portugal	16	8	0
		84	

home. The EC countries use a variety of energy sources (see Figure 1). Most countries use what they have available in their country. Italy for example, uses a large amount of hydroelectric power. This is because the Alps provide the fast flowing streams needed for its generation. The Netherlands uses a large amount of gas because there are large gas fields in the north-east of the country. France chose to develop nuclear power after the oil crisis in the 1970s which made the import of oil very expensive.

Energy sources like coal, oil and gas are **fossil fuels** which will eventually run out. These are called **finite** resources. Other energy sources like hydroelectric, wind and solar power will not run out. These are called **renewable** sources of energy. In the EC, most of the countries rely upon the finite energy sources. How will they obtain their energy in the future?

Many EC countries are not **self-sufficient** in energy. This means that they must import energy and this is expensive. The European Community imports 48% of all its energy needs although the amounts vary from country to country.

The EC countries are thinking about their future energy needs and 'keeping Europe going'. The European Community has planned an energy policy which has several aims:

- Energy conservation to reduce the wastage of energy.
- A reduction in the use of oil to reduce the need for oil imports.
- A target of 75% of energy to come from coal and nuclear power.
- Research into renewable forms of energy such as hydrolectric, wind, wave, tidal and solar.

Figure 2 Coalmine

Figure 3 Electricity pylons

Figure 4 Hydro-electric barrage

Figure 5 Animal power

Activities

1 What kinds of fuel and power do you use at home?

2 How would your life be different if you did not have electricity?

3 On an outline map of Europe plot the information in Figure 1. Draw a bar for each country and place it on or close to the country on the map. Draw each bar 1cm wide and 5cms long. Print the name of each country below your bar. Each bar represents 100%. Divide up each bar according to the amount of each fuel a country uses. Remember your scale is 1cm=20%.
Use a different colour for each energy type and add a key to your map. Add a title – The energy sources of the EC countries.
 a Which fuels supply the EC with most electricity?

b Why does Italy use 25% hydroelectric power but the Netherlands 0%?
c Why does France use 40% nuclear power?
d Which EC countries have no nuclear power? List all the reasons you can think of as to why some countries have no nuclear power.
e Are the main energy sources finite or renewable? What is the difference between the two?
f Why are more renewable forms of energy not being used?

8.3   Case study – energy in the UK

The UK uses a great variety of energy sources to meet the needs of its population of 56 million. The UK is almost self-sufficient in energy. There are supplies of coal, oil and gas. Some hydro-electric power is produced in the upland areas and several nuclear power stations have been built. The map in Figure 1 shows the distribution of the UK power sources.

Most of the UK's energy comes from the fossil fuels, the rest from nuclear and hydro-electric power (see Figure 2). The UK has very rich oil fields in the North Sea which produce enough oil for some to be exported. Nuclear power stations use uranium which the UK imports mainly from Canada. At the moment, more research is going into the use of renewable forms of energy, for example, a tidal barrage in the River Severn Estuary.

The generation of energy in the UK is of vital importance. Figure 3 shows the main uses of power, but, today people are worried about the damage being done to the environment. There is concern about acid rain, the threat of a nuclear accident and the damage to the land by opencast mining, oil spills and wind farms.

Figure 1
UK coal, oil, gas and nuclear resources

Key
● coal-fired power station
● oil-fired power stations
● HEP stations
☢ selected nuclear power stations
○ major oil refineries

oil fields
gas fields
coalfield

Figure 2
Primary energy use in the UK 1990

Figure 3
The use of energy in the UK 1990

other 13%
industry 27%
transport 33%
households 27%

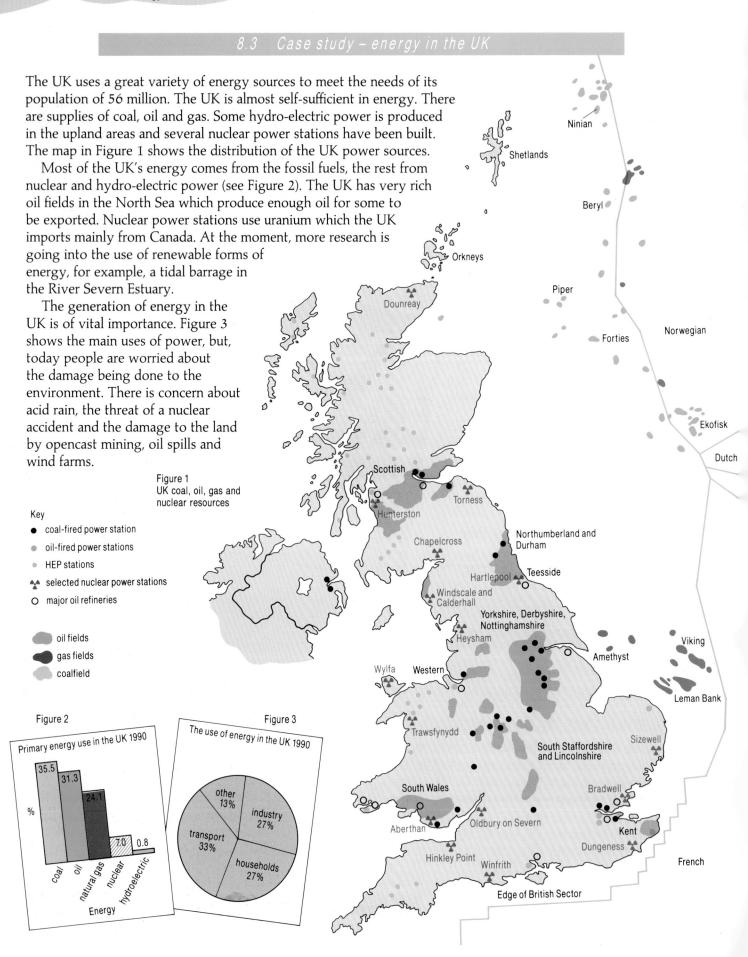

Activities

1 Tops and tails.

Match the correct statements, one from the left and one from the right. Use the map in Figure 1 and your atlas to help you.

Tops	Tails
a Most coalfired power stations are	in the mountainous areas
b Two North Sea oil fields are	at a port location
c Most hydro-electric stations are	on the coalfields
d Two North Sea gas fields are	Piper and Forties
e Most oil fired power stations are	Viking and Amethyst

Figure 4   Coal-fired power station

2 Most nuclear power stations are on the coast but away from main cities. Can you explain why?

3 Which nuclear power station is not on the coast? Look up its location in your atlas. Why do you think it is located at that point?

4 Describe the location of the hydro-electric power stations. Use a relief map in your atlas to help. Why are the HEP stations found in these parts of the UK?

5 Power stations are found in different areas because their needs are different. A coal or oil fired power station has different needs from HEP stations. Study the list below and copy down what you think are the five most important things needed by a coal fired power station. Study Figure 4, the photograph of a coal fired power station, to help you.

pretty scenery	iron ore nearby	hilly land
airport nearby	railway close	forest nearby
town nearby	open space	river nearby
motorway close	flat land	coalfield nearby

6 Imagine that National Power wants to build a power station at the place shown on the map in Figure 5. The station will burn coal.

a Some people do not want the power station to be built. In pairs discuss the reasons why. Write a report for your local radio station explaining why.

b Look again at the good and bad points of building the station. Which side would you take? Give reasons for your choice.

7 Read the newspaper article in Figure 6.

a What is geothermal power?

b What are its advantages and disadvantages?

c Why could geothermal power not be a possible energy source for all of the country?

8 Draw up a questionnaire with five questions to ask people about their views on power generation. For example, are they in favour of nuclear power, do they like the idea of wind farms and would they mind a power station being built within five kilometres of their home?

Collect all the class results together and draw some bar charts to show the results.

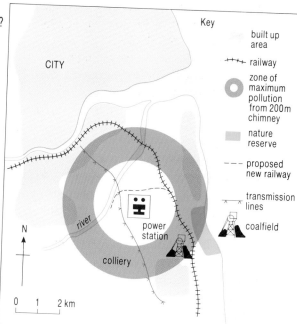

Figure 5   Proposed site for a coal-fired power station

Figure 6

THE DAILY TELEGRAPH, WEDNESDAY, DECEMBER 6, 1989

Project to harness geothermal power

By Roger Highfield Science Editor

AN APPEAL for £250,000 has been launched by Gateshead Council, the first step in a project to harness heat locked deep underground and turn it into a power source for the North East.

The British Geological Survey has identified Rowlands Gill, near Gateshead, as offering Britain's best prospect for "geothermal" heat and power, said Mr Ray Shenton, deputy director of architectural services of Gateshead Metropolitan Borough Council.

"It is a superb idea because it is a green energy source," he added. In hot dry rocks there is enough potential electricity production to keep the United Kingdom going for five years.

"Whether or not we can develop it is another question because it is such an expensive prospect," he added. "We are trying to raise £250,000 to extend the work which has already been conducted by the British Geological Survey to give us more information."

At depths of seven kilometres the temperature of the granite is predicted to be as high as 230 degrees Celsius, hot enough to produce superheated steam for local heating and to drive turbines to produce electricity to meet the needs of the North East "for the forseeable future," said Mr Shenton.

Gateshead is trying to raise the necessary money through grants from the Department of Energy, local industry and the European Community. Two boreholes at seven kilometres could in theory produce some 40 megawatts of energy, five megawatts of which could be turned into electricity.

Hot rocks research is already under way at the Cambourne School of Mines in Cornwall which has attracted £33 million Department of Energy funding.

The North Sea is a wonderful resource not just for the UK but for many countries which surround it. People use the sea in many different ways; including fishing, swimming, shipping, the extraction of oil and gas and water. The diagram in Figure 1 shows the different uses of the North Sea.

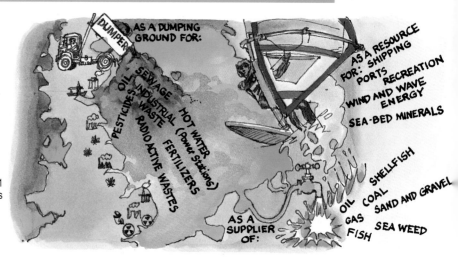

Figure 1
the North Sea – uses

Figure 2

1 Fishing

The North Sea has a rich marine life which has been fished for centuries. In the UK many ports e.g. Hull, Grimsby and Aberdeen have grown and thrived because of the fishing.

In recent years the fishing industry has declined. In the UK in the mid 1970s there were over 500 deep sea fishing trawlers, today there are less than 100. This decline is due to several reasons:

- Countries have put 200 mile fishing limits around their coasts which prevent boats from foreign countries fishing within those limits.
- The EC has put restrictions on the amounts of certain fish that can be caught; these are called **quotas**. The quotas are used to protect fish stocks from overfishing. Herring, haddock, cod and mackerel all have quotas.
- In recent times trawlers have become larger and refrigerated; fish tracking sonar and better navigation mean more fish are able to be caught and so fish stocks have decreased.
- Pollution of the North Sea has reduced catches.
- Large factory ships allow the trawlers to stay out at sea much longer.
- Competition from other countries such as Canada with cheaper fish to sell.

THE DAILY TELEGRAPH, MONDAY, MARCH 19, 1990

How trawlers are raking the North Sea to death

Heavy commercial fishing is not only dramatically cutting fish stocks, it is also posing a bigger threat to the ecosystem than pollution. Dr. Han Lindeboom calls for a halt to fishing in one quarter of the sea

THE North Sea is sending out more and more signals that it is truly ill – but the greatest threat is not from pollution. The effects of commercial fishing are almost certainly greater than all the problems of contamination.

The facts are startling. It is now a long time since dolphins or porpoises have been found near the Dutch coast. The catching of herring and mackerel has had to be banned, the numbers of cod are declining, and quotas are required for sole and plaice.

This disturbing state of affairs has prompted a study of the short-term effects of beam trawl fishing.

Beam trawl fishing, which is popular among Dutch fishermen, involves the use of two large nets held open by beams, which are dragged along the sea bed. Shoes, designed to glide over sea bed sediment, are mounted on the beam and linked by heavy chains which force fish into the nets. The complete apparatus, with a total weight under water of about 5,000 kg, is towed along at a speed of five or six knots.

In the recent Dutch research, when an area was trawled three times, 50 per cent of the heart urchins, starfish and certain polychaete worms disappeared, while 20 per cent of small crustaceans and shellfish were killed.

Research by RIVO has also shown that every square metre of the Dutch part of the North Sea is trawled at least once a year, and that there are several areas which are fished three to five times a year.

Danish research has shown that at least 600 sea mammals drown in Danish nets annually, while some 3,000 dolphins and porpoises also perish.

What is happening in the North Sea is that the fishing industry is causing a diverse ecological system to break down into one where only fast-growing, easily reproduced small organisms can survive. Large, slow-growing bivalves are disappearing and worms are taking their place. Slow-reproducing fish, such as sharks and rays are already more or less extinct in large parts of the North Sea, as are the big cod. Smaller, fast-growing species are on the increase.

And although some people blame pollution for the disappearance of the porpoises and dolphins in the North Sea, it is more likely that the fishing industry has played the key role. Besides drowning these animals in fish nets, fishermen have wiped out their most important prey – herring and mackerel.

Dr Han J. Lindeboom is Head of the Department of Applied Scientific Research a the Netherlands Institute for Sea Research in Texel, Holland.

2 Oil and gas in the North Sea

Oil and gas have taken millions of years to form. Plants and the dead bodies of tiny animals fell to the bed of the sea. They were mixed with and covered by mud and sand. Gradually the plants and animals rotted to form oil and the mud and sand were compressed into hard rocks. Figure 3 shows how the oil was formed.

The tiny droplets of oil were spread throughout the rocks. Earth movements have often crumpled the rocks to form concentrations of oil and gas called **traps**, as shown in Figure 4. It is these traps that the oil and gas companies want to find.

The oil and gas are found in **porous** rocks (rocks containing holes) and they are trapped by being surrounded by **impermeable** rocks, through which liquids cannot pass.

Once the oil has been discovered it is necessary to drill and force the oil to the surface. Huge oil rigs are used to extract the oil from under the ground. An oil rig like the one in Figure 5 will have about 140 people living and working 'on board'. There are dining rooms, a games room, a library and television and video facilities. The telephone system is very efficient as communication to the UK at all times is very important. There is a helicopter pad and lifeboats. The men who work on the rigs work 12 hours on and 12 hours off, 7 days a week. They stay on the rig for 10 to 14 days and then return home on leave. They must work whatever the weather. Their wages can be very high, often over £500 per week.

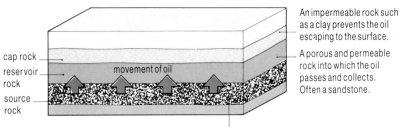

cap rock
reservoir rock
source rock
movement of oil

An impermeable rock such as a clay prevents the oil escaping to the surface.

A porous and permeable rock into which the oil passes and collects. Often a sandstone.

Usually a black shale representing mud laid down on the sea bed. Plankton trapped and buried in the the mud turned to oil as the result of bacterial action.

Figure 3   Formation of oil

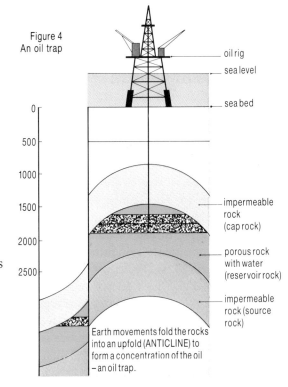

Figure 4
An oil trap

oil rig
sea level
sea bed

impermeable rock (cap rock)

porous rock with water (reservoir rock)

impermeable rock (source rock)

Earth movements fold the rocks into an upfold (ANTICLINE) to form a concentration of the oil – an oil trap.

Figure 5a   An oil rig

Nelson's Column

Figure 5b   Oil rig

The oil is called **crude oil** and it is thick, heavy and black. The crude oil is taken to an oil refinery either by pipeline or tanker. It is then **refined** to make it light for petrol, plastics and other products. At the refinery, the oil is heated in a column and different products are separated out at various temperatures.

In the North Sea, gas was discovered in 1965 and oil in 1970. Up until then the UK had been importing all its oil from the Middle Eastern countries. Today, the UK exports oil because the fields are so large. The largest gas field is the Leman Bank and the two main oil fields are Forties and Brent. The map in Figure 6 shows the North Sea gas and oil fields.

3 The North Sea or the Dead Sea?

The North Sea does not belong to one country and many share the resources it provides. There have been several International Conventions to try to control the use and the pollution of the North Sea. In November 1987 the UK Government hosted the Second North Sea Conference. At this conference it was agreed to end the dumping of harmful industrial wastes and to stop incineration at sea. The Third North Sea Conference was held in The Hague in March 1990 when further measures were agreed to protect and improve the condition of the North Sea. Figure 7 shows many of the problems of the North Sea.

The southern part of the North Sea and the waters closest to the shorelines are the worst affected. The pollution in the North Sea is from a variety of sources:

● Heavy metals like iron, zinc and mercury.
● Inorganic wastes e.g. pesticides, chlorine.
● Oil from rigs, spillages and land runoff thought to be 400 000 tonnes per year.
● Radioactive wastes e.g. those washed around the coast from Cap de la Hague in France and from Sellafield.
● Domestic sewage from pipelines. The UK is the only country to dump this at sea.
● Rubble and harbour dredgings.
● Incinerated wastes – these are wastes burned at sea which release gases into the atmosphere and wastes which fall to the sea bed. Many of these wastes are toxic.
● Effluent from the rivers flowing into the North Sea e.g. the Rhine, the Tees, the Thames and the Scheldt.
● Fertilisers which contain a lot of nitrogen and phosphates.

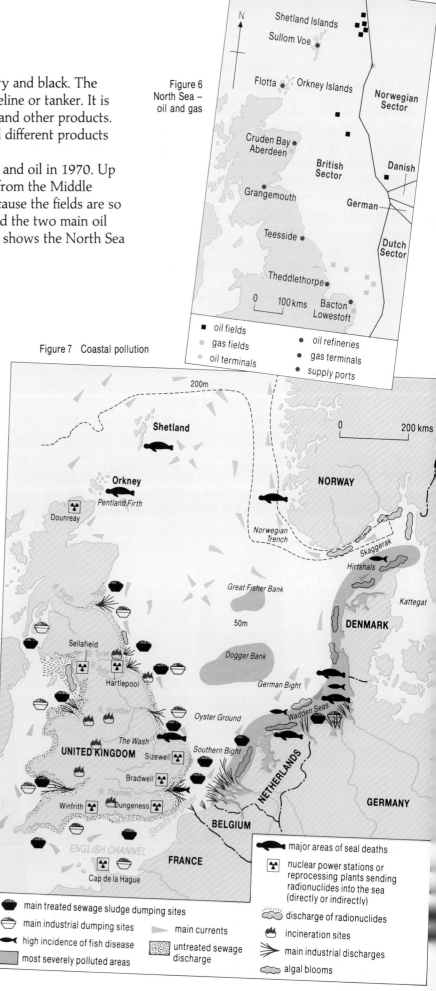

Figure 6 North Sea – oil and gas

Figure 7 Coastal pollution

The European Blue Flag Campaign

The European Blue Flag Campaign is sponsored by the EC and was launched in 1987 during the European Year of the Environment. The Campaign's aim is to have clean, safe beaches and water around our coasts. A Blue Flag (see Figure 8) is awarded for one year only and the stretch of coastline must reach very strict standards; one of the most important is water quality. Figure 8 describes the standards a coastline must meet to be given an award. Blue Flags may also be given to ports which have a high environmental quality.

In 1991, the UK succeeded in having a record number of Blue Flags since joining the scheme (see Figure 9). Yet many more beaches failed because of the persistent dumping of sewage and industrial waste. Figure 10 describes some of the problems of the dirty beaches.

Figure 8

CRITERIA FOR THE AWARD OF THE EUROPEAN BLUE FLAG FOR BEACHES 1989

The allocation of the Blue Flag to a bathing beach depends on its meeting a series of requirements.

Water and coastal quality
- No industrial or sewage discharge into the beach area.
- Reliable and frequent monitoring of bathing water.
- No visible oil pollution.
- Emergency plans to cope with oil or other pollution incidents.
- No algal materials growing or decaying in the beach area (except during or after storms, or on rocks).

Environmental education and information
- Prompt public warning of danger or major pollution.
- Laws covering beach use put on public display.
- Information on protected sites and/or rare or protected species publicly displayed and included in tourist information.
- Information on water quality publicly displayed.
- Education courses and activities or lectures for the public on the natural environment.
- Environmental Study Centres or Ecology Centres.

Beach area management and safety
- Beaches to be cleaned daily during the bathing season.
- Litterbins in adequate numbers, regularly emptied.
- Strict control of domestic animals in the beach area.
- Driving or vehicle racing on the beach prohibited.
- Adequate and clean toilet facilities with controlled sewage disposal.
- Adequate and operational life-saving equipment.
- First-aid post and life-guard.
- Safe access.
- Drinking water and telephones.
- facilities for handicapped persons.

Figure 9b

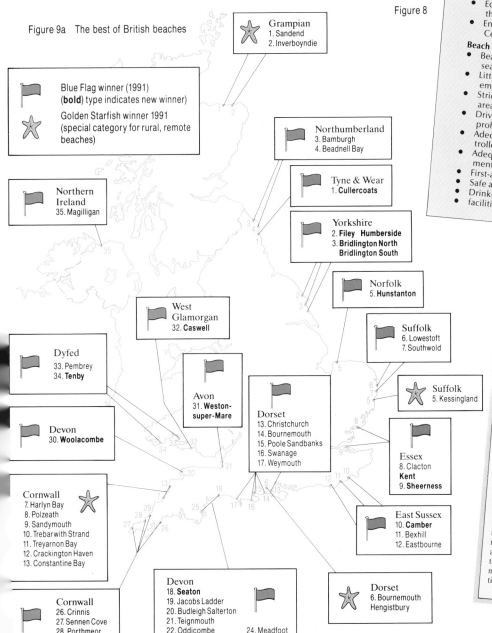

Figure 9a   The best of British beaches

Put out more Blue Flags

THIS week's announcement that 35 British beaches have been awarded European Blue Flags – a record number for Britain during the five years it has been taking part in the scheme – might appear to be cause for rejoicing.

The award of a Blue Flag, sponsored by the Commission of the European Communities and supported in Britain by the Tidy Britain Group and the English Tourist Board, is made to beaches with a high standard of water quality and which are cleaned daily during the bathing season and have good facilities, toilets, life-saving equipment and first aid. Blue Flag-winning beaches impose bans on dogs and prohibit driving or racing; there is also provision for environmental education, public information and safety.

While there is widespread satisfaction among environmental groups that a growing number of local councils and water authorities have finally begun to take action to clean up Britain's beaches, most people agree that there is still much more to do.

Britain's total of 35 Blue Flag beaches this year, for example, compares with more than 100 beaches in France that won Blue Flags last year, and over 130 in Spain. Critics point out that while 35 beaches were successful this year, this represents little more than half the 63 beaches that sought approval. The 35 flag winners are also just a small proportion of the 450 British areas designated as "bathing beaches" under the European Community's Bathing Water Directive.

Independent 8.6.91

Figure 10

Activities

1 Look at Figure 1 showing how we use the North Sea. Choose one of the uses and see if you can find out more information. You could combine your research with the rest of the class to produce a file or wall display.

2 a Draw a graph to show the following information. Write a sentence below to explain what the graph shows.

   UK haddock quotas: 1988 128 500 tons
   1989 54 400 tons
   1990 32 000 tons

   b The fish landings at Aberdeen were 100 000 tons in 1970 and 40 000 tons in 1989. Explain why the fish landings have declined.

3 Read the newspaper article in Figure 2.

   a Describe the method of fishing called **beam trawling**.

   b Write a list of the ways beam trawling is upsetting the North Sea **ecosystem**. (See Chapter 5 for more on ecosystems.)

4 Describe how North Sea oil was formed. Use the text and Figure 3 to help you.

5 Study the oil trap in Figure 4. Copy the following sentences fitting in the correct word from the diagram:

   The oil is trapped in the .... rock surrounded by impermeable rocks. The rocks in the trap bend .... and this is called an anticline. In the trap .... and .... are also found. The oil and gas are .... metres below sea level.

6 Make a large, neat copy of Figure 5a and using Figure 5b to help add the following labels in the correct place.

helideck   lifeboat   steel ballast tanks   living quarters   flare boom
drilling shafts   drilling derrick

7 a Nitrogen pollutes our rivers, lakes and seas. In recent years farmers have been applying more nitrogen fertilisers to the land. When it rains excess nitrogen is washed out of the soil into the rivers. The rivers carry the nitrogen into the North Sea. The following table gives you the amounts:

Nitrogen	
Thames	32 000 tonnes per year
Humber	41 000
Elbe	150 000
Weser	88 000
Rhine	420 000
Scheldt	60 000

Use these figures to draw flow lines from each river into the North Sea. The width of each line represents the amount of pollution. Use a scale of 1 mm = 20 000 tonnes per year. Colour in your flow lines and add a key.

b Have a close look at an atlas map of the rivers. Can you explain why the Rhine produces so much pollution?

8 a Figure 8 gives the criteria for the Blue Flag Award. Study Figure 10 and write down as many reasons as you can as to why the beach would fail the Blue Flag test.

b Imagine that this beach was awarded a Blue Flag in the year 2000. Draw a sketch of the beach in the year 2000, showing all the improvements to it.

9 Study Figure 9 and use an atlas to help you answer the following:

a In 1991 which counties could you visit if you wanted to swim at a Blue Flag beach?

b Describe the location of the UK's Blue Flag beaches. Can you suggest any reasons for the pattern?

c Suggest some reasons why there will be no Blue Flag beaches:
  i in North-West Scotland
  ii in Merseyside

8.5   Mineral resources in the EC

The countries of the European Community use a great variety of minerals and rocks for industry and construction. The mining and quarrying of the minerals are also important industries which employ a large number of people.

In the UK 23 000 people are employed in the quarrying of aggregates (crushed rock, sand and gravel). Quarrying produces 320 million tonnes of rocks a year most of which is used in the construction industry. One kilometre of motorway needs over 100 000 tonnes of aggregate and every house built needs 50–60 tonnes. The Channel Tunnel project will need about 10 million tonnes of aggregate. Most of the quarrying is done in the rural areas where employment is often limited. In the Peak District National Park 1 200 people are employed in 16 quarries. This is 10% of the Park's working population.

1 Case study: Quarrying dolomite, Ferryhill in the UK

The Thrislington Works shown in Figure 1, is near Hartlepool in County Durham. It is one of several works owned by the Steetley Quarrying Company, a large **multinational** company with interests throughout Europe and the rest of the world. **Dolomite** is quarried (Figure 2) by blasting. It is then loaded onto trucks by mechanical diggers. The blasting takes place at certain set times to reduce the disturbance to the local people. The trucks take the rock to be crushed, graded and burnt in a kiln. The end product is **dolime** which is taken by rail to Hartlepool, 25 kilometres away. The quarry also provides rock for the construction industry and the fine dolomite is used as agricultural lime. At Hartlepool the dolime is further processed into its final products to be sent for use in the chemical and steel industries.

Figure 1

Figure 2

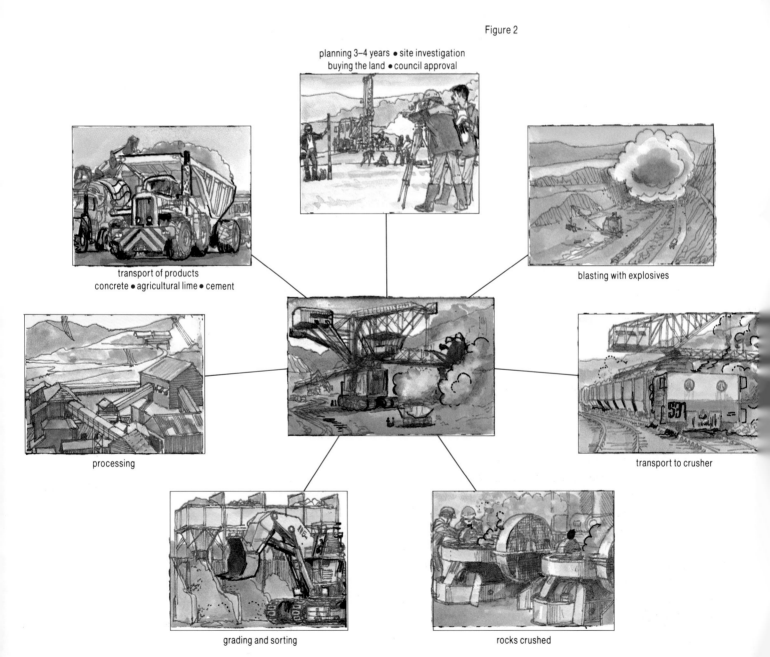

planning 3–4 years ● site investigation
buying the land ● council approval

transport of products
concrete ● agricultural lime ● cement

blasting with explosives

processing

transport to crusher

grading and sorting

rocks crushed

2 Case study: Quarrying bauxite in France

Bauxite is a very important metal ore. From bauxite we obtain **aluminium** which has many industrial uses. In the EC there are important bauxite mines in France and Greece. Many EC countries have an aluminium smelter using imported ores.

Bauxite is a clay with a large amount of aluminium in it. It is found near the surface so it is quarried in large open pits. The ore is purified near the quarry to form **alumina**. This reduces the volume of the ore by half and so it is less bulky and cheaper to transport. The alumina is then smelted. This process needs a large amount of electricity so aluminium smelters are located close to a large and cheap source of power.

France produces about 5% of the world's bauxite mostly from the south-east of the country (see Figure 3). The bauxite is mostly located in the valley of the River Argens. The quarried rock is sent by road to Gardanne and La Barasse where it is made into alumina. It then goes to the smelters powered by HEP in the Alpine valleys or to the ports of Toulon and St Raphaël for export.

France is increasing the amount of alumina it imports as its own reserves are used up and the demand for aluminium continues to grow. A new aluminium smelter is being planned at the coast near Dunkirk in Northern France.

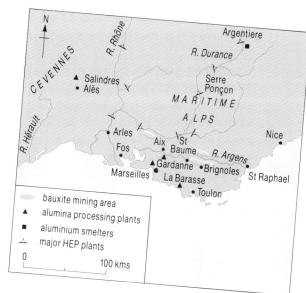

Figure 3
Bauxite deposits of south-east France

Activities

1 The diagrams in Figure 2 show the stages in quarrying but they are all mixed up. Copy the diagrams putting them in the correct order. Describe what is happening in each diagram.

2 Copy the graph in Figure 4 and complete a line graph using the figures below for crushed rock production in the UK.

1960	25 million tonnes	1982	85 million tonnes
1973	130 million tonnes	1984	115 million tonnes
1977	90 million tonnes	1985	120 million tonnes
1979	110 million tonnes	1988	160 million tonnes

   a Is the general trend of the graph up or down? Can you suggest reasons for this trend?
   b What might be the reasons for the fall in production in the mid 1970s and early 1980s?

3 Make a copy of the map in Figure 3 of south-east France.
   a Mark on your map, using three different colours, arrows to show:
     i the route of the bauxite to the alumina processing plants.
     ii the routes of the alumina to the aluminium smelters.
     iii the routes of the alumina to the ports for export.
     Now use three different colours for your arrows and add them to the key.
   b Is the alumina processing plant at Gardanne in a good location? Why?
   c Is the aluminium smelter at Argentière in a good place? Why?
   d If you were planning to build a new aluminium smelter in south-east France where would you build it? Give reasons for your answer.

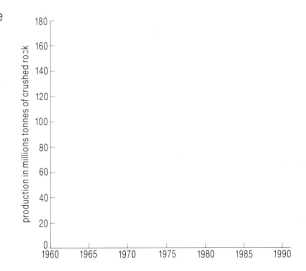

Figure 4

4 Find out as many uses as you can of aluminium. Complete a spider diagram like the one in Figure 2 to show the uses.

5 a Study the series of photographs in Figures 5 to 7. Write down the ways in which the quarry owners try to lessen the effects of the quarrying on the local people and the surroundings.

b Once quarrying is complete, the company **restores** the site. Figure 8 shows some of the uses of reclaimed quarries. Study Figure 9 which shows a plan of a quarry site. In pairs or small groups, design a **restoration plan** for the site. Use a large sheet of paper to draw your scheme. Write some paragraphs explaining your proposals.

Figure 5

Figure 6

Figure 7

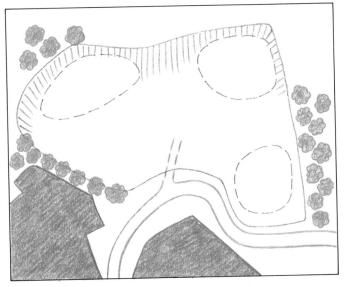

Figure 8

Figure 9
Plan of a quarry site

KEY

deepest parts of quarry

housing

Extra Information

The council owns ⅔ of the quarry land and wishes to build houses to expand the village. The council also needs a new LANDFILL site to dispose of household rubbish.

The other third of the quarry site is owned by a local farmer. He wants his land back to grow crops.

Dictionary

anticline rocks bend upwards
finite resource a resource which will eventually run out
fossil fuels oil, gas or coal
impermeable does not allow liquids to pass through

multinational operating in several countries
oil trap where oil is caught in porous rock surrounded by impervious rock

porous full of holes such that liquids can pass through
renewable or **alternative resource** a resource which will not run out

Imagine life without roads, railways or canals. How would we travel from place to place? Across Europe there is a vast **network** to make our journeys easier. A transport network consists of a series of **links** (roads, rail) and **nodes** (towns, junctions). On a map a road network looks like that in Figure 1. It is often easier to show the same information on a **topological** map using straight lines to represent the curved roads (see Figure 2.) The London Underground is a simple topological map (Figure 3).

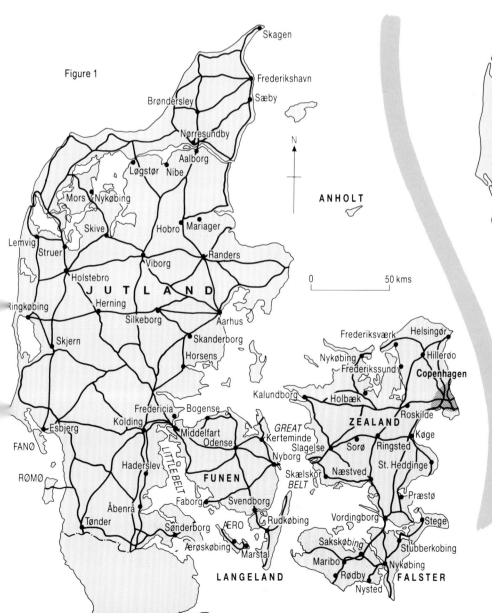

Figure 1

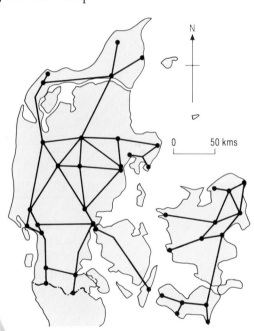

Figure 2a
Simplified topological map
of main road network in Denmark

$$\beta \text{ index} = \frac{4 \text{ links}}{4 \text{ nodes}} = 1$$

$$\beta \text{ index} = \frac{5 \text{ links}}{4 \text{ nodes}} = 1.25$$

This network is better connected
as it has a higher value

Figure 2b

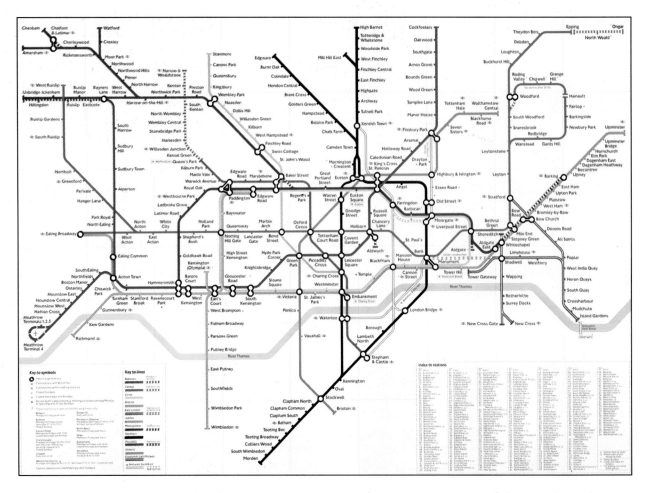

Figure 3
The London
Underground
network

Studying a network helps you to work out which places are the most **accessible**. If the number of links between places is added up, the **Shimbel index** can be calculated. The place with the lowest number is the most accessible.

It is also possible to work out how well **connected** the network is. This depends on the number of links compared with the number of nodes. It is known as the **beta index** (β index), and is calculated as:

$$\frac{\text{number of links}}{\text{number of nodes}}$$

The higher the value, the better connected the network. Look at the example in Figure 2b. See what happens to the beta index if an extra link is added to the network.

Networks in the EC

Generally there are a large number of links between the major cities in the EC. However, there are some parts of the EC where the networks are poor. This may be because of physical or economic factors. Physical barriers include mountains or large expanses of water.

In 1993, the Channel Tunnel link between the UK and France is due to open. This will considerably improve connectivity in Europe. Before the building of the tunnel, the British rail network was not connected to the rest of Europe so people and goods had to be moved by air or sea.

The major economic barrier is the lack of money to build or improve transport networks. The EC has a transport policy which aims to improve connectivity in the network in order to make it easier to travel within the EC. Money is made available for various projects from central funds, although some projects like the Channel Tunnel have been privately financed.

There are several different methods of transport used for people and freight in the EC. The cost of the different methods varies as you can see by looking at the graph in Figure 4. The lengths of road, rail and waterway vary quite a lot between countries of the EC as shown in Figure 5. Compare the figures for West Germany and the UK, for example. Which do you think is the main waterway in West Germany? (The figures for the whole of Germany are not yet available.)

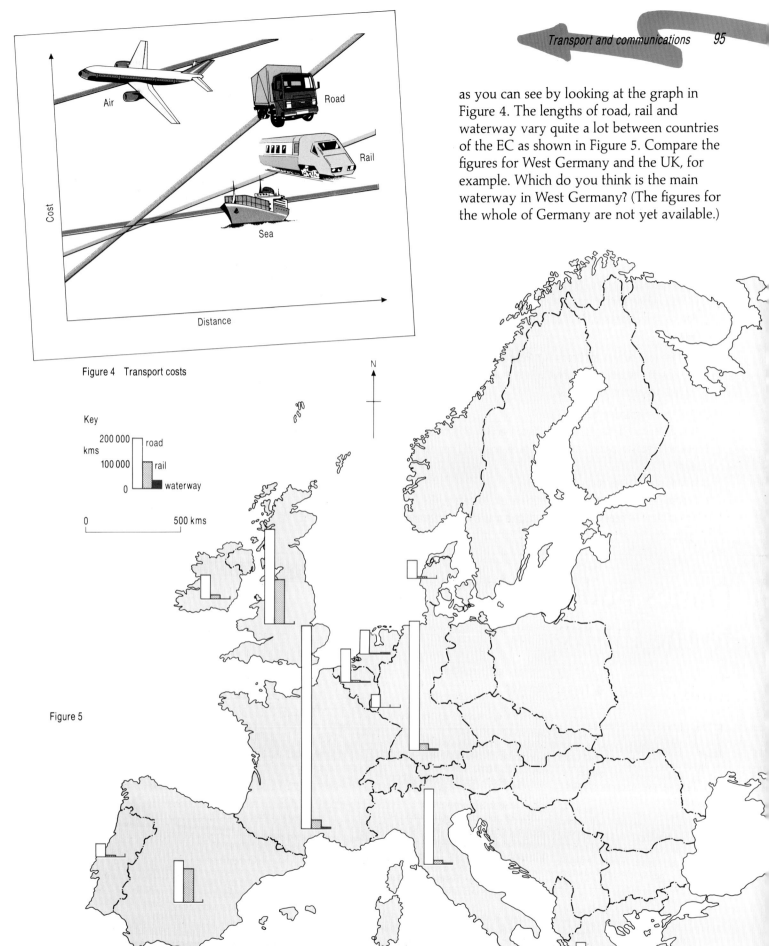

Figure 4   Transport costs

Key

200 000 road
kms
100 000 rail
       0 waterway

0   500 kms

Figure 5

Activities

1 a Look at Figure 6 which shows a topological diagram. Part of the accessibility matrix has been done for you. Make a copy of the diagram and complete the matrix. You should record the least number of links between places.

  b Add up the totals for each row. This is known as the Shimbel index. Which node is the most accessible in the network?

  c Work out the beta index for the network.

  d i How could you improve the accessibility of A and D? Draw another diagram to show your proposals.
    ii Complete an accessibility matrix.
    iii Work out the shimbel index and the beta index.

  e How do your answers to d i–iii differ from those in b and c? Have you improved the network?

2 Look at the road network for Denmark in Figures 1 and 2. Find a map of Denmark in your atlas. Does the network for the whole country look well connected to you? Use your atlas to suggest reasons for your answer.

3 Look at the newspaper article in Figure 7.

  a How is Denmark aiming to improve the connectivity of its network?

  b How will Denmark benefit from the future changes? Will any other countries benefit and how?

  c Why do some Danes doubt the plans?

  d Choose *one* of the schemes in the article and produce a publicity document on a single side of blank A4 paper. You should include a map and diagram and some written points saying why the scheme should go ahead. Think of a snappy title for your work.

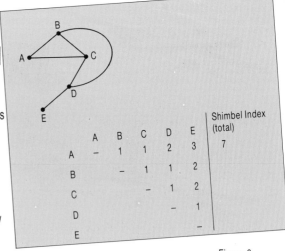

	A	B	C	D	E	Shimbel Index (total)
A	–	1	1	2	3	7
B		–	1	1	2	
C			–	1	2	
D				–	1	
E					–	

Figure 6

4 Look at the graph in Figure 4.

  a Which method of transport is used to move goods quickly?

  b Which method is the cheapest over a long distance?

  c Which method is the most expensive?

  d Try to suggest what type of goods you would transport by air.

  e For short distances, which is the cheapest method of transport?

  f Why do you think motorways have improved road transport?

  g Why has it become easier in the present day to transport large volumes of goods?

Figure 7

Danes build bridges to the future

Three mammoth projects will link Zealand to the European mainland COPENHAGEN ● Terkel Svensson

DENMARK will face the challenge of growing European unity by building three huge bridges which will end the isolation of the island of Zealand and the nation's capital, Copenhagen.

The link across Great Belt is already being built and will carry trains from 1993 and cars from 1996.

For half of the distance motor vehicles will drive on the longest bridge in the world, 6.8 metres above water. Trains will cross through two tunnels.

For the other half of the journey, trains and cars will cross on a 6.6 kilometre bridge. The toll for cars will be the same as presently charged for the ferry.

About 13,000 vehicles are expected to use the four-lane motorway each day, taking about 11 minutes; today the ferry takes about an hour. The 200 daily trains will cross in only seven minutes.

The Danes have had doubts over the plans for a fixed link to Germany; some people fear that a 23.6 kilometre tunnel or bridge from Rødby to Puttgarden on the German Island of Fehmern would endanger the viability of the Great Belt link.

There is also anxiety that the link might become a Swedish motorway link to the European single market, effectively bypassing Denmark and thus being of no benefit to the country.

Building these three fixed links will make not only Copenhagen but the whole of Scandinavia and Northern Germany an area of growth.

THE EUROPEAN – Weekend June 29–July 1, 1990

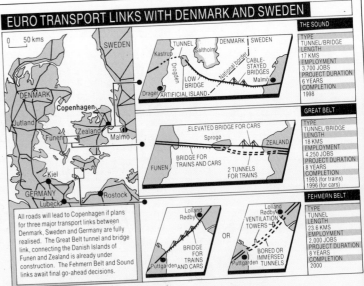

'The links will make the whole of Scandinavia an area of growth'

9.2   Motorways

Dual carriageways have been built extensively in Europe since the 1930s. Motorways, however, still only form a small proportion of the total road network in the EC (see Figure 1). It seems likely that as car ownership continues to grow, more and more motorways will be built.

In the early 1990s the British Government put forward its plans to improve the road network. Look at Figure 1. Some of the new roads will be privately financed and others may be **toll roads** where drivers pay for the use of some of the road. Elsewhere in Europe, as some of you will know, toll roads are common e.g. the autoroutes in France.

Part of the UK road network links up (via ferry) with the rest of Europe. The **Euroroute motorway network** is shown in Figure 2. Notice that it links major cities and ports.

Many cities also have a well developed system of **ring roads**. London has the North and South Circular roads which are inner ring roads. Since 1987 the M25 outer ring road has been completed. Paris too has an important ring road; the 'périphérique'.

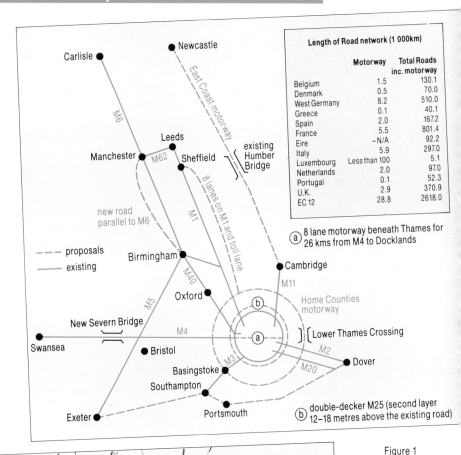

Length of Road network (1 000km)		
	Motorway	Total Roads inc. motorway
Belgium	1.5	130.1
Denmark	0.5	70.0
West Germany	8.2	510.0
Greece	0.1	40.1
Spain	2.0	167.2
France	5.5	801.4
Eire	–N/A	92.2
Italy	5.9	297.0
Luxembourg	Less than 100	5.1
Netherlands	2.0	97.0
Portugal	0.1	52.3
U.K.	2.9	370.9
EC 12	28.8	2618.0

(a) 8 lane motorway beneath Thames for 26 kms from M4 to Docklands

(b) double-decker M25 (second layer 12–18 metres above the existing road)

Figure 1

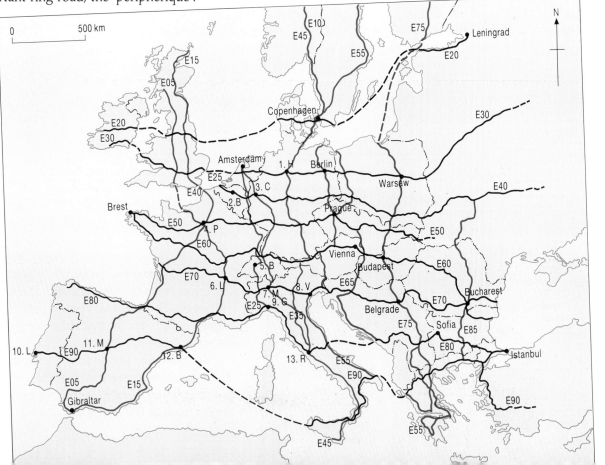

Figure 2 Euroroute network

Activities

1 a Draw a map of the Euroroute network using Figure 2.
  b Name and locate on your map the major cities of Europe.
  c What do ------ mean on the map?
  d Which route connects Spain, Italy and Greece?
  e Which route would you travel on to drive from the UK to Spain?
  f The E25 and E35 cross the Alps. How do you think this is made possible? Give a reason for your answer.
  g Write a summary paragraph describing the network in the EC. Say which countries are well connected and which are not.

2 a On an outline map of Europe and using the data in Figure 1, draw proportional bars to represent the total length of motorways in each country. Each bar should be the same width. Work out a suitable scale (for example, you could use 0.5cm for every 1000km of road).
  b Which country has the shortest total length of motorway?
  c Which country has the greatest total length of motorways?
  d Suggest reasons to try to explain the answers to *b* and *c*.

3 Suggest reasons why towns and cities like London and Paris have had to develop a system of ring roads.

4 Traffic jams are one of the reasons why businesses lose money as people and goods take a long time to get from one place to another. In pairs, suggest some ways in which congestion on the roads could be reduced. Refer to actual examples in operation near where you live. Now design a poster to illustrate how congestion could be reduced.

9.3   Railways

In 1986 the transport ministers of Belgium, Netherlands, West Germany and France agreed to prepare a plan for the construction of high speed rail links between Paris, Amsterdam, Brussels and Cologne. This plan was aimed at improving cross European railway links which have tended to be less well developed than motorway networks. Some of the journey times will be very fast when the planned high speed links are completed.

Figure 1
TGV train

The French TGV

France has had high speed trains (TGV – train à grande vitesse) since the 1970s. (See Figure 1.) The trains travel at 200 to 300 kilometres per hour and have cut journey times considerably between major cities. They are designed as passenger trains and there are no level crossings or tunnels. Although the network is not extensive, the trains are fast and comfortable. Congestion on some roads has been eased, although the air companies do not like the competition! There has been considerable local opposition to the building of new TGV lines as you can see by reading the article in Figure 2.

Provence defends itself against high-speed train

The sleepy little town of Lambesc is the unlikely nerve centre of a campaign against the TGV. JOHN MOYNIHAN reports

MARKET DAY in the sleepy Midi town of Lambesc near Aix-en-Provence invariably inspires a fusillade of gossip in nearby cafés about the state of a neighbour's rabbit breeding, the wine harvest, the progress of OM Marseille football team, a failed hijack on a motorway or a love affair between a boy and girl whose families have not spoken to each other for years.

Recently, however, the tranquil chatter surrounding the wine and food stalls has been transformed into mass indignation directed towards an emerging threat to this pretty hamlet. An SNCF (French Railway) plan to build a new TGV high-speed train track linking the Channel Tunnel, Paris and the south of France, has gained instant enemies in the Bouche-du-Rhône region because it will cut through some of the most beautiful areas of the region where Paul Cézanne once trudged with his canvases to paint.

The proposed arrival of this orange-coloured monster of rail technology has resulted in thousands of protesters pouring into the centre of Aix – the town in which Cézanne lived and worked – to demand that SNCF change its mind about tearing up the landscape. And 33 mayors in the region have sent a petition to the French Government demanding a grievance interview in Paris.

Co-ordination of resistance is being led not by a local man or woman but by a British painter, Francis Canvass, who lives and works in a farmhouse outside Lambesc.

He feels it is "a duty to protect a landscape which has inspired some of the finest artists including Cézanne, Van Gogh, Picasso, Matisse and Bonnard.

Members of Mr. Canvass' organisation recently stopped a TGV train shortly out of Marseilles running on the existing track. "It was all very peaceful," he said. "Travellers on their way to Paris were handed bottles of wine and leaflets. They didn't seem to mind. We don't want any violance though some farmers are demanding a hotting-up of the protest."

"Many houses are going to be up for sale because of the incredible noise – 100 decibels – caused by the orange monster roaring past," said Mr. Canvass. "Mind you, I'm not totally against the train. I admire it. But only if it goes in specified areas which will not destroy natural beauty.

The mayor of Lambesc, looked into Mr. Canvass' office: "The mayors have done a tremendous job in rallying support. Thirty years ago people could not have cared less about railways cutting through here. Now Midi people are very aware of the environment.

That is why we have a petition signed by 33 local mayors demanding an interview in Paris. We certainly do not want to see the train going through our back gardens every 15 minutes – Le TGV passe – une région trépasse…"

Mr. Canvass drove out of Lambesc to the local Chateau Beaupre of Baron Blanc whose family have owned the estate since 1855. The TGV line cutting through to Italy and linking Marseilles, could destroy vineyards.

Mr. Canvass pointed out where the track had been planned: "The TGV will go straight through this forest. The area is known as La Trévaresse which is one of the last green belts in the region. The helicopter surveyors made sure they didn't come down here on dry land. They would have been lynched."

Baron Blanc, 86, explained why the news of the TGV had shattered him: "Industrialists and politicians may be keen on the idea of the train because of the speed factor but personally, it is the end of everything I have worked for to build a reputation in the wine trade."

He exports 40 per cent of his produce. "My son and daughter have built houses on the estate but the track linking Italy, France, Spain, Germany and Britain would decimate our land.

THE EUROPEAN Weekend May 25–27, 1990

Figure 2

The Channel Tunnel

The building of the Channel Tunnel will further improve the links. Look at the information in Figure 3. There are some problems with the link because at the present time, trains will travel rapidly on the European mainland but will be much slower in the UK. There have been plans for a high speed rail link from London to Folkestone but high costs and environmental opposition led to plans being shelved in 1990. Some people feel that until there is a high speed rail link the UK will not benefit as much as it could.

Figure 3

Set for a meeting in mid-channel

THE construction of a 50km tunnel from Folkestone to Coquelles, with a 38km stretch passing directly under the Channel, is the biggest engineering project ever undertaken in Europe. At its height, it will employ 15,000 construction workers.

The tunnel is made up of three separate, parallel, bore holes. Trains will use two of them, each 7.6m in diameter. The third will be a service tunnel, about 5m in diameter, which will be used to provide routine maintenance and ventilation.

Conditions underground, where a convoy of machinery led by the boring machine stretches back 250 metres, are hot, damp, noisy and dangerous. Locomotives remove spoil from the tunnel face and deliver linings and other building materials.

The main engineering challenge is having to drill through fractured chalk saturated with water. The problem is particularly acute on the French side, where tunnellers are only expected to progress at about half the speed of their English counterparts.

Much of the technology is tried and trusted. For example, the laser beam guides used to ensure that the tunnel is following the correct course, were used on the Mersey tunnel 20 years ago. But the electronic "target" which intercepts the laser employs the latest technology. The gadget can calculate exactly where the machine is and which way it is pointing. It is one of the main reasons why Eurotunnel is confident that the French and English tunnellers will meet in the middle.

The tunnel itself is not straight, but dips up and down and swings from side to side in order to bore through the most suitable chalk.

Eurotunnel's technical director, is confident that work will be completed on time. "There are always teething troubles but once machinery is working well and people get used to the system of working, the tunnelling picks up at a phenomenal rate," he said.

Andy Gliniecki

INDEPENDENT Friday 26 May 1989

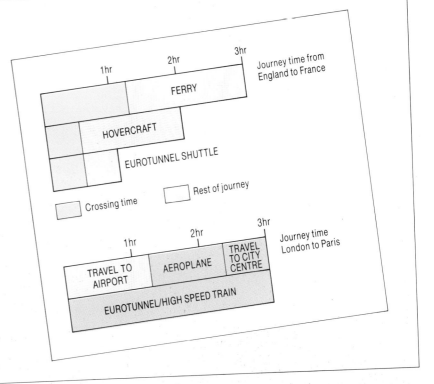

Activities

1 a Using the information in Figure 4, draw two bar graphs to show the changes in predicted volumes of traffic across the English Channel 1983 to 2013. You should draw them using grids of the same scale which will allow you to compare the results more easily.

b Which type of traffic is expected to increase the most after the Channel Tunnel opens in 1993?

c Suggest some reasons for your answer to *b*.

2 a In pairs, discuss the arguments 'for' and 'against' the Channel Tunnel.

b Either

  i design a poster, or

  ii write a newspaper article

to put forward either the benefits or the problems associated with the tunnel. Can you add any more points to the information in Figure 5?

3 Figure 6 is a topological map of the main international railway network in Belgium.

a Draw up an accessibility matrix to discover the most accessible place in Belgium. Remember to record the smallest number of links between places.

b Work out the beta index for Belgium.

c Which place is likely to be the most accessible?

4 Divide the class into seven small groups each one taking the role of one of the following:

- Baron Blanc and family
- Mr Canvass
- M. Labor, an industrialist in Aix
- M. or Mme Maison, house owners in Lambesc
- M. le Maire, mayor of Lambesc
- M. Vitesse, worker from SNCF
- M. Parler, a Parisian politician

a Read the extract in Figure 2 to assess the characters' point of view. You may add ideas of your own and the text in this unit will help you. Each group should prepare a speech to put forward your characters' viewpoint to the rest of the class.

b Discuss as a class whether or not the new TGV track should be built.

c Individually produce a cartoon showing either the advantages or the disadvantages of the scheme.

Actual and projected volume of traffic across the channel.				
	1983	1993	2003	2013
Passengers (millions)	46	67	94	119
Freight tonnes (millions)	53	84	123	170

Figure 4

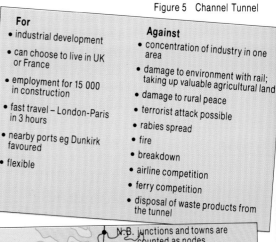

Figure 5   Channel Tunnel

For
- industrial development
- can choose to live in UK or France
- employment for 15 000 in construction
- fast travel – London-Paris in 3 hours
- nearby ports eg Dunkirk favoured
- flexible

Against
- concentration of industry in one area
- damage to environment with rail; taking up valuable agricultural land
- damage to rural peace
- terrorist attack possible
- rabies spread
- fire
- breakdown
- airline competition
- ferry competition
- disposal of waste products from the tunnel

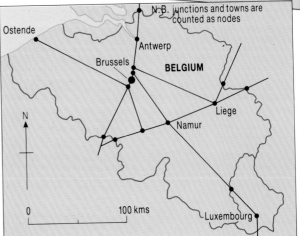

Figure 6
Topological map
of the main
railway network
in Belgium

9.4   Waterways and ports: Rotterdam 'Gateway to Europe'

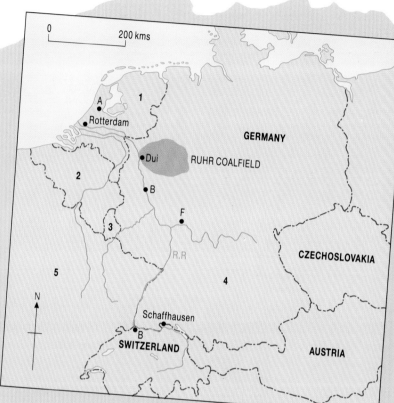

Figure 1

The river Rhine is navigable for over 800 kilometres from Rotterdam to Schaffhausen and is, therefore, an important international routeway. Look at the map in Figure 1. Notice that Rotterdam is at the mouth of the Rhine and Maas (Meuse) rivers.

Rotterdam–Europort FACT FILE:

● Rotterdam is the world's largest port (see Figure 2).

● The port has a large **hinterland**. This is the area a port serves. As you can see from the map in Figure 1, the hinterland of Rotterdam is extremely large, covering almost 50% of the EC countries. Most of the trade goes between the Netherlands and West Germany.

Import and export of goods in millions of tonnes, 1988	
Kobe	166.7
Singapore	158.0
New York	146.4
Yokohama	114.6
Antwerp	96.9
Marseilles	95.8
Rotterdam Europort	273.5
Vancouver	71.3
Hamburg	58.7
Le Havre	50.0
Genoa	45.2
London	44.2
Dunkirk	35.7
Brenen	30.1
Amsterdam	28.0
Ghent	24.3
Trieste	22.3

Figure 2

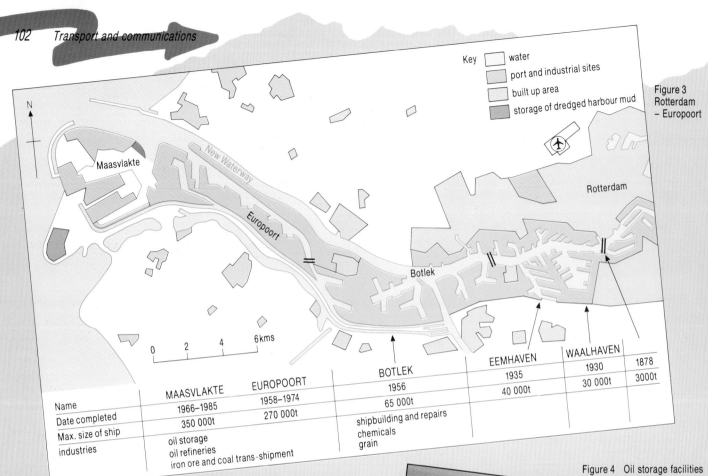

Key
- water
- port and industrial sites
- built up area
- storage of dredged harbour mud

Figure 3
Rotterdam
– Europoort

Name	MAASVLAKTE	EUROPOORT	BOTLEK	EEMHAVEN	WAALHAVEN	1878
Date completed	1966–1985	1958–1974	1956	1935	1930	3000t
Max. size of ship	350 000t	270 000t	65 000t	40 000t	30 000t	
industries	oil storage oil refineries iron ore and coal trans-shipment		shipbuilding and repairs chemicals grain			

Figure 4   Oil storage facilities

- The area of the port extends over 30 kilometres (Figure 3). Dutch engineers have improved the facilities of the port by building the New Waterway to connect Rotterdam to the North Sea. Land has been reclaimed from marshes and the sea to create Europort and Maasvlakte mainly for storage for the oil industries. (See the photograph in Figure 4.)

- Each year 190 000 ships pass through the port carrying a variety of different cargoes. A dredged (deepened) channel allows the largest ships of up to 350 000 tonnes (oil 'supertankers') to enter the Maasvlakte area nearest the sea. Enough mud to fill 70 supertankers is dredged every year! Of this 43% is too polluted to be used to improve the soil or for reclamation. Therefore, it is stored in two dumps in the Maasvlakte area. These will be full in the early 2000s. The Dutch hope that the new plans to reduce pollution along the Rhine will mean that in the future dredged material can be used and not dumped.

Figure 5   A push barge

● The river is not deep or wide enough for large ships to travel upstream from Rotterdam. Therefore, any cargo they are carrying has to be transferred onto smaller ships or barges (look at the photograph of the push-barges in Figure 5). Cargo may also be transferred to trains, lorries or pipeline. This is known as **trans-shipment**. As you can see from Figure 6, a wide variety of cargoes are carried through Rotterdam.

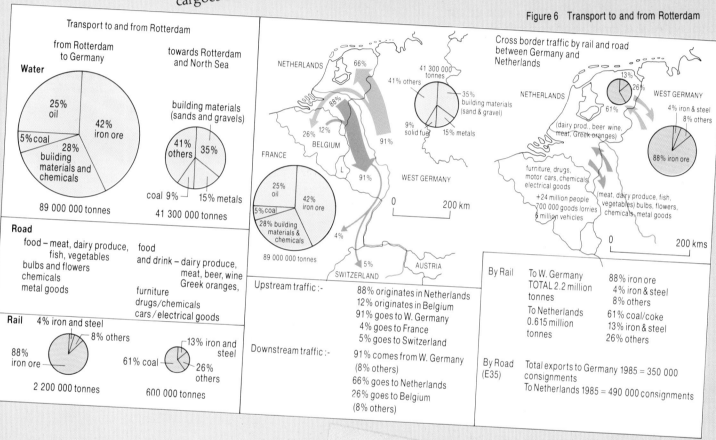

Figure 6   Transport to and from Rotterdam

Transport to and from Rotterdam

from Rotterdam to Germany

Water

25% oil
42% iron ore
5% coal
28% building materials and chemicals

89 000 000 tonnes

towards Rotterdam and North Sea

building materials (sands and gravels)

41% others
35%
coal 9%
15% metals

41 300 000 tonnes

Road

food – meat, dairy produce, fish, vegetables bulbs and flowers chemicals metal goods

food and drink – dairy produce, meat, beer, wine Greek oranges, furniture drugs/chemicals cars/electrical goods

Rail

4% iron and steel
8% others
88% iron ore

2 200 000 tonnes

13% iron and steel
61% coal
26% others

600 000 tonnes

NETHERLANDS 66%
88%
26% 12%
BELGIUM
91%
L
91%
FRANCE
25% oil
42% iron ore
5% coal
28% building materials & chemicals
89 000 000 tonnes
4%
5%
SWITZERLAND AUSTRIA
WEST GERMANY

41 300 000 tonnes
41% others
35% building materials (sand & gravel)
9% solid fuel
15% metals

Upstream traffic :-
88% originates in Netherlands
12% originates in Belgium
91% goes to W. Germany
4% goes to France
5% goes to Switzerland

Downstream traffic :-
91% comes from W. Germany (8% others)
66% goes to Netherlands
26% goes to Belgium (8% others)

Cross border traffic by rail and road between Germany and Netherlands

NETHERLANDS
13% 26%
61%
WEST GERMANY
4% iron & steel
8% others
88% iron ore

(dairy prod., beer wine, meat, Greek oranges)

furniture, drugs, motor cars, chemicals electrical goods
+24 million people 700 000 goods lorries 6 million vehicles

(meat, dairy produce, fish, vegetables) bulbs, flowers, chemicals, metal goods

0   200 kms

By Rail	To W. Germany TOTAL 2.2 million tonnes	88% iron ore 4% iron & steel 8% others
	To Netherlands 0.615 million tonnes	61% coal/coke 13% iron & steel 26% others
By Road (E35)	Total exports to Germany 1985 = 350 000 consignments To Netherlands 1985 = 490 000 consignments	

0   200 km

● Modern equipment and the use of **containers** (look at Figure 7) help easy transfer. Most cargo is transported in containers of standard sizes. They are easy to stack, load and unload. As they are made of aluminium they also protect the cargo by reducing theft and damage. Containers can travel by train, ship or lorry.

Figure 7   Containers

Canals

Artificial waterways were important especially in the 19th century. They have helped to increase the navigable lengths of rivers. In Belgium, for example, there have been extensive 20th century improvements to allow the canals to take larger ships and push tugs of up to 9000 tonnes. (Remember these are still very much smaller than ocean going ships.) As it is rare to find perfectly flat areas, **locks** have to be constructed. One of the most modern locks is located at Ronquières. Once there were 20 locks here. Now, ships are moved by means of giant lifts. Look at the photographs in Figure 8. Locate Ronquières in your atlas.

Often canals are constructed to link major rivers. There are many examples of these in the EC, for example Rhône–Saône, Scheldt–Rhine, Rhône–Rhine, and Seine–Maas.

Figure 8 Ronquières

Activities

1 Make a copy of Figure 9. Using the data from Figure 2, draw a bar graph to show the data for the *European* ports only. The first bar has been done for you. (You may need to look up the ports in an atlas to check which ones are European. You should only have 12 ports on your graph.) Colour in the bars according to the country they belong to and include a key.

2 a Look at the information in Figure 3. When was Rotterdam originally developed as a port?

  b What did you think were the initial advantages of the port?

  c i Did the port expand upstream or downstream from Rotterdam?
    ii Why did the port have to expand in this direction?

  d Why do you think Rotterdam is known as the 'gateway' to Europe?

  e Why does 'trans-shipment' have to occur at Rotterdam?

3 Study Figure 6.

  a What type of goods are transported by road?

  b Why are food products not sent by river?

  c Name two important types of cargoes transported by ship.

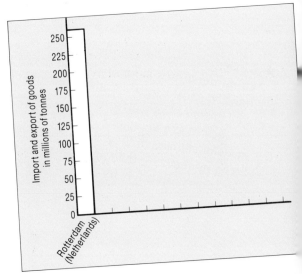

Figure 9

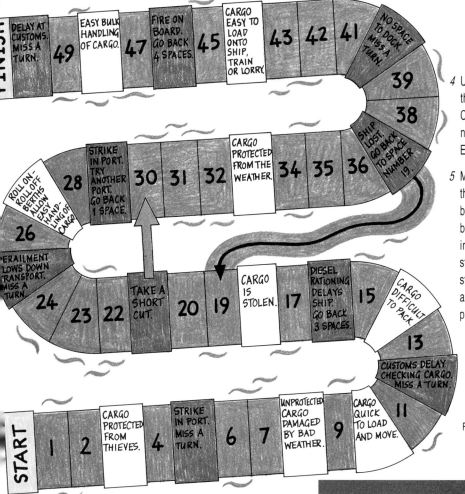

4 Use an atlas to find the location of the canals mentioned in the text in this section. Look up the major rivers of Europe. Considering the EC as a whole suggest reasons for the large number of canals in Central Europe compared with Southern Europe. (Consider the relief and rainfall of the two areas.)

5 Much of the cargo transported now is in containers like those in the photograph in Figure 7. Make a copy of the board in Figure 10. Decide which of the statements in the boxes are advantages (good) or disadvantages (bad). Add instructions such as 'move forward 2 spaces' from good statements and 'move backwards 2 spaces' from bad statements. (Move between one and four spaces only into an empty space. Now play the game, using a die, with a partner.)

Figure 10

9.5   Airports

Each EC country has a variety of airports. Some deal with internal traffic and others with international traffic. Look at the map of UK airports in Figure 1. Notice that there are a range of types of airports with international, regional or local status. Within the EC there are also some airports which are more important than others (see Figure 2).

Key
■ Main International airports (over 1 million passengers per year)
● Airports with over 100 000 passengers per year
● Airports with under 100 000 passengers per year

Figure 1
Major airports of the UK

Europes largest airports in 1989			
	Passengers × 1 million		Freight × 1000 tonnes
London	62.6	Frankfurt	1079.3
Paris	45.0	London	932.3
Frankfurt	26.7	Paris	832.8
Rome	16.5	Amsterdam	582.6
Amsterdam	15.7		

Figure 2

With increasing numbers of passengers using the airports it is important that expansion and new building takes place. London's airports have expanded in size and more changes are planned as you can see in Figure 3. Advertising also helps to increase the passenger use of airports by putting over some of the advantages of air travel.

Figure 3

London's third airport will be second to none.

The new terminal complex at Stansted opened in March of 1991, 10 years and £400,000,000 in the making it is just part of BAA's £2 billion investment programme.

When you enter the terminal you will be struck by the simplicity of the design.

Everything you need is on one level.

Stansted is ideally located just a short drive off the M11 and M25. By train, it will take just 40 minutes on the direct rail link from Liverpool street.

Nothing could be easier. But then making life easier for the passenger is what BAA is all about, and that takes careful planning.

INDEPENDENT 8 April 1990.

LUTON

STANSTED

HEATHROW

GATWICK

New terminal for passengers and cargo planned. Holiday and charter flights important. 1995 will handle 5 million passengers. Too close to Stansted to expand too much as the air space is conjected.

1988 terminal four opened. Rail link to Paddington being developed. Fifth terminal proposed on site of Perry Oaks sludge works. If not, Paris and Frankfurt may replace London as Europe's main gateway.

Gatwick 'needs 2nd runway'

By John Harlow

A SECOND runway at Gatwick airport and the splitting in two of the Civil Aviation Authority is proposed in an all-party Transport Select Committee report into air safety, published yesterday.

Residents' organisations around Gatwick immediately protested, saying they were promised that a second runway would not be built before the year 2019.

But Mr. Edward Townsend, of BAA, said: "I just do not see where another runway would go. It is impossible to contemplate where to put it. We would have to be bulldozing people's houses, and who would accept that?"

"The only possible site is blocked by the new north terminal," he said.

A pressure group, National Policy for Britain's Airports, said a second Gatwick runway could wreck the small community of Charlwood.

Some 800 homes could be destroyed and 2,000 residents uprooted, said Mr. Jim Bailey, the organisation's co-ordinator.

Case study — Schiphol airport, Amsterdam

Site: Flat land reclaimed from Haarlemmermeer (Haarlem Lake) in 1852.

Passengers: Flights began in 1919 after the airport had been used for military purposes. The airport was destroyed in the Second World War but a new modern airport was built and completed in 1967. It is estimated that it will handle 25 million people in the year 2000.

Industries: Develop nearby e.g. aircraft construction, banking and transport companies. There are strong links with the bulb and flower growing areas in the Netherlands.

Communications: Excellent air, road and rail links in the area. In the future, Amsterdam may also be connected to the high speed rail network in Europe.

The airport is located in the Green Heart of the Netherlands, (similar to a green belt in the UK where building is restricted) but in the 1980s and 1990s some developments of industry and housing were allowed near the airport. At present, therefore, economic development has priority.

Noise pollution: Many of the noisiest areas are not near settlement. Plans to change the direction of one of the runways so that planes would not fly over built up areas were too expensive. Quieter aircraft have been introduced. Noise levels may be a problem in the future as aircraft numbers increase.

Figure 4

Communications

Noise pollution

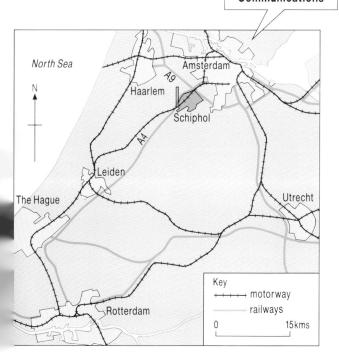

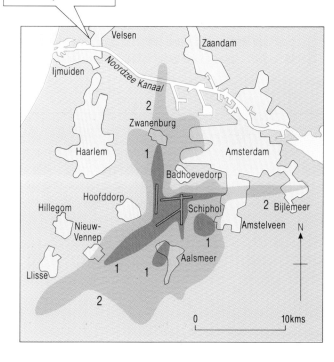

Activities

1 a Using Figure 1 plot the location of the main international airports on an outline map of the UK

b Draw on and name the major conurbations (large cities) of

   i Greater London,

   ii West Midlands (Birmingham),

   iii Greater Manchester,

   iv West Yorkshire (Leeds, Sheffield),

   v Merseyside (Liverpool),

   vi Tyneside (Newcastle),

   vii Clydesdale (Glasgow).

c What do you notice about the location of the major airports?

d Look at Figure 1 again. Which regional airports are more than 100 kilometres away from a conurbation?

e Suggest one advantage and one disadvantage of locating an airport close to a conurbation.

2 a Using Figure 1, which is your closest International airport?

b Which one would you go to if you wanted to

   i fly to London or Edinburgh?

   ii fly to Australia?

   iii have a trip in a light aircraft?

3 Look at the information on Schiphol airport in Figure 4.

a When was the new Schiphol airport built? Why?

b Using Figure 4 estimate the area the airport covers. Give your answer in square kilometres.

c Why do you think trees have been planted around the airport?

d Copy the sketch of the airport shown in Figure 5 and add the following labels in a suitable place to describe the site and location of the airport.

flat land   open space for buildings and runways   space for industrial development
green belt land   away from centres of population   good transport network
A9   A4   easy access to the capital – Amsterdam.

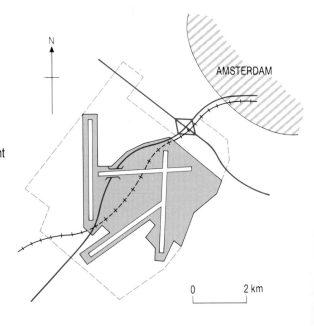

Figure 5

 Schiphol Airport

Runways

Main roads

Schiphol railway

Boundary of the Schiphol zone

Built up area

4 Such large airports have many problems. Divide yourselves into small groups and discuss the following questions: Record your results as you go.

a The airport is growing – should further expansion into the green belt be allowed or should another airport be built elsewhere? Give your reasons.

b The airport produces noise pollution. How should nearby areas be protected?

c The airport attracts industry and other developments e.g. housing which add to the road congestion, noise and sprawl over the green belt. Should such economic development be allowed to take place, or are environmental concerns more important?

Within your group there may be conflicting opinions, but record all the reasons. Now, discuss the questions as a class. Did each group have similar answers to the problems? Note down any ideas your group did not include.

Using the information from the activity choose *one* of the following:

● Imagine you live in Aalsmeer (Figure 4), an area suffering from severe noise pollution. Write a letter of complaint to your local newspaper.

● You work for the Airport Authority and are in favour of proposed expansion of the airport. Write a report to be presented to the local radio.

● You belong to the local conservation group. Write a poem or design an informative poster about the disadvantages of the airport to the environment.

7 There are 16 forms of transport hidden in the wordsearch (Figure 6). Put the words you find in the table.

P	L	A	N	E	E	G	R	A	B	B	A
M	G	H	F	O	E	A	D	L	C	G	K
H	O	V	E	R	C	R	A	F	T	L	N
E	J	I	Y	R	R	O	L	B	J	I	P
L	U	T	S	V	W	X	I	R	Q	D	Y
I	M	V	U	U	T	K	A	S	A	E	Z
C	B	K	J	B	E	L	R	I	B	R	C
O	O	I	N	H	E	G	O	E	F	D	Y
P	J	O	I	L	T	A	N	K	E	R	M
T	E	Q	A	P	R	O	O	N	R	E	F
E	T	R	R	S	A	D	M	E	U	V	W
R	B	A	T	C	M	T	F	Z	Y	X	G

TRANSPORT BY RAIL   BY WATER   BY ROAD   BY AIR

1.

2.

3.

4.

Add more methods of transport to the lists.

Figure 6

Dictionary

hinterland the area a port serves
link a line (road, rail, canal, river) joining places in a network

lock confined section of a canal where the water level can be changed to raise or lower boats to the level of the next section of canal

network a transport system made of links and nodes
node a settlement or a junction in a network
trans-shipment transferring goods from one method of transport to another

10.1 Where does our food come from?

We tend to take for granted our supply of food. It is usually available for us to buy at a local supermarket or grocery shop. The food that we eat comes from a variety of sources as it is impossible to produce everything we want to eat and drink in the UK. Look at Figure 1 which shows the source of food in a traditional 'English' breakfast.

We grow a surplus of some foods and, therefore, we **export** these goods. Food that we do not have enough of we have to **import**. Many of the foods we eat in the UK are products imported from other member countries of the EC.

Agriculture, or farming, helps to make a country **self-sufficient**. The UK, for example, can produce enough of certain foods (wheat, barley, veal) without having to rely on other countries. Farming also provides jobs and raw materials for industries.

In the EC there are several different types of farming (see Figure 2).

Farming can be **intensive** where there is a high output per hectare (yield) or **extensive** where the output is low. Yields are increasing for many products as a result of modern technology. Machinery, fertilisers (see graphs b and c in Figure 3) and high yielding crops are responsible for this increase. In 1900 a farmer could feed 4 people; by 1950 a farmer could feed 10; and by 1990 the same farmer could feed 40 people. Look at the information in Figure 4. Notice how the yields have increased yearly. These graphs show data for the EC as a whole and hide the great variations between countries (see Figure 5).

Figure 1 The great 'English' breakfast

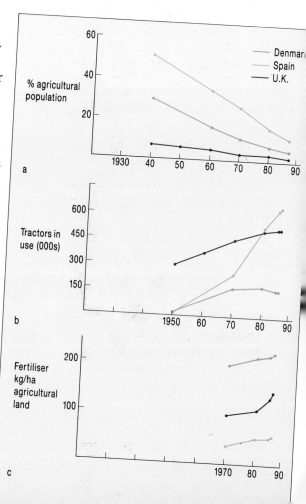

Figure 3

Figure 2 Different types of farming

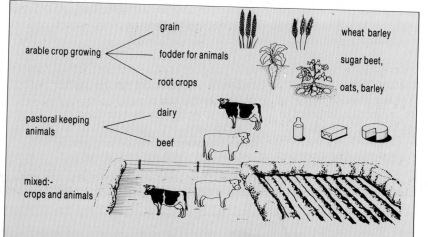

a)

yield per cow

milk production

number dairy cows

1977 = 100

b)

EC production of meat (1000 tonnes)

c)

EC production of cereals (1000 tonnes)

Figure 4

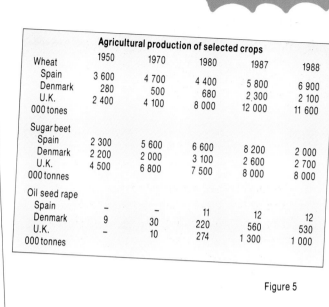

Agricultural production of selected crops					
	1950	1970	1980	1987	1988
Wheat					
Spain	3 600	4 700	4 400	5 800	6 900
Denmark	280	500	680	2 300	2 100
U.K.	2 400	4 100	8 000	12 000	11 600
000 tones					
Sugar beet					
Spain	2 300	5 600	6 600	8 200	2 000
Denmark	2 200	2 000	3 100	2 600	2 700
U.K.	4 500	6 800	7 500	8 000	8 000
000 tonnes					
Oil seed rape					
Spain	–	–	11	12	12
Denmark	9	30	220	560	530
U.K.	–	10	274	1 300	1 000
000 tonnes					

Figure 5

Activities

1 Look at the information in Figure 1 about the source of food for a typical 'English' breakfast.

 a Which products can be obtained from the UK?

 b Which products can be obtained from non-EC countries? Give a reason why most of these could not be produced in the EC. (You could also make a record on a tally chart of what you have eaten during one day or one week. Work out those products which came from animals; those which came from crops grown in the UK and those from crops grown abroad and imported.)

2 Name some typical food/drink products we import from the following countries (the list below may help):

- Denmark
- Netherlands
- Spain
- France
- Germany
- Greece
- Belgium
- Eire
- Portugal
- Italy

 wine, butter, cheese (Brie, edam, Danish blue), pasta, chocolates
 beer, fruit (oranges, tomatoes), bacon

3 Conduct a survey either at home, or a local supermarket to see where food products come from. The country of origin is often labelled on the packet/tin or the name might help. (If you choose to do this at a local shop it is easier to choose just a small section like fresh fruit or canned fruit or dairy products. Try to look at about 20 items.

 i Make a list or tally chart of the products and where they come from.

 ii Draw a bar graph or pie chart to show the number of products from each country.

 iii Work out what percentage of the products come from EC countries.

 iv Draw a map to show the origin of the products.

 v Write a paragraph about your results. Try to suggest some reasons why the food at home or in the local shop comes from different countries.

4 Look at the graphs in Figure 3.

 a What has happened to the percentage of agricultural population?

 b What has happened to the numbers of tractors used?

 c Explain the relationship between graphs a and b.

 d What has happened to the amount of fertiliser used per hectare of agricultural land?

5 a Look at the graph for EC cereal production in Figure 4. Describe the general trend.

 b Why does cereal production tend to vary so much from year to year?

6 a Using the information in Figure 5 draw a graph similar to one in Figure 3. Choose *either* wheat, *or* sugar beet *or* oilseed rape. Make sure you choose a different crop from the people sitting near you. Draw *one* graph with three lines on it for Spain, Denmark and the UK. Compare your graph with the others.

 b Comment on the general trends you can see.

 c Suggest a reason for these trends.

10.2   Farming patterns in the EC

On a small scale, such as within the UK, it is easier to see that there are regional variations in the types of farming. Look at Figure 1. Notice that the UK has quite a varied pattern of farming although it is possible to detect a dominance of arable crops in the east and animals in the west. This pattern is largely the result of climatic variations.

Figure 1
Farming land-use patterns in the UK

Key
- Sheep
- Cattle – beef/dairy
- Arable
- Mixed
- Horticulture
- City

Sheep: found in upland areas in the west and north. They can survive the harsh climatic conditions and rugged relief.

Cattle – beef and dairy: found mainly in the west where the climate is mild and wet – perfect for grass! It is expensive to feed cattle indoors (stall feeding) so most are left out to grass. Cattle like the good quality grass found on lowlands. Rough higher pastures are suitable only for sheep. ·

Arable: cereal and root crops are grown where soils are fertile and the land is flat to enable machines to operate. A sunny climate helps quick growth and ripening.

Mixed: most farms in the U.K. keep animals and grow crops wherever there are suitable conditions for both activities.

Horticulture: Fruit, vegetables and flowers are grown intensively where the maximum is gained from the land by using fertilisers and machines. Sometimes crops are grown in glasshouses where the climate can be carefully controlled. Horticulture tends to occur close to cities.

0   100 kms

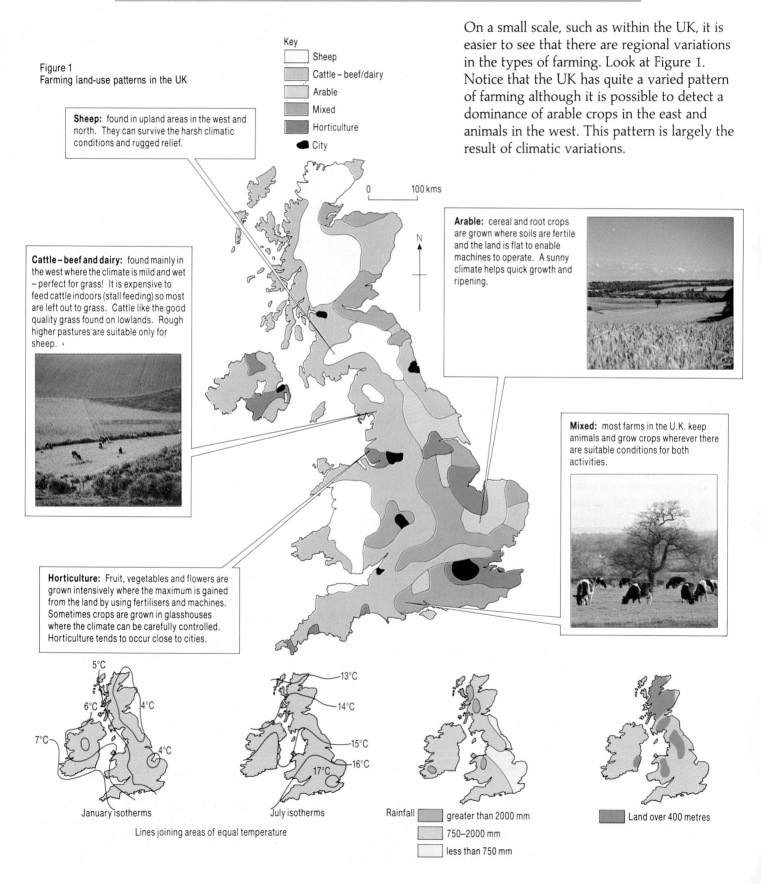

January isotherms

July isotherms

Rainfall
- greater than 2000 mm
- 750–2000 mm
- less than 750 mm

Land over 400 metres

Lines joining areas of equal temperature

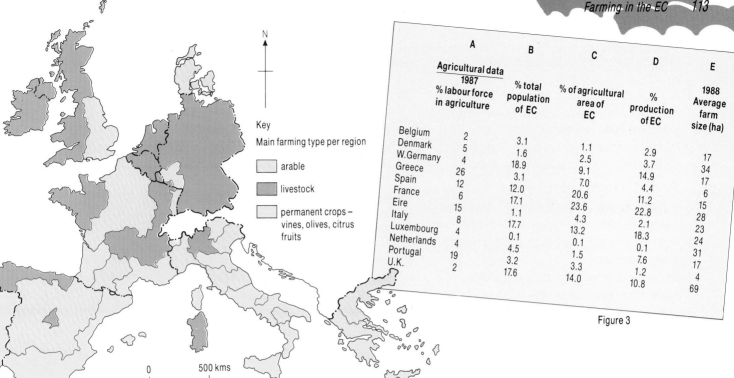

	A	B	C	D	E
Agricultural data 1987	% labour force in agriculture	% total population of EC	% of agricultural area of EC	% production of EC	1988 Average farm size (ha)
Belgium	2	3.1	1.1	2.9	17
Denmark	5	1.6	2.5	3.7	34
W.Germany	4	18.9	9.1	14.9	17
Greece	26	3.1	7.0	4.4	6
Spain	12	12.0	20.6	11.2	15
France	6	17.1	23.6	22.8	28
Eire	15	1.1	4.3	2.1	23
Italy	8	17.7	13.2	18.3	24
Luxembourg	4	0.1	0.1	0.1	31
Netherlands	4	4.5	1.5	7.6	17
Portugal	19	3.2	3.3	1.2	4
U.K.	2	17.6	14.0	10.8	69

Figure 3

N.B. Regions shaded according to main type of agriculture. It may not be the only type.

Figure 2
Main farming type
per region

There are, of course, many other factors that affect what is grown on a particular farm – these include the cost of labour and machinery and the type of market nearby.

Most of the farming in the EC is intensive, although this varies from very high yielding arable farms in the UK to lower yielding farms in the southern part of the EC. Figure 2 shows you the major farming types in the EC.

The workforce employed in farming varies from country to country (see Figure 3). The UK and Belgium have only 2% of their workforce employed in agriculture whereas some other countries such as Greece have a much higher percentage.

Activities

1 a Make a careful copy of the map of UK farming in Figure 1. Use different colours to show the different farming land uses.
  b Use an atlas to name the cities.
  c Copy and complete the following sentences using the words given below:

arable   horticulture   sheep   intensive   glasshouses
machines   west   east   over
2000mm   5°C   16°C   4°C
stallfed   decrease   climate

The map of farming land use patterns shows that most cattle are kept in the north and .... of the UK. This is mainly because the climate being wet (rainfall of ....) and mild (temperatures are over .... in winter) favours all-year-round grass growing. This means that animals do not have to be kept indoors or .... for much of the year. As temperatures .... with height, the higher land and rough grazing are suitable only for .... farming.

.... farming is where the land is ploughed and crops are grown. Much of this land is flat so that large .... can be used. Most of this type of farming is carried out in the .... of the UK where high temperatures of over .... in the summer help to ripen the crops. Temperatures may drop to .... in winter, but frosts help to break up the soil and kill pests.

The cultivation of flowers and vegetables is called .... This involves expensive inputs and concentrates on getting the most out of a plot of land – this is .... farming. Sometimes .... are used as they allow the .... to be controlled.

2 a Give some examples of horticultural products grown in the UK.

b Why do you think horticulture tends to be close to cities?

c Why might some farmers invest large sums of money in glasshouses (large greenhouses)?

d The most important horticulture area is in Lincolnshire and Cambridgeshire. Try to discover the name of this area and why it is such a good area for horticulture.

3 Look again at the map you drew for activity 1. Mark on the area where you live.

a According to the map, what type of farming is found in or near your area?

b Use your atlas, or knowledge of the local area to suggest some reasons for this type of farming.

4 Study the data in Figure 3 (columns A, D, E and F) and answer the following questions:

a Which country has the largest percentage of the population in the EC?

b Which country has the largest percentage of agricultural area?

c Which country has the smallest percentage of agricultural area?

d Give a reason for your answers to b and c.

e Which country has the greatest percentage of the labour force employed in agriculture?

f Which country has the lowest percentage employed in agriculture?

g Which countries have the highest percentage of agricultural production?

h Suggest two reasons for your answer to g.

i Which country has the highest average farm size?

j Which country has the lowest average farm size?

5 a Use the information in column A of Figure 3 and an outline map. Show the percentage of people employed in agriculture by drawing pie charts or individual bars for each country.

b Comment on the final result. Although agriculture is not the main source of employment in the EC, where is it important?

6 a Describe the general pattern of farming types in the EC using Figure 2 or a similar map available in your atlas.

b Use your atlas to suggest some reasons for the pattern you observe.

10.3   Mixed farming in the UK

Farm case study – Carrsides Farm in County Durham, England

Since 1928 the Wilkinson family have been running Carrsides farm. Look at the map in Figure 1 to show the location of the farm. Although it is a **mixed** farm of 155 hectares dairy cattle are the main enterprise. Crops are grown mainly to feed the livestock – such crops are called **fodder crops**. Other crops on the farm are sold. Look carefully at Figure 2 as it details the activities on the farm.

One of the important processes on the farm is **crop rotation**. Crops, such as wheat, barley and oil seed rape, remove minerals from the soil which the farmer has to replace by using fertilisers. Usually it is not good to grow the same crops in each field year after year. The farmer, therefore, rotates the crops grown in each field. Grazing animals are also rotated on pasture so that they do not eat all the grass in one go!

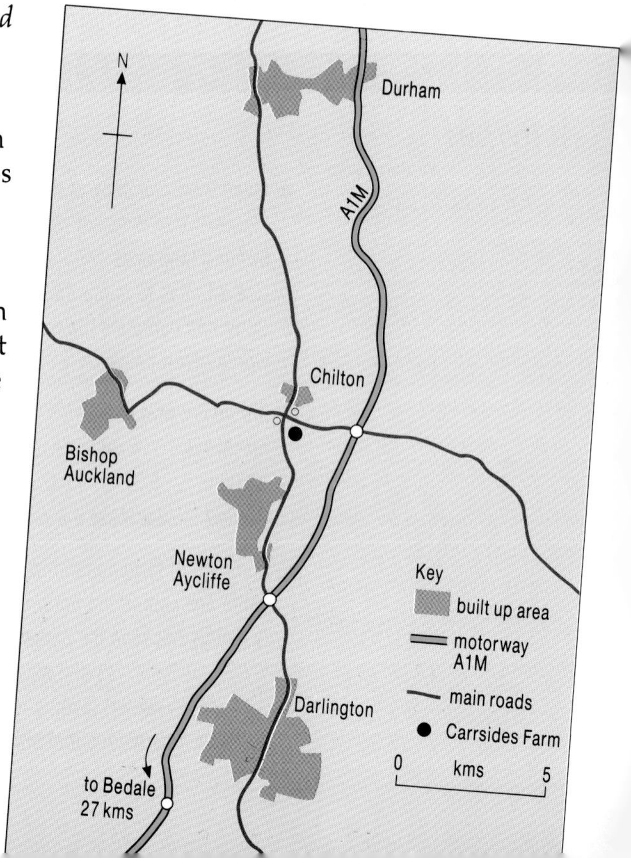

Figure 1
Location of Carrsides Farm

INPUTS

PHYSICAL

soil: boulder clay and loam
relief: gentle
temperatures: 4° C in winter
               15° C in Summer
rainfall over 750mms

HUMAN

2 full-time
3 part-time (family)
casual labour at harvest

ECONOMIC

wages repairs
machinery; fuel
veterinary bills
feed – protein pellets
seeds
fertiliser
livestock

PROCESSES

	DAIRY CATTLE	BEEF CATTLE	ARABLE/GRASS	MISC	MAINTENANCE
J	calving	calving	maintenance of machinery		defrost water troughs look at all 24 buildings
F	calving	calving	buy fertiliser		check machinery
M	calving cull few cows	calving	fertilise	14 ewes lambing foaling of mares	checking
A	calving check fences	selling	fertilise spray check electric fences		service tractors
M	calving cows out	selling	prepare silage pit		prepare silage pit
J	cows out	selling heifers out bulls in	cut hay for silage fertilise grass		trim verges check harvesting machinery
J	cows out	selling heifers out bulls in	check machinery buy fertiliser cut silage		painting and building
A	spray cows with insecticide cows out	heifers out bulls in	harvesting baling, ploughing sowing	4 pigs farrowing	check cultivating machinery hedgecutting
S	cows in	all cattle in	finish harvest ploughing, sowing sheep arrive to eat grass		hedgecutting
O	calving	extra calves bought	ploughing, sowing, fertilising		store summer equipment hedgecutting
N	cull cows not in calf calving	calving	finish sowing		hedgecutting
D	calving	calving	sheep return to hill farm		general maintenance

OUTPUTS

STOCK

cattle → Darlington
          Bishop Auckland
          Bedale

poultry → Darlington for
            chicken paste

milk → Durham

CROPS

wheat ⎱
barley ⎰ → Darlington

oil seed rape → Humberside

eggs → Durham
        Darlington
        Bishop Auckland
        Chilton

Figure 2

Activities

1 Look at the information in the 'processes' section in the systems diagram (Figure 2). Choose dairy cattle or beef cattle and produce a diagram similar to that in Figure 3 to show the farmer's year.

2 a How many full time and part time workers are there in total on the farm?

   b How does Mr Wilkinson manage in the summer when there are many extra jobs to do?

3 a Make a list of all the animals the Wilkinsons keep

   b Try to suggest a reason why movable electric fences are used in the grazing areas.

   c Try to suggest a reason why culling of cows takes place during the year.

   d Why do you think sheep visit the farm between September and December?

4 Choose one of the seasons of the year. In groups produce a poster to show the farmer's work at that time.

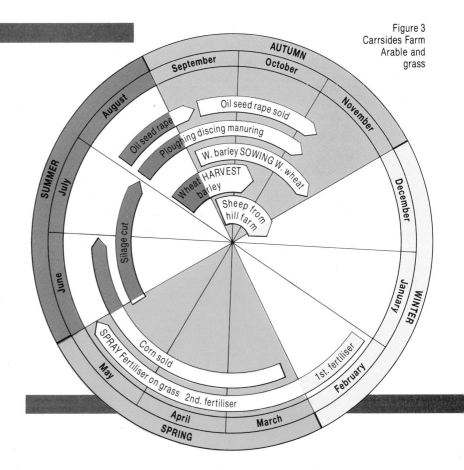

Figure 3
Carrsides Farm
Arable and
grass

10.4 Mediterranean agriculture

The southern countries of the EC are all involved with agriculture which is typical of the Mediterranean region. Look at Figure 1. Much of the agriculture involves the growing of permanent crops such as grape vines, olive and citrus fruit trees. They require years of cultivation before giving good yields. These crops like the climate typical of the Mediterranean. (Look at details of the climate in Chapter 3.)

Viticulture in the Rioja region of Spain

Growing vines (**viticulture**) is common in many areas of Spain. The Rioja region is in the North East of Spain (look at the map in Figure 2).

You have already come across the idea that farming can be regarded as a **system** with inputs and outputs. Certain physical, human and economic **inputs** are necessary for farming to take place. During the year a farmer will carry out various activities and

Key
(lemons – Sicily and Greece; grapefruit – Spain)
——— northern limit of oranges
- - - - northern limit of olive producing area

0 _____ 500 kms

Figure 1

Figure 2 Rioja region of Spain

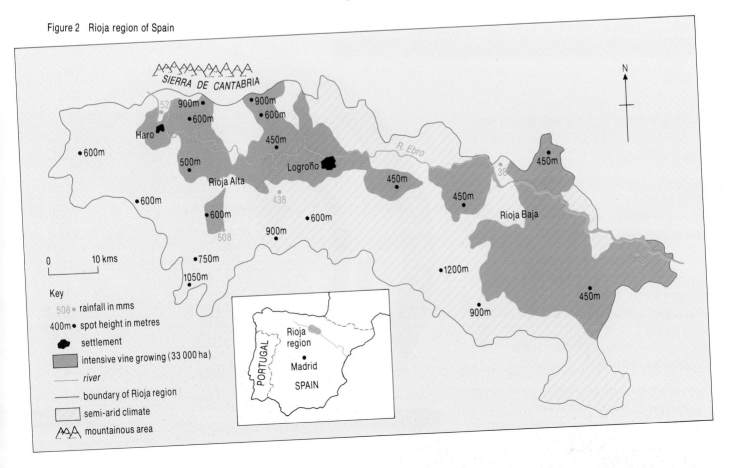

Key
508 ● rainfall in mms
400m ● spot height in metres
● settlement
▨ intensive vine growing (33 000 ha)
——— river
——— boundary of Rioja region
▨ semi-arid climate
▲▲▲ mountainous area

INPUTS

PHYSICAL

Temperature: 10°C average all year.
Summer over 22°C.
Winter not less than 30°C.
Frosts can kill; stoves lit in fields on frosty nights.

Soil: Gravelly, chalky with good drainage but retains some moisture

Sunshine: Lots needed. Much more sunlight on south facing slopes. 1400 hours but too much sun makes too much sugar in the grape. Doesn't make good wine.

Rainfall: Approx: 500 mms per year. Hail a major hazard Western Rioja area produces higher quality wine.

Relief: Slopes allow better drainage 500m+ in altitude good.

Shelter: From wind.

HUMAN AND ECONOMIC

Labour: Family with part-time help at harvest time.

Machinery: Buildings: Press and other wine making equipment.

Fertiliser: Bordeaux mixture helps growth.

Sprays: Against aphids which eat roots.

Netting: To keep off birds.

Plants: New stock needed each year to replace a few old plants 20–30 years old. Plants will give good harvest after 3 years old.

PROCESSES

FARMERS YEAR

J	P						
F	P	N					
M	P	N	F	Plo	Pla		
A		N		Plo	Pla		
M					Pla	S	Frost
J	PT		F			S	
J						S	
A	PT					S	
S	Ripening						Birds Wasp
O							H
N				Plo			H
D			F	Plo			

P: Pruning; wire up vines
N: Preparation in nursery
F: Fertilisers
S: Spray
M: Harvest

PT: Trim shoots
Pla: Plant replacement vines from nursery
Plo: Plough   Spring to expose root base
Winter to protect roots

Rack wine in barrels.
↓ Keep topping up as wine evaporates. Bottle some wine.

↓

Fill empty casks with water so that they do not dry out.

Prepare tools, clean barrels etc.

Press

Press
↓
Fermentation

OUTPUTS

– Grapes for the local Co-operative

– Pressed grapes for the local co-operative

(Bottled wine – if the grower produces enough grapes)

(Grapes are usually picked & crushed on the same day)

Wine aged in oak barrels for a minimum of 2 years

EC wine:-
67.3% human consumption
20.4% distilled for surplus
7.3% distilled for vinegar
5% exported

Figure 3

these are known as **processes** in the system. There will also be **outputs** from the farm consisting of the products the farmer grows or makes. Study the systems diagram in Figure 3 and the photographs in Figure 4 carefully as they show you the main features of vine growing.

Figure 4a
A vineyard

Figure 4b Vine protection from frost

Many businesses rely on vine growing, for example:

- specialised producers of port, vinegar, grape seed oil, wine making equipment (presses, barrels, bottles)
- cellars for maturing and storage of the wine (Figure 5)
- transport, distribution and marketing the product.

However, there is **overproduction** of wine in the EC leading to the development of an increasing 'wine lake'. Like other types of farming, yields of grapes and the amount of wine made have increased because of the high inputs of fertilisers and specially bred vines. The graph in Figure 6 shows this increase in the world wine production since 1910. Notice from the inset table that the actual amounts do vary from year to year.

The EC consumption of wine, however, is falling as alternative drinks are becoming popular. Wine lakes are costly and the distilled alcohol cannot be sold cheaply as it would compete with other sources.

Figure 5   Wine storage

World wine production (1000 hectolitres)							
	1909–14	1930	1950	1965	1980	1986	
World	141134	162540	192961	283659	354305	330116	
Europe	125357	132550	148965	225976	281590	268162	

Figure 6

EC & world wine production (1000 hectolitres)						estimate
	1981	1982	1983	1984	1985	1986
World	310988	365812	311692	322848	301237	330116
EC 12	184021	219675	207964	190498	185504	200103
of which France	57311	79093	67894	63418	69349	70157
Italy	69700	71948	81500	70170	63340	71600
Spain	33667	38251	31238	34179	33103	35500
+ Greece West Germany Luxembourg Portugal						

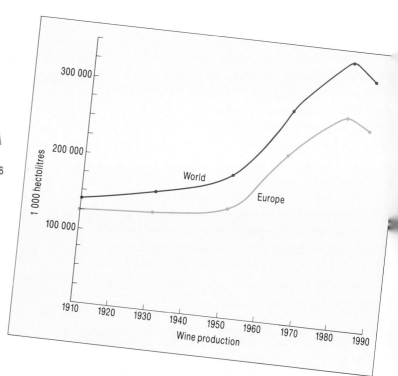

Solutions to the wine lake

Between 1982 and 1990 there was a ban on the replanting of new vines in the hope that this would reduce outputs from vineyards. Research is being carried out into alternatives for the grape such as in the production of low alcohol drinks, animal fodder and grape extracts for medicines. Older farmers are being encouraged to sell their land, but there are several economic and social problems associated with abandoning too many farms in one area.

Activities

1 a Use an atlas to describe the climate of the Mediterranean.

  b Draw a climate graph for Athens using the following information:

	J	F	M	A	M	J	J	A	S	O	N	D
Precipitation	62	37	37	23	23	14	6	7	15	51	56	71mm
Temperature	10	10	12	16	20	25	28	28	24	20	15	11°C

(Look in Chapter 3 for information on how to draw a climate graph.)

  c Compare this climate with the UK – consider total rainfall and seasons and the range in temperature throughout the year.

2 Using the information in the systems diagram of a vineyard in Spain (Figure 3) answer the following questions:

  a Make a list of all the problems a wine grower has to face during the year.

  b Try to suggest a possible solution for three of these problems.

  c Why are large amounts of capital (money) needed to set up a vineyard? How do you think co-operatives would help the small-scale farmer?

  d Why is the vineyard a long term investment for the farmer?

  e What percentage of the EC wine is not distilled for vinegar or for surplus?

3 Copy and complete the following simplified systems diagram based on Figure 3. Make your diagram interesting to look at by organising the layout carefully and by using colours.

Inputs	Processes	Outputs
Temperatures over	Pruning	G ....
.... in winter and	F	W ....
.... in summer.	S	
Rainfall	H	
.... soil	P	
Family	P	
M		
F		
New		

A	P	L	O	U	G	H	I	N	G	B	C	G
D	L	P	E	E	K	A	L	E	N	I	W	N
H	A	R	V	E	S	T	I	N	I	F	G	I
G	N	U	H	I	O	G	J	T	Y	K	L	Z
R	T	N	N	R	R	N	M	N	A	O	P	I
E	I	I	A	O	L	I	V	E	R	L	F	L
E	N	N	Q	R	M	N	O	S	P	N	Y	I
C	G	G	R	A	P	E	T	J	S	I	U	T
E	V	W	X	Y	Z	P	L	A	A	A	B	R
C	B	O	T	T	L	I	N	G	D	P	E	E
F	L	A	G	U	T	R	O	P	G	S	H	F

Figure 7

4 a Using Figure 6 describe the changes in wine production from 1910. When did production increase most rapidly? What seemed to be the trend for production in the 1980s?

  b Look at the data about wine production in Spain. What can you say about the production from 1981 to 1986?

  c How would the trends you identified in *b* affect a small-scale farmer dependent on vines for a living?

5 What problems might the farmers or the villages which rely on farming experience because of the EC policy to reduce the output from each vineyard?

6 Do the Mediterranean word search in Figure 7. There are 18 processes, products, and countries in the table.

10.5 Case-study – Denmark

Farming in Denmark is highly specialised and intensive. Many of the farms deal in both crops and animals, but an increasing number specialise in one or the other. Look at the pie charts in Figure 1 which show the variety of animal produce and crops which are important in Denmark.

Figure 1

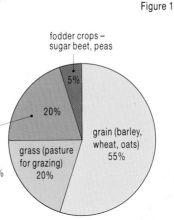

fodder crops – sugar beet, peas 5%
industrial crops (fodder, sugar beet for exporting) 20%
grass (pasture for grazing) 20%
grain (barley, wheat, oats) 55%
Danish crop production by % 25%

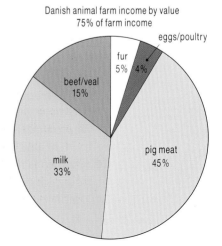

Danish animal farm income by value
75% of farm income
eggs/poultry
fur 5% 4%
beef/veal 15%
pig meat 45%
milk 33%

The success of Danish farming is due to the **co-operative system**. Families working their own farms get help through the co-operatives in all aspects of farm life. Look at Figure 2. There are also special agricultural schools where children can go at 16 years of age to learn farming techniques alongside basic school subjects. At the age of 19, colleges offer a 3 year management course. This is compulsory for all those who wish to buy a farm and/or receive state aid for their farm.

Several changes have taken place in Danish farming. Some of these are shown in Figure 3. Notice that changes in one section, for example number of farms, will have an effect on other sections.

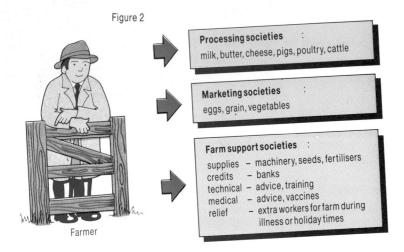

Figure 2

Farmer

Farm information				
	1960	**1970**	**1980**	**1990**
Number of farm units	196 076	140 197	119 155	79 338
Average farm size (ha)	16	21	27	35
Number of farms				
< 10 ha	91 486	44 038	36 196	14 408
10–30 ha	81 153	68 625	51 688	32 228
30–50 ha	17 087	18 868	19 506	16 689
50–100 ha	5 123	7 055	9 619	12 287
> 100 ha	1 227	1 611	2 149	3 727
Workers:				
Full-time	3000 000	161 200	159 400	
Part-time	128 300	34 100		
% population employed in agriculture	16	9	7	–
Number of tractors	111 321	174 600	189 426	162 555 *

* Although the number of tractors has fallen, the capacity of each one has increased.

Figure 3

The farming system in Denmark

Physical inputs:

● **Soils** in Denmark are glacial in origin (see Chapter 4 for further details) and they affect the type of crops the farmer can grow. Look at Figure 4. Notice that the east of Denmark is more suitable for arable crops. Fertilisers are added to increase the yields and replace the minerals which the plants take out of the soil. Usually the crops are **rotated** on the farm so that every year each field will have a different crop grown in it. Permanent grazing grass needs careful treatment.

● **Relief** is not a problem in Denmark as most places are either flat or with gentle hills. Machinery is easy to use on gentle slopes especially where field sizes are large.

● **Climate** Rainfall averages 664mm per year (about the same as London). This is fairly well distributed and is sufficent for arable crops. The soil with its clay content helps to retain some of the available moisture. In Western Denmark where the soils are drier because they contain more gravel, **irrigation** is sometimes used. Temperatures are approximately 0°C in the winter. Frosts are useful in helping to break up the soil. Summer temperatures reach an average of 16°C which is needed to ripen the crops. In the winter cattle are brought indoors and fed on fodder crops either bought or grown on the farm.

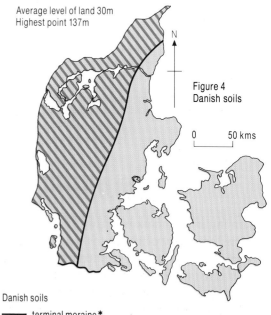

Average level of land 30m
Highest point 137m

Figure 4
Danish soils

0   50 kms

Danish soils

—— terminal moraine *

▨ outwash plain * Lighter sandy soils suitable for pasture. Some of the land is irrigated. Cattle and pigs common.

▦ boulder clay * Darker, heavier soils suitable for arable crops like wheat, barley. Grain growing and pigs are the most important types of farming.

* Look again at Chapter 4 to remind yourself of the meaning of these glaciation terms.

Human and economic inputs

● **Labour** Family run farms are common.

● **Capital** Farm buildings are important especially in pig and poultry farms where the animals are kept indoors all year so they can be easily watched and fed. (See the photograph in Figure 5.) Chickens have individual compartments in large buildings where the right amount of food is automatically given to each hen. This is an example of **factory farming** and it produces very high yields.

● medical care and quality fodder are needed for the animals.

● fertilisers, pesticides and irrigation may be needed for the crops. Research is carried out to keep improving the yields and qualities of the crops and animals.

Figure 5
Intensive farming, Denmark

Activities

1 a Look at Figure 1. What percentage of the farming income comes from:
   i Cattle
   ii Pigs
   iii Poultry
  b What percentage of the farming income comes from selling fodder crops?
  c Why are fodder crops grown?

2 a Why is the co-operative system in Denmark so successful?
  b How are the high quality products maintained?

3 Look at the changes in Danish farming in Figure 3.
  a What has happened to the number of farm units
  b What has happened to
   i the average farm size
   ii the number of farms <10ha
   iii the number of farms >50ha
  c Suggest a reason for the changes noted in *a* and *b*.
  d What changes have taken place in
   i the number of workers on farms
   ii the numbers of people employed in agriculture
  e Suggest a reason for your answer to *d*.

4 a Cattle and pig farming is common in Denmark.
   Figure 6 shows you the density of cattle (dairy and beef) and pigs in each county of Denmark. Work in pairs to complete a different map from your neighbour.
   Using an outline map of Denmark. For either cattle or pigs, complete a choropleth map to show the densities of the animal populations. (Remember, the darkest colour is the highest density.) Suggested categories are:

   cattle   0–40; 41–80; 81–120
   pigs   0–150; 151–300; 301–450; 451–600

Figure 6

		1990	
		Cattle	Pigs
1–3	Capital Region	34	201
4	Vestsjaelland	37	304
5	Storstrøm	42	294
6	Bornholm	39	335
7	Fyn	54	320
8	Vejle	55	348
9	Århus	48	319
10	Sønderjylland	79	418
11	Ribe	76	265
12	Ringkøbing	73	368
13	Viborg	62	290
14	Nordjylland	66	297
	Denmark average	61	318

   Use an atlas and discuss the following with your neighbour.
  b Describe the map you have produced. Are there high density and low density areas in certain parts of the country, or is the distribution even?
  c Describe the difference in the general distribution of cattle and pigs.
  d What type of farming do you think will be carried out in areas where cattle and pig farming is not so common?
  e Suggest a reason why pig farming is more widespread than cattle farming. Think about the different way in which the two types of farming are carried out.

5 Use the information in the unit to produce a systems diagram to show mixed farming in Denmark. Carefully plan your layout and use colours and drawings to make your diagram look attractive.

10.6   The Common Agricultural Policy

The EC has various policies designed to help with parts of the economy. The CAP or the **Common Agricultural Policy** is one such example. As you saw in section 1.2 (Figure 3), agriculture takes up a very large proportion of the annual budget.

The aims of the CAP are to:
- increase farm outputs to help self-sufficiency
- reduce the imports of food
- keep food prices at a reasonable level
- allow a fair standard of living for farmers

All this is possible through loans, grants, training and modernisation of the farms and methods. Many of the small farms have joined up into larger more efficient units. Self-sufficiency is important because it stops the EC from relying on other countries. The CAP was outlined in the 1960s when memories of food shortages in the Second World War were still evident. However, there are both advantages and disadvantages of the policies. These are summarised in Figure 1.

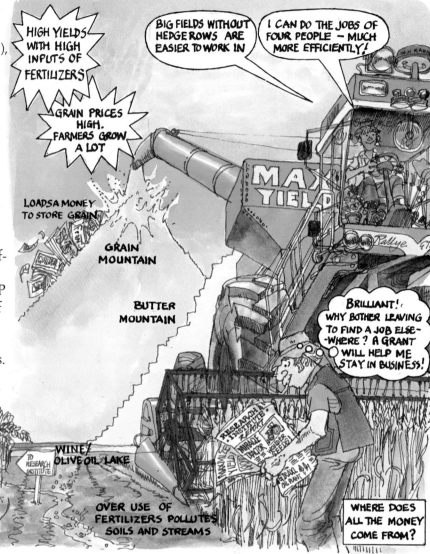

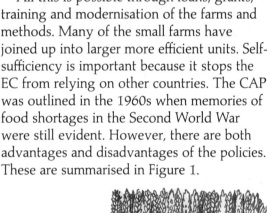

Figure 1
Some of the effects of agricultural overproduction in Europe

Figure 2   Grain store

Food mountains and lakes

One of the main criticisms of the CAP is the surplus food that has been created through encouraging the farmers to produce as much as they can. For example, wheat farmers were guaranteed that the EC would buy their crops at a set price if it could not be sold elsewhere. The crops could then be stored in warehouses similar to those in Figure 2. Some storage is good in case there is a bad harvest one year, but too much stored grain is very expensive to look after. Sometimes products are stored to wait for a price rise. The scale of the surpluses has caused great concern.

What can be done about the surpluses?

Several solutions have been suggested, some with problems of their own. Two important solutions have been:

Quotas – limits placed on the production of milk from dairy farms since 1984. Many farmers in the UK, for example, have had to reduce their herds as excess milk is not bought by the Milk Marketing Board.
Set aside policies – farmers have been compensated for agreeing not to plant crops in certain fields. They can plant woodland instead. Some farmers are encouraged to use traditional methods of farming without chemical fertilisers where the outputs would not be so great.

Activities

1 a What does CAP stand for?
  b What are the aims of the CAP?
  c What effect has the policy had on farm outputs?
  d Using the information in Figure 1, list three advantages and three disadvantages of the CAP. Give reasons for your answers.

2 a Look at the data in Figure 3. A value of 100% indicates that the EC is self-sufficient in that product. In how many of the eight products were the EC countries self-sufficient in 1968/9?
  b In how many of the products were the EC countries self-sufficient in 1973/4?
  c Describe the degree of self-sufficiency since 1984/5.
  d Has the degree of self-sufficiency gradually increased in all cases? Give a reason for your answer.
  e What do you think happens to the surplus products?

3 a Draw line graphs to show the surpluses of food (except for cereals) using the data in Figure 4.
  b Choose an alternative method to show the data for cereals. You could draw a bar graph or a pictogram.
  c Describe the changes in food surpluses between 1979 and 1988.
  d i Discuss in pairs how you would reduce the surpluses in the EC. Think about the possible problems of your solution. Discuss the views with the rest of the class.
    ii Imagine you work for the EC Commission. Prepare a statement to present at a meeting about the problems of wine lakes in the EC and how to solve them.

Figure 3

Degree of self-sufficiency in the main agricultural products

	1968/69	EC9 1963/74	EC10 1984/85	1985/86	EC12 1986/87
Total cereals	86	91	118	119	111
Wheat	94	104	129	120	119
Sugar	82	100	101	126	127
Fresh fruit	80	82	83	88	85
Butter	92	98	134	130	105
Cheese	99	103	107	106	106
Beef	95	96	108	106	108
Sheep meat & Goat meat	56	66	76	80	80

Figure 4

	1979	1983	(EC10) 1986	(EC12) 1987	1988
Surpluses (1000 tonnes)					
Cereals	2.67	9.54	14.71	13.76	10.75
Olive oil	0.53	0.12	0.28	0.32	0.40
Alcohol (1000 hecto litres)			0.66	1.09	2.89
Butter	0.29	0.68	1.3	0.88	0.22
Skimmed milk powder	0.21	0.95	0.86	0.72	0.14
Beef	0.31	0.41	0.67	0.69	0.72

Dictionary

arable farming   crop growing
co-operative   a group of people working together buying and selling goods

extensive farming   low inputs giving low yields per area
intensive farming   high inputs giving high yields per area

marginal farming   on land which is barely suitable
mixed farming   crop and animal farming
pastoral farming   keeping animals

The word 'industry' usually conjures up images of a large factory making chemicals or cars or perhaps the smaller factories you have seen on an industrial estate. Whilst we would all agree that these are industries, the word 'industry' really means **work**. Anyone who works such as miners, teachers, factory workers, office clerks are all involved in industry. Figure 1 shows some examples of industry.

Industry can be divided up into three main types:

● Primary industries – these produce **raw materials** for other industries.
● Secondary industries – these **manufacture** or make products.
● Tertiary industries – these provide a **service** to people or other industries.

There is a rapidly developing fourth type called quaternary industries – these include some of the new **high-technology** industries which are involved in research and development. They provide information and expertise in areas such as microchips and telecommunications.

In the EC countries the percentage of the working population in different types of industry varies; this is shown in the table in Figure 2. These figures can be used to indicate how **developed** a country is.

The more developed countries of Europe e.g. Germany, France and the UK often have a low percentage working in primary industry (e.g. farming) but a high percentage in services. The less well developed countries e.g. Spain, Greece and Portugal have a higher percentage in farming but

Figure 1

Figure 2

EC Country	% of the working population		
	Primary	Secondary	Tertiary
Belgium	3	30	67
Denmark	7	27	66
Germany	6	41	53
Greece	29	27	44
Spain	17	32	51
France	8	33	59
Eire	16	29	55
Italy	11	34	55
Luxembourg	4	33	63
Netherlands	5	28	67
Portugal	24	34	42
United Kingdom	3	32	65

a lower percentage in services. The developed countries have efficient farming methods. The use of tractors and combine harvesters requires little labour yet the yields are high. This contrasts with the **labour intensive**, primitive methods of farming in the poorer countries of the EC.

Industry in the more developed countries produces a massive range of products to be sold both at home and abroad. Manufacturing is efficient and earns high profits. To support the manufacturing and to cater for the needs of the populations of these developed countries many service industries are required. In the less well developed countries, industry is not as well developed. Many people work in craft industries such as pottery and weaving and there are fewer large industries. The people are poorer and do not demand the range of services.

Activities

1 In the different countries of the European Community the number of people who work in each type of industry varies.

a Use the table in Figure 2 to draw divided bar charts for each country. The graph has been started in Figure 3.

b Read through the following statements. There is an 'odd one out' in each of the bracketed lists. Can you spot each one? Use your graph from 2a to help.

   i Countries with the highest percentage in primary industry are (Portugal, Greece, Luxembourg, Spain)

   ii Countries with the lowest percentage in primary industry are (UK, Eire, Belgium and Netherlands)

   iii (Belgium, Denmark, Netherlands, Portugal) have a high percentage in tertiary industries.

   iv (Greece, UK, Spain, Italy) have a lower percentage working in tertiary industry.

2 On an outline map of Europe, construct a choropleth (shading) map to show the figures for primary industry. Use the following key.

   Key 0–5%   6–15%   over 15%
          yellow   orange   red

   On your map, label the EC countries.

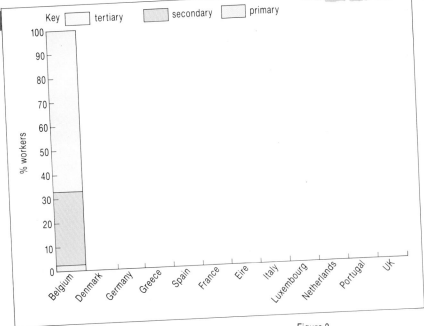

Figure 3

3 In Chapter 6 you learnt about the **core** and **periphery** in the EC. Look back at the map on page 52. Using your completed map, describe the pattern on your map.
Describe the links between:
● 'more developed' countries, numbers in primary industry and the **core** of the EC.
● 'less developed' countries, numbers in primary industry and the **periphery** of the EC.

11.2   The manufacturing industry system

Manufacturing is the 'make it' industry.

Figure 1 shows how manufacturing industry can be shown as a **systems** diagram. The industries need raw materials. They also need money, labour, power and machines to operate their processes. These are the **inputs** to the industry.

The inputs are used to manufacture the end product. The final product such as a computer or a pair of jeans, may be sold in a shop or it may be a raw material (or **component**) for another industry. For example, the iron and steel industry produces steel for other industries to make into products such as ships and cars. In the processing, **waste materials** may be formed. The products and the wastes are the **outputs** of the industry. Another output is the profit that the company makes when it sells its products.

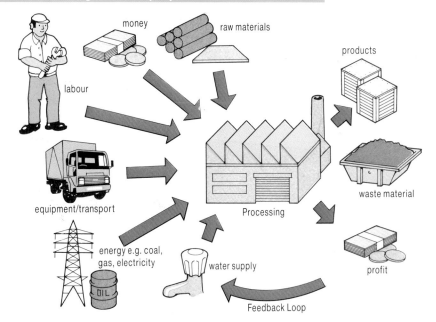

Figure 1   Systems diagram for a manufacturing company

Manufacturing industries make a wide variety of goods (see Figure 2). Products like steel, ships and cement are made by **heavy** industries. They use bulky raw materials and make heavy, bulky goods. Industries which make shoes, watches and fizzy drinks are examples of **light** industries. They use small, light raw materials to produce goods which are light and small.

Some industries need to locate close to their raw materials; these are called **fixed** industries e.g. cement manufacture, iron and steel making. An iron and steel works uses iron ore, coal and limestone in its processing. All of these are bulky and expensive to transport so the industry is located close to them to reduce transport costs.

Other industries have freedom to choose where they locate; they are called **footloose** industries. An example of a footloose industry is computer manufacture. The industry uses small and light components which are quite cheap to transport and the industry uses electricity which is easily available from the **National Grid**. The end product, computers, are also light and easy to transport.

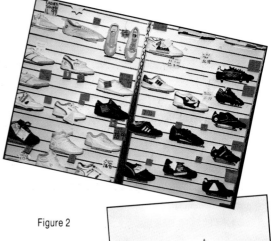

Figure 2

Activities

1 a Figure 3 shows information about Rolls Royce Aeroengines. Produce a systems diagram like the one in Figure 1 for the industry.

  b Choose a product of your own, or use one of the suggestions in the photographs in Figure 2. Decide what the inputs, manufacturing and outputs will be and draw a second systems diagram for your product.

2 The Rolls Royce Aeroengines factory at Sunderland relies upon other industries for its raw materials. It also supplies other industries with components. This is called industrial **linkage**. Give two examples of industrial linkage from the Figure.

Rolls Royce Aeroengines (UK) Ltd
Sunderland, Tyne and Wear has just one of many Rolls Royce factories employing 700 people. The factory uses computerised machines to shape steel into components for aeroplane engines.

Main inputs
- steel forgings from Doncaster, Blaenaravon and Cincinnatti (USA)
- labour force from the local area
- machine tools from Birmingham and Germany
- chemicals from Teesside
- paint from Birtley

Outputs
- components for aeroplane engines sent to Derby and East Kilbride
- scrap metal sent to Gateshead or returned to the foundries at Doncaster and Blaenarvon
- dirty water, treated and put into River Wear

Figure 3

3 *a* Study the photographs in Figure 2 showing a variety of products from manufacturing industry. Copy and complete the table below to show whether the industry will be light or heavy, fixed or footloose. An example has been done for you.

Industry	Light or heavy?	Fixed or footloose?
Shipbuilding	Heavy	Fixed

b Copy and complete the paragraph below using your table and the photographic evidence.

Industries using bulky raw materials are called .... industries. They must locate close to their raw materials so they are .... industries. Two examples of these industries are .... and .... Some industries are not tied to their raw materials and use electricity for power such as .... and .... These are .... industries, free to locate in many areas. Their products are less bulky and use smaller raw materials; they are called .... industries.

4 *a* Study the information in Figure 4 about the Ford Car Company. On an outline map of Europe mark and label all the places mentioned. Use an atlas to help you locate the places accurately. Draw a red arrow going to the factory for each input and mark a blue arrow going from the factory for each output. Label the arrows with the actual input or output.

b Is Ford Europe a fixed or footloose industry? Explain your answer.

Ford Europe

The Ford car company is a MULTINATIONAL with vehicle plants throughout the world.
- Ford Europe is an independent part of the company
- The largest single assembly plant is in Cologne in Germany. Here they assemble Fiesta, Capri and Granada cars using COMPONENTS from all over Europe.

Inputs
- engines from Spain and Wales
- axles and transmissions from France and England
- glass from UK and Spain
- brakes from France
- alloy wheels from Italy
- headlights from Germany, UK, Italy and Spain

Manufacturing   assembly of components, paint spraying, quality control

Outputs
- cars sold on the local market and exported to all the EC countries

Figure 4

11.3   The location of manufacturing industry in the EC

The core of the EC has most of the wealth, the largest cities and the major industrial areas of the EC.

The map in Figure 1 shows that industry is not evenly spread in the EC. Why do you think some areas are more attractive for industry than others?

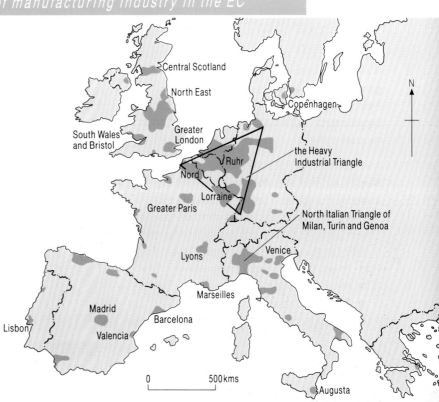

Figure 1
Major industrial areas in the EC

The older heavy industrial areas are mostly located on the coalfields. These are shown on the map in Figure 2. The coalfield areas became important for industry during the **Industrial Revolution** in the late 19th century. The coal was important as a source of power and as a raw material. Industries like iron and steel and chemicals set up on the coalfields because the coal was bulky and expensive to transport. Industrial areas linked to coalfields are called **resource** locations.

Other industrial areas are linked to large towns and cities. The large number of people creates a big demand for goods. The industries in capital cities such as Paris, London and Amsterdam are examples of these **market** locations.

Industry is always changing. New technology is developed, new products are made and the raw materials alter. Some older industrial areas have lost industry and declined whereas other areas are growing and gaining industries.

Many industries today rely on the import and export of goods so the **port** location has become important. There is often plenty of cheap, flat land in coastal areas for a large modern factory to be built.

Since the 1980s there has been a growth in the **high technology** industries such as electronics and computers. These industries have grown together in certain areas called **Business Parks**. These Parks tend to be near good transport links such as motorways and

Key
1 NW Spain
2 Nord Pas-de-Calais
3 Sambre-Meuse
4 Campine and Limburg
5 Ruhr
6 Aachen (lignite)
7 Lorraine-Saar

0   500 kms

Figure 2   EC coalfields

close to University towns which provide a skilled labour force. Most Business Parks are located in pleasant environments away from the hustle and bustle of city life.

Activities

1 The main industrial areas in the EC are either in resource locations, market locations or port locations.
  For each of these locations write down three examples of each from the map in Figure 1. Explain why each location is a good site for an industry.

2 Figure 3 gives some information about different factories. In pairs read the information carefully. Each factory is going to be built somewhere on the map shown in Figure 4. Decide where you would locate each factory. Copy the sketch map and add the name of the factory at the chosen location.

3 After 1992 the EC will become a single market. This will have a great effect on European industry.
  a Imagine that you are a company director. Your firm already sends goods abroad by lorry as well as selling them in the UK. What benefits will your firm feel after 1992? Can you see any disadvantages? Prepare a report for the next Board Meeting outlining:
  ● the benefits to your company
  ● any disadvantages or problems
  ● a five point plan for your company that will improve its chances of competing in Europe.
  Take turns to present your reports.

Figure 3   Factory sites

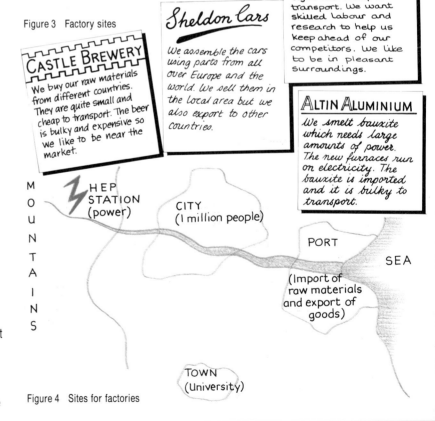

CASTLE BREWERY
We buy our raw materials from different countries. They are quite small and cheap to transport. The beer is bulky and expensive so we like to be near the market.

Sheldon Cars
We assemble the cars using parts from all over Europe and the world. We sell them in the local area but we also export to other countries.

CDC COMPUTERS
Our components are light and cheap to transport. We want skilled labour and research to help us keep ahead of our competitors. We like to be in pleasant surroundings.

ALTIN ALUMINIUM
We smelt bauxite which needs large amounts of power. The new furnaces run on electricity. The bauxite is imported and it is bulky to transport.

MOUNTAINS

HEP STATION (power)

CITY (1 million people)

PORT

SEA

(Import of raw materials and export of goods)

TOWN (University)

Figure 4   Sites for factories

11.4 Case study – the heavy industrial triangle

Most of the coalmines, steel making and engineering in the EC are
located in a central part of North West Europe called the **heavy
industrial triangle**. The area includes the Ruhr coalfield in Germany,
the Nord coalfield in France and the Lorraine iron ore field. Locate
these places on the map in Figure 1. The area produces 95% of EC
coal and 50% of the steel in Europe.

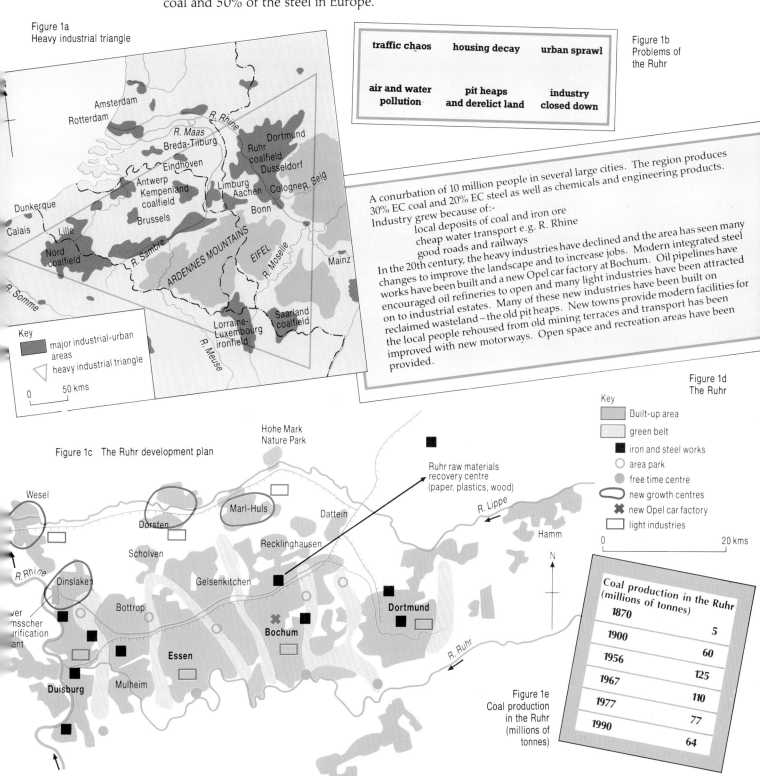

Figure 1a
Heavy industrial triangle

Figure 1b
Problems of
the Ruhr

| traffic chaos | housing decay | urban sprawl |
| air and water pollution | pit heaps and derelict land | industry closed down |

A conurbation of 10 million people in several large cities. The region produces
30% EC coal and 20% EC steel as well as chemicals and engineering products.
Industry grew because of:-
    local deposits of coal and iron ore
    cheap water transport e.g. R. Rhine
    good roads and railways
In the 20th century, the heavy industries have declined and the area has seen many
changes to improve the landscape and to increase jobs. Modern integrated steel
works have been built and a new Opel car factory at Bochum. Oil pipelines have
encouraged oil refineries to open and many light industries have been attracted
on to industrial estates. Many of these new industries have been built on
reclaimed wasteland – the old pit heaps. New towns provide modern facilities for
the local people rehoused from old mining terraces and transport has been
improved with new motorways. Open space and recreation areas have been
provided.

Figure 1d
The Ruhr

Key
  Built-up area
  green belt
  iron and steel works
  area park
  free time centre
  new growth centres
  new Opel car factory
  light industries

Figure 1c   The Ruhr development plan

Figure 1e
Coal production
in the Ruhr
(millions of
tonnes)

Coal production in the Ruhr (millions of tonnes)	
1870	5
1900	60
1956	125
1967	110
1977	77
1990	64

The Ruhr is the largest coalfield in the EC. Mining began in the 19th century. Iron ore was available from the hills to the south and soon the region became an area of **heavy industry** with iron and steel, chemicals and engineering industries. Many cities grew in the area including Essen, Bochum, Duisberg and Dortmund (see Figure 1c).

The coal was both a fuel and a raw material for the industry. Many of the industries were **linked**. For example, the mined coal was used in steel making and car manufacturers, such as Volkswagen, provided a market for the steel.

Today there has been some decline but the Ruhr remains a very large and important industrial area. This is partly due to **industrial inertia**. In the Ruhr, steel industries located to use the local coal and iron ore. Today, the coal is more expensive than imported coal from the USA or Poland. The iron ore is imported as local supplies are exhausted. The Ruhr is no longer the best place to have the steelworks, but the industry survives. This is what is meant by industrial inertia.

The older, small steelworks have closed and new large works have been built on the banks of the Rhine – a **waterfront** location. There are still many steel using industries in the Ruhr area so there is a **market** for the steel. The Government has given **subsidies** to the steel industry so that it can buy Ruhr coal more cheaply.

Figure 1 describes some more characteristics of the heavy industrial triangle in the EC.

Activities

1 Use Figure 1 and an atlas to help you answer the following questions.
  a Which countries form a part of the heavy industrial triangle?
  b Which capital cities are located in the heavy industrial triangle?
  c Which three important industrial areas form the corners of the triangle?
  d Why is the 'heavy industrial triangle' a good name for the area?

2 Study Figure 1c, showing a map of the Ruhr area.
  a Work out the area that the Ruhr region covers. Do this by working out the distance:
  ● from north to south
  ● from east to west
  ● multiplying your two results together. Your final result will be in square kilometres.
  b How many iron and steel works are there in the Ruhr?
  c Describe the location of the steel works, e.g. are they mostly in the west? or the north? are they close to the River Lippe? or the River Rhine?
  d What were the advantages for the steel industry setting up in the Ruhr region?
  e New steel works in the Ruhr have been built close to the River Rhine – can you think why? (Hint – most iron ore is imported now.)

3 a Draw a line graph to show the figures for coal production in the Ruhr (Figure 1e). Add the following labels to your graph in the correct place:
  coal discovered   peak of production   decline begun   output steady
  b Write some sentences explaining how each of the following have helped the Ruhr to stay an important industrial area:
  market   steel using industries   the Government

4 a Study the problems of the Ruhr area (Figure 1). Draw sketches and add labels to explain and illustrate each problem.
  b Some of the solutions to the problems of the Ruhr are shown in Figure 1c. Design your own sketches for each of the solutions shown. Write a sentence below each sketch saying what the solution is and which problem it will solve.

5 Using Figure 1c answer the following questions:
  a How many green belts divide up the Ruhr area? In which direction do they go?
  b How many Area Parks and Free Time Centres are located in the Ruhr?
  c Where are the Free Time Centres located and how is this different from the Area Parks?
  d If you lived in Marl-Huls, how far is it and in which direction would you travel to the nearest:
  ● Nature Park
  ● Area Park
  ● Free Time Centre?
  e Explain why the Ruhr Raw Materials Recovery Centre and the River Emscher Water Purification plant are in good locations.

6 Imagine you work in the advertising department of the Ruhr Planning Authority. Design a poster to attract new industry to the Ruhr region.

11.5   Industry in the UK

In the UK today, only 3% of people work in the primary industries such as farming and mining. During this century there has been a massive reduction in the numbers of miners and farmers. The main reasons have been increased mechanisation and the use of modern machines and the closure of mines due to **exhaustion** of the coal reserves.

Over 95% of the workforce in the UK have jobs in manufacturing and the service industries. These industries are mainly found in towns and cities where 80% of the people live. Figure 1 shows the main industrial areas in the UK.

In the UK the 20th century has seen many changes in industry. The **type** of industry has changed and the **location** of industry has changed. A study of north-east England will show many of these changes.

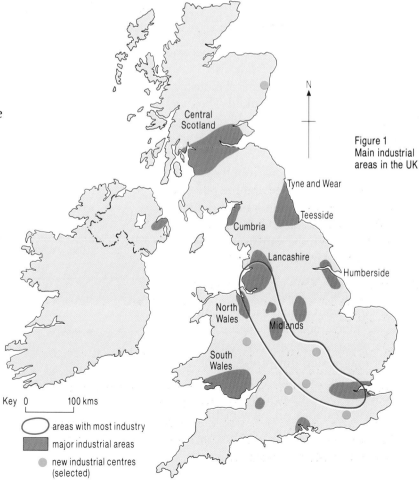

Figure 1
Main industrial areas in the UK

Key 0   100 kms

⬭ areas with most industry

▨ major industrial areas

● new industrial centres (selected)

Case study – the north-east of England

What is your **perception** of the north-east of England? Where does it start and end? What image do you have of it? Figure 2 shows some images other people have of the area. Study them carefully. What do you think, can you see any errors in the map?

The region has seen great changes in recent years. Let's now explore the region.

Industry in the north-east of England grew in the 19th century during the Industrial Revolution. A large coalfield was discovered – the cross-section in Figure 3 shows the extent of the coalfield. Coal mining began in the west on the **exposed** coalfield. Here the coal was close to the surface and easily mined. At the time the north-east coalfield supplied London with most of its coal. People and money flooded into the region and other industries grew.

The presence of the coal attracted iron and steel making especially in Middlesbrough and at Consett. Shipbuilding located at the mouths of the Rivers Tyne, Wear and Tees and other steel using industries e.g. engineering and railway equipment became established in the area. Teesside also developed an important chemical industry.

These industries are all **linked**. They are located together on the coalfield to reduce the costs of moving the coal and other raw materials.

Today, most of the coal from these early mines has been exhausted and the pits closed. There is still mining in the west of the region but it is opencast mining. This method removes coal from the narrower seams which were untouched by the earlier deep mines. The diagrams in Figure 4 show the different methods of mining coal.

The **concealed** coalfield in the east of the area was mined much later. Figure 3 shows the coal seams in the east covered by a thick layer of **magnesian limestone**. In the 19th century, mining methods were primitive and the coal was too deep below the limestone for pits to be established. New methods of mining deeper coal were needed before mining could move east.

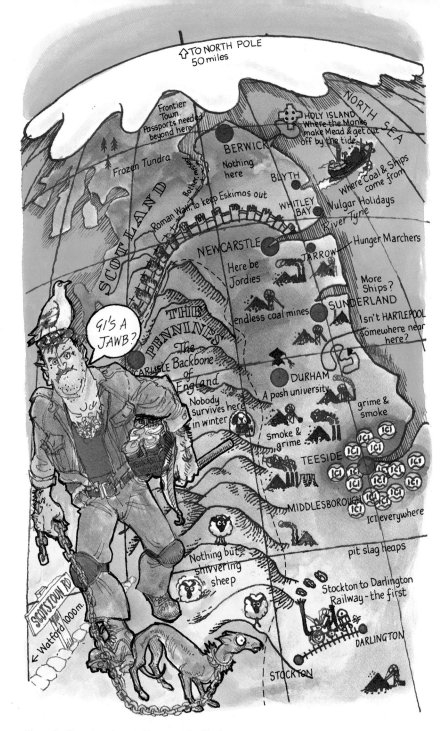

Figure 2   Stereotyped mental image of the North

Figure 3   Cross section of the North East

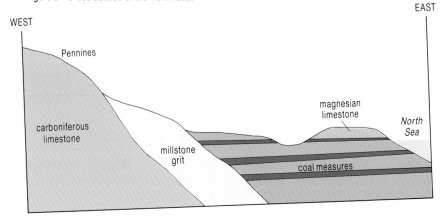

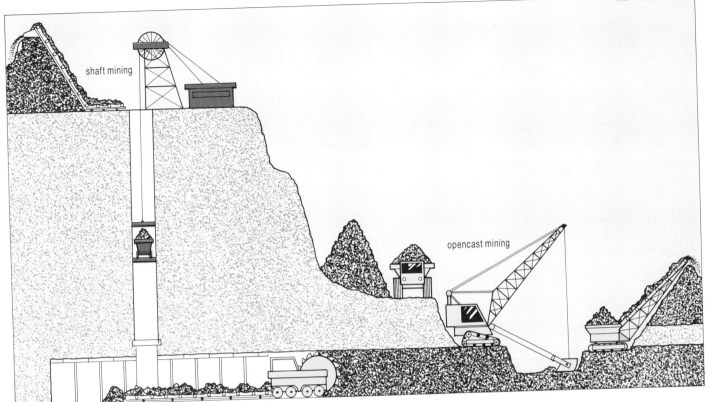

Figure 4 Methods of mining coal

Today, the north-east coalfield is nearly exhausted and only a few pits remain. These are modern collieries located at the coast e.g. Easington and Dawdon which are mining coal up to five miles under the North Sea.

In the 1960s and 1970s, many industries closed in the north-east causing **decline** and massive unemployment. The landscape was littered with derelict buildings, closed shipyards, old mine workings, pit heaps and decaying villages.

Today the region has begun to recover from the decline. The Government and the EC has given the region special help by designating it as a **Development Area** and by creating three **Enterprise Zones** (see page 134). The region receives loans and grants to help attract industry. Figure 5 shows the benefits the area receives in more detail.

The Enterprise Zones were created after 1980. They are quite small areas (50–400 hectares) with severe problems of decay. Each zone has land available for light industry and warehousing and the companies in the zone receive massive benefits (see Figure 5). In the north-east, Hartlepool, Middlesbrough and Tyneside each have an Enterprise Zone. Part of the Tyneside Enterprise Zone was used as the Garden Festival site in 1990 (see page 72) reclaiming a derelict and polluted industrial area.

The region has been successful in attracting **foreign investment**. The site chosen was in the Development Area and Nissan received £100 million in Government grants. By 1989 there were six Japanese firms in the north-east and in 1990 Fujitsu announced plans to build a factory at Newton Aycliffe (see Figure 6).

Government aid to the region

Development Areas	Enterprise zones
Government built factories available at low rents and rates, up to 2 years rent free	rate free factories for 10 years
factory building – up to 45% grant	maximum grants for machinery and buildings
government loans available	no development land tax
85% grant to reclaim derelict land	no charge for industrial training
£10 per week training grants	100% allowances for consultation, extension or improvement of factories
grants for training centres	no industrial development certificates needed

Figure 5

Other developments like the MetroCentre (see page 66) have improved the image of the region. The MetroCentre is the largest indoor shopping and leisure complex in the EC, and it attracts visitors from all over the country. The Centre was built with the help of Government grants and reclaimed 40 hectares of derelict land.

Elsewhere in the region, pit heaps have been landscaped e.g. the Elemore Colliery site and new roads have been built such as the A69 trunk road connecting the MetroCentre and buildings renovated like Holmside Hall. Figure 7 shows these and other improvements taking place around the region.

Japanese to create 900 new North jobs

By IAN CAMERON
Industrial Editor

JAPANESE electronics company Fujitsu will today unveil plans for a huge North-East plant creating more than 900 new jobs.

The announcement will herald one of the biggest ever overseas investments in the region.

The news marks the end of months of talks between development agencies in the region and Fujitsu which is looking for a site to make computer components.

The North-East is believed to have beaten off stiff competition from other UK and European sites.

As well as direct employment, the arrival of Fujitsu will provide valuable spin-off jobs for local sub-contractors.

Apart from Sunderland car maker Nissan, which hopes to employ 2,500 people by the end of the year, it is felt that Fujitsu is the most important Far East investment in the region so far.

The Journal 12.4.89

Figure 6

Figure 7

CONSETT 10 YEARS ON ...

CONSETT'S Number One Industrial Estate was purchased in 1981 and, following the demise of the steelworks, has been the focal point of industrial development in Derwentside.

The development is now fully occupied with 105 factories occupied by 70 companies employing 1,396 people.

Phase two, covering the remaining 45 acres, incorporates a high tech scheme as well as advance factories and fully serviced sites. About five acres remain undeveloped.

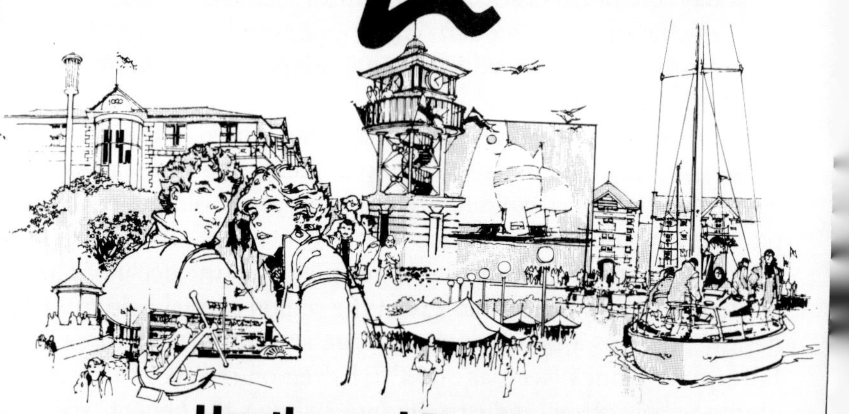

A high quality, low cost operating environment, and professional business support measures have now helped some 200 companies to create 4,500 new jobs in fields as diverse as precision engineering and biotechnology, food production and supermicro computer manufacture.

Significantly these firms are forecasting they will create 1,600 additional jobs over the next two to three years.

Derwentside District Council now runs with the slogan, "An environment for Success", reflecting the area's semi-rural location, rapid access to major city conurbations and international ports, a committed labour force, and an outstanding business support package which can significantly improve profitability, rates of return and payback periods.

Business in the district can qualify for European finance, and financial aid from central Government.

This can be added to with grants from Durham County Council and Derwentside District Council.

Durham Advertiser,
Thursday, October 26, 1989

TEESSIDE

HOME OF THE UK'S MOST EXCITING NEW WATERFRONT DEVELOPMENT

... Hartlepool Renaissance A Marina and Much More

Houses, shops, restaurants, bars, a prestigious hotel, a business park all situated around Hartlepool's Maritime Heritage, this is Hartlepool Renaissance.

A mile of waterfront, a two hundred acre site complete with infrastructure and services just waiting for the development schemes that will make Hartlepool the most exciting location in the north east of England.

Hartlepool Renaissance is a marina and much more. It is an exciting new waterside environment in which people can live and work. With berths for over 400 boats, public spaces like the Hoe and the Piazza that will give people exciting new recreational and community facilities and sites for businesses which can benefit from a waterfront location.

Teesside Development Corporation through Hartlepool Renaissance is spending £51m on land acquisition, site preparation and provision of infrastructure; repairing harbour and sea walls, installing new lock gates, putting in access and distribution roads, car parks, public spaces and services to the site, and so developers have a fully prepared site to move onto.

Lead developers, Lovell Partnerships, have already started work on their prestigious home development, on Warrior Quay. Other developers are invited to submit their schemes now.

Hartlepool Renaissance is happening now, come and be part of it, contact Duncan Hall, Chief Executive, Teesside Development Corporation, Tees House, Riverside Park, Middlesbrough, Cleveland TS2 1RE. Tel 0642 230636. Fax 0642 230843

TEESSIDE

Initiative Talent Ability

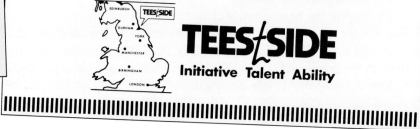

Activities

1 *a* Make a copy of the map in Figure 1, marking on the main industrial areas. Using an atlas and the map on page 82 (UK coalfields) decide which areas are linked to coalfields and which are linked to cities and ports. Use two different colours or shading to show the coalfield areas and the ports and cities. Add a key to explain your colours.

  b Using your atlas mark and label one main city in each of the coalfield areas shown.

  c Choose an industrial town or city near where you live. Mark and label it on your map.

2 Figure 8 shows a map of industrial areas in a city. Copy the map leaving out the letters. Replace the letters on the map with the correct label from the list below.

  old inner city industry
  industry close to raw materials
  industry (services) in the CBD
  port industries
  hi-tech industries
  industrial estates near main roads

3 *a* Work in pairs and use your local knowledge and a map of your local area. Recognise where the industry is on your map.
    What type of industry is found in each area?
    Can you recognise any of the types of industrial area in the list in activity 2? Copy the list and write the name of a local example alongside.

  b Hold a class discussion about your local industries. Use the following themes to guide your discussion:
    Where are the oldest industries in your local area? How many examples can you think of?
    Are there any new industries in your local area? Where are they located? Name some examples.
    Are there any new retail parks planned or built? What do they contain?
    Has a local city centre seen any redevelopment? What has been cleared and what is it being replaced by?

  c Using the results of the discussion and activity 3a produce a labelled sketch map of your area to show the location of the industrial areas. Use the list of types of industrial area given in activity 2 to help you label your sketch map.
    (Refresh your memory on sketch maps – look back to page 12.)

Figure 8   Industrial areas in a city

4 Imagine that you are to lead the talks with a Japanese firm which is trying to decide where to locate a new factory. The firm will want to know:

  a Details of the problems the region has had in recent years.

  b Any Government help which may be available.

  c How the region has recovered from the decline and the advantages it now has for industry.

  In small groups, produce a brochure to present to the company at the talks. Include some pictures, maps and diagrams as well as written work.

6 *a* What is your 'mental map' or perception of the north-east now? Study Figure 2 again. What are the **misconceptions** of the artist? Can you explain why people have these images of the north-east?

  b Try drawing your own mental map of a different area in the UK. Check how accurate you have been by using an atlas and other books.

11.6   Case study – high-tech and service industries in the UK

The 'hi-tech' and service industries are examples of **growth** industries. Since the 1980s these industries have expanded. Many new companies have been formed and the growth has created many new jobs. Hi-tech industries tend to locate in clusters called Science Parks and Business Parks. They are found throughout the UK (see Figure 1).

Notice that three **hi-tech corridors** can be recognised in Figure 1:

● the M4 corridor including Sunrise Strip (Slough–Reading–Swindon)
● Solent Strip – Southampton–Portsmouth
● Silicon Glen – Glasgow–Edinburgh

Hi-tech industries are light industries which need less space than the heavy industries. The raw materials are small so that transport costs are less important. They are **footloose** industries and free to locate almost anywhere. The factors which affect the location of the hi-tech industries are:

● links with universities
● availability of skilled labour
● electronics firms nearby
● government help
● pleasant environment
● good transport and access to an airport

Figure 1

Key

areas with most high-tech industries

+ some new industrial centres and business parks

0   100 kms

N

Silicon Glen in Scotland

Silicon Glen is the name given to the Central Valley of Scotland where hi-tech industry is located. The industries employ 46 200 people and the total exports from the companies are greater than those of whisky! Many of the companies are **foreign multinationals** e.g. the American companies IBM and Compaq. One of the attractions of the area has been the grants given by the SDA (Scottish Development Agency).

In the suburbs of Glasgow the SDA has developed the West of Scotland Science Park. The Park is closely associated with the Universities of Glasgow and Strathclyde. Industrial units have been built and companies are researching into computers, silicon chips and laser technology. The site is only 20 minutes from Glasgow city centre and the airport and the setting is more like a country estate than an industrial estate.

Activities

1 Study the location of the 'new' industrial areas in the UK shown on the map in Figure 1.

  a Copy and complete the sentences below using the map.

  Most of the new industrial centres in the UK are in the (north/south) of the country. Many are close to ...., the capital city. The three most important areas are .... in Scotland, the .... Corridor going north of London to Cambridge and the .... which follows the M4 west of London. Some of the hi-tech areas are in New Towns e.g. .... while others are in the older industrial areas e.g. .... and ....

2 a Trace the outline map of Scotland from Figure 2. Draw bars to show the totals of electronics firms for each region. Place each bar carefully on your map. Plan it first so that the bars do not overlap. Use a scale of 1mm equals one firm. Either label the regions on your map or add a key for them.

  b Describe the pattern shown on your map. Where are most of the factories and why? Where are there least factories and why? You may find it useful to look at a map of Scotland in your atlas showing the relief of the land and transport routes.

3 Figure 3 shows some comments made by people living and working in Silicon Glen. Read them carefully.

  a Write a list of the advantages and a list of the disadvantages of Silicon Glen.

  b Imagine such an industrial area was to be built near you or perhaps there already is one! Your work for the local newspaper which is to run a front page article on the development. Decide whether you are in favour or against the idea and write an article explaining your point of view.
  Join up with someone else in the class of the opposite point of view to you and design your front page with headlines, newspaper title etc. If you can why not produce your front pages using computer software?

4 What do the hi-tech industries make? Do some research on your own and collect pictures out of old magazines and newspapers of hi-tech products. You could draw pictures of those products you can't find. As a class or in small groups, produce a large poster for your classroom advertising the products of hi-tech industry.

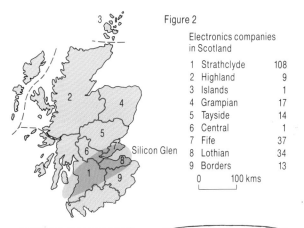

Figure 2

Electronics companies in Scotland

1	Strathclyde	108
2	Highland	9
3	Islands	1
4	Grampian	17
5	Tayside	14
6	Central	1
7	Fife	37
8	Lothian	34
9	Borders	13

0   100 kms

Figure 3   People of Silicon Glen

Dictionary

Business Park   a collection of hi-tech firms, offices, shops, hotels, and leisure facilities on land privately developed by a commercial firm

Enterprise Zones   areas which receive large grants and other help to attract industry and reclaim wasteland

heavy industrial triangle   concentration of coal, steel, chemicals and engineering industries in the EC

industrial linkage   industries receiving products and giving products to other industries

manufacturing   changing raw materials into end products

raw materials   goods which are used by other industries to make a product

Science Park   a collection of hi-tech firms and offices with direct links to universities

services   tertiary industries like teaching or banking

Less than 40 years ago very few people had holidays. If they did they were often unpaid. People earned lower wages and few could drive let alone afford to own a car. Most people did not travel further than their nearest town or city.

In the 1980s over 50% of the people in the European Community went away on holiday either to another EC country or elsewhere in the world. Many more spent their holidays in their own country.

Tourism is an industry and the tourist is the person who travels for recreation. The tourist industry is very important within the European Community. It employs 7.5 million people – 6% of the working population and it provides 5% of the Community's wealth. The EC countries earn more from tourism than they spend on it!

Tourism is a **service industry**; it earns the EC countries money and creates many jobs in transport, hotels, catering and recreation activities. The EC countries also earn money through **foreign exchange**, when the tourists exchange their money for the currency of the country they are visiting.

The countries of the European Community recognised the importance of tourism by making 1990, **European Year of Tourism**. During that year the Community had several aims:
- to encourage 'off-season' tourism
- to develop cultural and rural tourism
- to promote travel especially by young people
- to make people more aware of different cultures and ways of life
- to promote the free movement of people within the Community

Activities

1 Using Figure 1 you can recognise three main types of holiday:
- 'sea and sand'
- cultural, historic and scenic
- winter skiing

a Write a few sentences to describe what the map shows about the location, climate and attraction of each holiday type.

b Conduct a classroom survey – what were the main holiday destinations of your class? Into which category of holiday did they fit? Complete a table to show the holiday details:

Country	Holiday Type			
	Sea and Sand	Cultural	Winter	Total
UK				
Other EC countries				
Spain				
Italy				
Greece				
Eire				
Germany				
France				
etc				
Other countries of the world				

c On an outline map of Europe, plot bars to show the total number of people who visited each country. Draw the bar for the rest of the world at the side of your map and label it. Divide each bar according to the number of each type of holiday. Use three different colours for the types and add a key and title to your map.

d Which was the most popular destination? Can you explain why?

e Which was the most popular type of holiday? Can you explain why?

2 Study the information in Figure 2 on EC tourism. Use different ways of plotting the information – a bar graph, pie chart and pictogram are three suggestions. Work carefully, make your diagrams neat and colourful, don't forget to label axes, add titles and keys if needed.

a Write one sentence giving the most popular **type** of holiday, the most popular **means of transport**, the most popular **time of year** and the most popular **accommodation**.

b Think of two possible holidays which would fulfil all the most popular features of holidays in the EC.

c 60% of UK holidaymakers travelling abroad use air transport. Why is this figure much higher than for most other EC countries?

3 Study the aims of the European year of tourism. Divide the class into small groups. Each group should choose one of the EC aims.

Imagine that your group is the EC Commission responsible for writing the aim. Discuss why the aim was needed and how best to put it into practice.

After your discussion, produce a large poster to show the aim, why it is needed and the best ways of achieving it. Use the poster to help your group explain to the rest of the class about your aim.

Discuss each one and at the end of the discussion add any extra points which you did not include at first. Your finished posters can then be displayed.

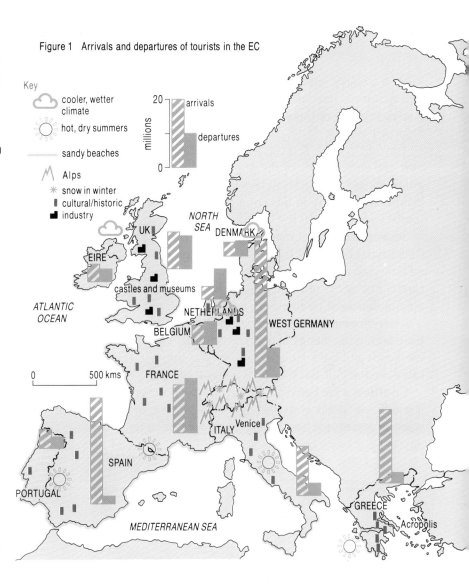

Figure 1 Arrivals and departures of tourists in the EC

Figure 2 EC tourism statistics

Type of holiday		Transport	
52% sea		68% car	
25% countryside		14% train	
23% mountains		13% aeroplane	
		5% boat	
Accommodation		**Holiday season**	
33% hotels		October–March	9%
22% relatives/friends		April–May	9%
17% renting		June	11%
16% camping/caravanning		July	28%
7% holiday homes		August	34%
5% lodging in private houses		September	9%

Some figures add up to more than 100% because some people go on holiday on more than one occasion.

12.2   Holidays in the UK

What a country — mountains, castles, National Parks, cities, winter skiing, forests, beaches, amusement parks — something for everybody? All of these **attractions** can be found in the UK (see Figures 1 and 2).

Tourism in the UK is big business — it earns about £9000 million a year and employs 6% of the population. Although more people are going abroad for their holidays than ever before, the majority of Britons still holiday in this country. There are also many foreign tourists who come to the UK for their holidays.

Some places attract many tourists — they are called **honeypot** sites. One tourist honeypot in the UK is London, the capital city. Over 40 million visitors come to London each year. Honeypots need very careful management to make sure the attractions we all want to enjoy are not damaged by the sheer number of people.

Overcrowding can be a problem at many tourist sites e.g. Blackpool, Stonehenge and in the National Parks, particularly at weekends and Bank Holidays during the summer. Car parks and cafés become full and the roads congested.

Conflicts arise between different recreation types. For example, it is difficult to mix water-skiing and swimming on lakes and hill walking and motor bike scrambling on the fellsides.

Key

National Parks

☒ main cultural and historical resorts

● main coastal resorts with sandy beaches

⊗ winter sports resorts

Figure 1
Location of major holiday resorts

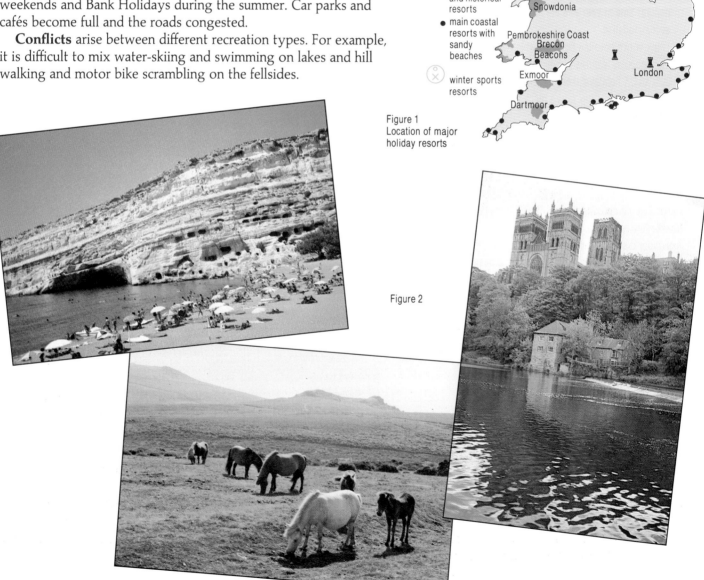

Figure 2

There are also conflicts between the **local** people and the tourists. Many local people do not like the invasion by tourists. Problems are caused by litter and noise. They are inconvenienced by the increased road traffic. New facilities built for the tourist (e.g. visitor centres or toilet blocks) may spoil the scenery and do not benefit the locals. Many cottages are being purchased as **second homes** which raises house prices. The local people find themselves unable to afford to buy a home and they are forced to move away.

Tourism can have advantages for the local community. Trade for local shops increases and jobs are created e.g. car park attendants, ice cream sellers, guides, waiters and waitresses in hotels, campsite attendants etc. New entertainments may be built, a particular benefit to the teenagers, and more money will come into the area.

But when winter comes the tourist attractions and resorts are quiet. Deck chair attendants, extra hotel staff and campsite workers are no longer needed. **Seasonal unemployment** is a major problem. Attempts are being made to lengthen the holiday season, for example, by offering other activities such as the Blackpool illuminations; using hotels for conferences or by offering cheaper winter breaks.

Activities

1 Work in pairs and use the map in Figure 1 and the photographs. Complete the table below with at least two examples. You may find an atlas useful.

Type of holiday resort	Examples
Sandy beaches near to large cities	
Coastal National Park	
Mountains, lakes and rivers	
Historic castles, cathedrals, birthplaces	
A resort with snow in winter	
Resorts with the warmest summer weather	

2 On an outline map of the UK, mark and name the examples you chose in activity 1. Use symbols and add a key to show the different types of holiday resort.

3 Holiday resorts often have a mixture of **natural** and **man-made** attractions. You can see examples of these in the photographs. The cathedral is man-made but the mountains and rivers are natural. Work in pairs or small groups and choose one of the four main types of holiday resort – National Park, historic, beach resort and winter resort. Identify which are the man-made and natural attractions you would find at your chosen resort. Produce a spider diagram for a class display. In the man-made section you could also include the **facilities** which are provided such as car parks, cafés etc.

4 Figure 3 shows the figures for visitors to the UK in 1988. Using an outline map of the world show the information using **flow lines**. Make the lines wider to represent large numbers of people and thinner to show small numbers. Start your arrow in the country of origin and finish it in the UK. Write on to your map the number of UK tourists who stayed in the UK.

Overseas visitors to the U.K. – the top 10 in 1988	
USA	2 620 000
France	1 969 000
W. Germany	1 830 000
Netherlands	881 000
Italy	661 000
Canada	651 000
Belgium & Luxembourg	586 000
Spain	509 000
Australia	481 000
Middle East	475 000
38 million British holidayed in Britain.	

Figure 3

a Name the countries from where the visitors have come.
b Lightly shade those countries which are in the EC in one colour and those which are Commonwealth countries in another. Add a key to your map.
c Try to explain the pattern of visitors to the UK as shown on your map.

5 Study the newspaper article in Figure 4.

   a Why is the British sightseer becoming 'greener'?

   b Explain why each of the following might cause
      a drop in tourist numbers.

      Use examples from the press cutting to illustrate
      your answers;

      ● narrow country roads leading to tourist sites
      ● the poor British weather
      ● a drop in the exchange rate making it
         expensive to holiday in the UK

   c How many of the 20 top attractions are in London?
      How can you explain this?

   d Which is the most popular attraction?

6 A competition is being held! The prize is an all
   expenses paid five-day holiday in London.

   You have to do one of the following:

   a Write a poem
   b Design a travel brochure
   c Produce a large poster

   The theme for all of these options is how to spend
   your five days in London. The information
   in Figure 5 will help you.

'Green' tourist sights in favour

By John Harlow

THE BRITISH sightseer is becoming "greener", with a growing interest in viewing animals in their natural habitat, rather than looking at them in cages, claims the English Tourist Board report on tourist attractions in 1988.

The number of visits to zoos and parks grew by seven per cent, far outstripping those to historic buildings, museums and art galleries, and despite the bad weather which characterised last year's summer.

Reserves devoted to particular animals, like monkeys or flamingoes, attracted record numbers of visitors, while the great churches like York Minster and St Paul's, slipped down the tourist board's list of "Top Ten" tourist attractions.

"Children have always loved animals, but now the older ones are putting animals into a 'green' context and wanting to see them in as natural an environment as possible," said a tourist board official yesterday.

"Some zoos, like Regents Park, have space constraints, but the new sanctuaries have new sites and are drawing families willing to drive two hours or more to get that 'authentic' feeling. They do not feel guilty, like they do when seeing animals in cages."

The number of visits to British tourist attractions increased by five per cent in 1988, which officials confidently predict will be topped when the 1989 figures are released next year.

"With more than £100 million spent on upgrading older sites or opening up 70 new attractions, the business got its house in order to take advantage of the boom summer this year," said the official.

"In 1988 and 1989, growth could have been much greater if the Government had put more money into improving roads. We are told that this is coming, so we are set to break even more records."

The report also lists reasons put forward by businesses which did not do so well. These included damage from the hurricane in October 1987, which still affected Kent parks the following summer, the drop in American visitors, and losses created by rising admission prices and reduced opening hours.

The Daily Telegraph 11.12.89

THE TOP ATTRACTIONS

Charged		Free	
1 Madame Tussaud's	2,705,000	1 Blackpool Pleasure Beach	6,500,000
2 Alton Towers	2,510,000	2 British Museum	3,859,000
3 Tower of London	2,182,000	3 Albert Dock	3,500,000
4 Blackpool Tower	1,478,000	4 Westminster Abbey	3,250,000
5 Natural History Museum	1,367,000	5 National Gallery	3,228,000
6 London Zoo	1,326,000	6 St Paul's Cathedral	2,500,000
7 Kew Gardens	1,181,000	7 Science Museum	2,436,000
8 Chessington World/Adventure	1,151,000	8 Yarmouth Pleasure Beach	2,250,000
9 Thorpe Park	1,028,000	9 Canterbury Cathedral	2,125,000
10 Flamingo Land	1,001,000	10 York Minster	2,100,000

Figure 4

Figure 5   Tourism in London

7. Study Figure 6, a press cutting about Stonehenge, just one of many honeypot sites in the UK.
Use the following as a guide:
- the problems for the local people living beside a tourist spot
- the problems for the visitors going to the site
- the damage to the environment caused by the visitors
- ways of coping with the needs of the visitors

8. Consider the plan to build the new road and visitor centre at Stonehenge.
  a What are the advantages of the scheme? Are there any problems the scheme may cause?
  b What have been the difficulties in getting the scheme off the ground?
  c Enter the architectural competition to design the new visitor centre.
  You could draw the exterior of the building as well as the plans for the inside. Remember the centre must be invisible from Stonehenge and must fit in with the character of the area.

Figure 6

£6m visitor centre is planned at Stonehenge

By Kenneth Powell
Architecture Correspondent

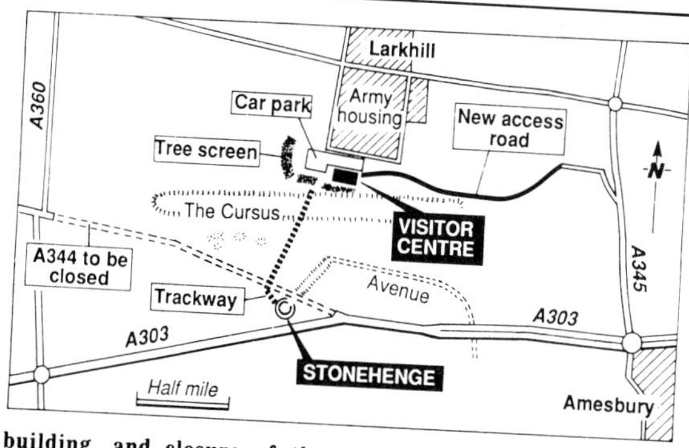

A VISITOR centre catering for up to one million visitors a year is to be built at Stonehenge after five years of discussions between English Heritage and the Ministry of Defence.

The MoD has agreed to sell the land needed for the building on a site north of the monument and close to Army married quarters at Larkhill. An architectural competition is likely to be held to select a design.

Visitors will walk to Stonehenge from the centre along a three-quarter-mile track which, says English Heritage, provides views "uncluttered by any 20th century intrusions".

Existing visitor facilities, close to the A344, will be removed and the road closed and grassed over, with traffic diverted via the A303.

The scheme was announced at the launch of English Heritage's annual report yesterday by Lord Montagu of Beaulieu, Chairman of English Heritage.

He said that plans for the building, and closure of the road, would be subject to planning approval.

He said: "There is a long way to go and our first task is to find people to work with us on this exciting scheme to draw up financial arrangements and to help us to plan it in detail".

The £6 million project is expected to take five years and English Heritage is considering a partnership with the private sector to provide funding.

It is likely that catering facilities and shop space would be leased.

The need for new visitor facilities at Britain's finest prehistoric monument was identified in 1984 but although the Ministry had agreed to surrender land for the visitor centre, the route of the access road remained in dispute.

An English Heritage commissioner said yesterday: "It was an uphill struggle. It seemed as if the whole defence of the West hinged on the fate of a few yards of officers' gardens".

The new centre will provide parking for 1,000 cars and space for 5,500 visitors.

English Heritage says it will feature the latest exhibition techniques but a full-scale replica of Stonehenge, suggested as a means of easing visitor pressure on the monument, has been ruled out.

The centre will be invisible from Stonehenge, but the choice of an architect will be a matter of some interest. English Heritage has been criticised for the intrusiveness of some of its buildings on historic sites and a modern design is unlikely to be selected.

THE DAILY TELEGRAPH, THURSDAY, NOVEMBER 2, 1989

12.3   Choosing a holiday abroad

Have you ever been abroad for your holidays? If I'd asked this question 50 years ago most people would have replied no! Today, more and more people are going **abroad** for their holidays.

Next time you are visiting some shops, have a look through the window of a travel agent. Notice the huge number of travel magazines. There are brochures for:
- Different **destinations** – the UK, the EC countries and all over the world.
- Different types of holiday – there are summer brochures for 'sea and sand' holidays; winter brochures for skiing holidays; there are mountain and lake holidays, cultural tours and cruises.
  The brochures include:
- a choice of **transport**, such as flying, cruising, train and ferry
- a choice of **accommodation** e.g. hotel, campsite or self-catering
  How do people decide where to go on their holiday abroad?

Figure 1 describes how different people decide on their holidays.

Notice all the reasons for their choice of holiday. They all want a certain type of holiday, for some the cost is important, for others the transport or accommodation. People consider many things before they book their holidays. This is **decision making**.

Dr. and Mrs Baxter

I HAVE A LONG SUMMER HOLIDAY AND WE LIKE TO TRAVEL AROUND CASTLES, CHURCHES AND MUSEUMS, AND SEE THE COUNTRY. MRS BAXTER DOESN'T LIKE FLYING. SHE COOKS AND RUNS THE HOUSE ALL YEAR, SO A GOOD HOTEL AND FOOD GIVES HER A REAL BREAK.

I'M 70 NOW, BUT I STILL LIKE A HOLIDAY, USUALLY APRIL, BEFORE IT'S TOO HOT FOR ME. I DON'T DRIVE, BUT I LIKE TOURING, SEEING NEW SCENES. I REALLY ENJOY THE MOUNTAINS WHERE IT'S COOL AND THE AIR IS FRESH

Mr. Asif

Figure 1
Decision-making

George

Jill and Gavin

WE'RE GETTING MARRIED THIS SUMMER, AND WE WANT TO GO ABROAD FOR OUR HONEYMOON. JILL LOVES SUNBATHING AND GAVIN LOVES SPORT- WINDSURFING AND GOLF. THE WEDDING IS AT 11 A.M. AND WE'D LIKE TO BE AT OUR DESTINATION THAT EVENING. WE'LL LOOK FOR SOMETHING CHEAPER THAN A HOTEL

I'M A FARMER, AND I CAN'T GET AWAY IN THE SUMMER, SO I HOLIDAY IN WINTER. I'M PRETTY FIT, AND A COUPLE OF FRIENDS AND I ENJOY SKIING, AND THE APRÈS-SKI TOO! I'M NOT MUCH OF A COOK, SO I BOOK A GOOD CENTRAL HOTEL AT THE RESORT. I DO SPEAK FRENCH, AND I LIKE TO PRACTISE WHILST I'M AWAY

Activities

1 Look again at Figure 1.
Write a list of all the factors the people have considered before they book.
Use the map on page 139, an atlas and a selection of holiday brochures to help you complete the table below.

Name	Destination	Transport	Accommodation
Dr and Mrs Baxter			
Mr Asif			
Jill and Gavin			
George			
Your choice			

2 a If you were going to book a holiday this year, what would you base your decision on? Write a list of all the factors you would consider. Put your list into order of importance.

 b Using your list in *a*, choose a country or area you would like to visit. Research your area or country using travel brochures and other resources to produce a small project. In your project include some details of the climate, scenery, facilities, accommodation, transport and cost.

12.4   *Holiday case studies*

1 'Sea and sand' holiday – The Algarve, Portugal

Where did you decide to send Jill and Gavin for their holiday? One choice could have been The Algarve in Portugal.

The Algarve is a province, (just like a county in the UK), in the far south of Portugal. It attracts many visitors every year because of its hot, dry, summer weather and its golden beaches. Figure 1 describes its attractions.

Portugal, like many of the Mediterranean countries, is an area where the standard of living is lower than other parts of the EC. Many of the people are poor farmers or fishermen. The growth of tourism has

brought many changes, some good and some bad. Figure 2 describes the changes which are taking place at Albufeira in the Algarve. This small fishing village has grown greatly to meet the needs of the growth in tourism.

Portugal earns a good income from tourism but the increase in visitors to the country leads to the demand for more facilities. New resorts are being built along the coast to cater for the demand. Some people call these developments **concrete jungles** and feel that they destroy the natural beauty of the area.

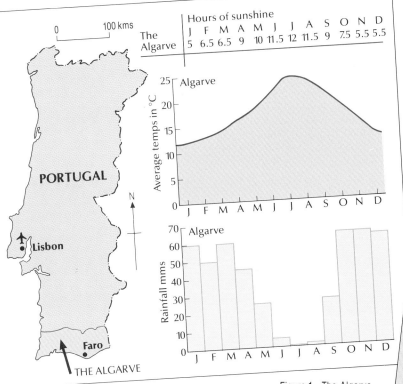

The Algarve	Hours of sunshine J F M A M J J A S O N D
	5 6.5 6.5 9 10 11.5 12 11.5 9 7.5 5.5 5.5

Figure 1 The Algarve

Hotel Dom Pedro Golf★★★★

An attractive modern hotel, situated near to the beach and marina at Vilamoura. The hotel has an extremely good reputation both for its accommodation and many facilities including a wide variety of sports such as tennis courts and reduced green fees at the nearby golf course, as well as many others. For the evenings there is a regular entertainment programme including dancing three nights a week and a poolside barbecue plus a folklore show weekly. The many shops, restaurants, bars, discos and the Vilamoura Casino are nearby.

Car hire is not essential.

Amenities:
★ Restaurant ★ Bars ★ Lounge
★ Games Room ★ Hairdressing
★ Tennis Courts ★ Shops
★ Many Sports Facilities
★ Children's Playground
★ Large Gardens
★ Swimming Pools ★ Sauna
★ Table Tennis ★ Darts
★ Air Conditioning

Entertainment:
★ Cocktail Evenings
★ Buffet Dinners
★ Live Music ★ Magic Evenings

★ Occasional Fashion Shows
★ Folklore Show ★ Bingo
★ Party Nights

Accommodation:
Twin bedded bedrooms, private bathroom/w.c., balcony with sea view. T.V.
Official Rating: 4 star
Price Includes: Bed and Breakfast. Taxi transfer from and to airport.
Bedrooms: 261

Figure 2 Tourism impact in the Algarve

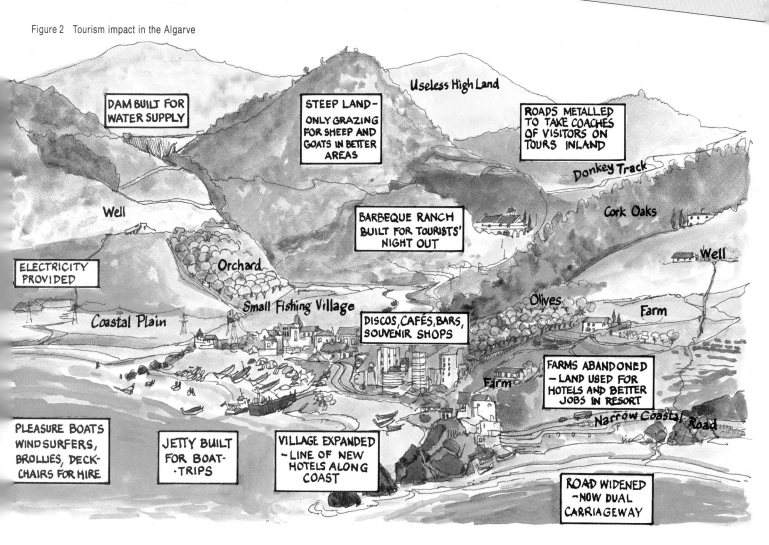

2 Cultural holiday – Venice in Northern Italy

Find Venice in your atlas – notice its **location**. Venice lies on the coast of north-east Italy, at the northern end of the Adriatic Sea. It is at the mouth of the River Po which is a **delta**. The city is built on over 100 islands split up by many canals. The largest of these is called the **Grand Canal**. Across the canals there are over 350 bridges such as the **Rialto Bridge** (Figure 3).

The site was chosen for a settlement because it provided a good defensive position. Later, Venice became a rich and powerful trading city, known as the 'Queen of the Sea'. Today the city is not as important although over 100 000 people still live there.

The city and the Venetian Empire were ruled by a Doge, the chief magistrate of Venice, and there were many wealthy merchants. The wealth was used to build fine buildings e.g. the **Ducal Palace, St Mark's Cathedral** and hundreds of towers called **campanils** Today the city attracts many tourists to see the great architectural and art treasures. Often the tourists outnumber the locals!

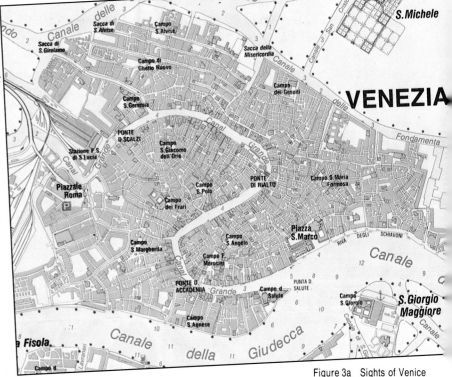

Figure 3a   Sights of Venice

Figure 3b   Satellite image of Venice

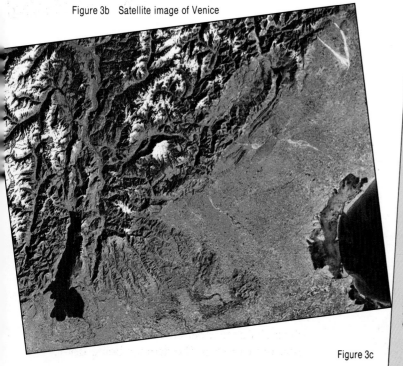

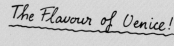

The Flavour of Venice!

Ride in a Gondola
50,000 lira for 50 mins.

Coffee   1500 lira

T-shirts of Venice
18,000 lira

Leather Gloves
17,000 lira

Pizza 4,000 lira

Motor Boat Trip around
the Grand Canal
3,000 lira

Seafood Risotto
16,000 l

Leather belts
8,000 l

Spaghetti Bolognese
6,500 l

Vaporetto (any distance)
1,000 l

Gondoliers Straw Hats
14,000 l

Silk Scarves
16,000 l

A brooch
16,000 l

Ice cream
1,500 l

Famous Venetian Handmade
Murano Glass
6 glasses - 80,000 l
Glass animal 12,000 l
Glass vase - 15,000 l

2,000 l = £1

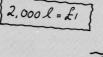

Figure 3c

The canals in Venice make travel by boat by far the easiest method of transport. Most people own a boat instead of a car, the buses are waterbuses or **vaporettas**, the police use fast motor launches, even the rubbish is collected by garbage boats and there are the famous **gondolas**.

The sea, which was once the reason for Venice's success, now seems to be the threat to the city's existence. The city suffers severe flooding and seems to be sinking into the lagoon. The salt water is **corroding** the buildings, eating away at the stonework, causing the mosaics to crumble and canvas paintings to rot. The floods are worst when there is an onshore wind and a high tide. The water piles up at the end of the Adriatic Sea.

Figure 3d

Figure 3e

Figure 3f

Figure 3g

There are other problems too. The city continues to lose population. There are problems of air and water pollution from the nearby chemical factories and the lagoon is being choked by seaweed. The famous churches and palaces are not being repaired fast enough. Venice is also at risk from the great numbers of tourists which choke the city. Many visitors only come for the day and try to see all the popular attractions, causing great overcrowding and damage.

An international fund called 'Venice in Peril' was launched to raise money to help pay for the restoration work which is needed. The building of a tidal barrage, like the Thames Barrier, across the lagoon has also been suggested to stop the flooding. In the future visitor numbers may have to be restricted to reduce the damage being done.

Activities

1 Look up Portugal in your atlas. Draw a sketch map of the province of Algarve and use the answers to the following questions to label your map.
   a Which ocean borders the Algarve on two sides?
   b Which country lies to the east of the Algarve?
   c Which range of mountains separates the Algarve from the rest of Portugal?
   d Which city is the capital of the Algarve and has the region's airport?
   e Which cape is the most southerly point in Portugal and the most south-westerly point in Europe?

2 a Draw a climate graph to show the temperature and rainfall figures for the Algarve (page 19 shows you how to draw a climate graph).
   b Study the graph. Which is the busiest season in Portugal?
   c Why would Gavin and Jill who live in London enjoy a holiday in the Algarve during the summer?

3 Figure 5 shows the figures for visitors arriving at Faro airport in the Algarve in June 1989.
   a Show these as segments of a pie chart. Convert the figures to percentages and then multiply by 3.6 to find the number of degrees for each segment.
   b From which continent do most visitors come? Write down any two reasons for this.
   c In June 1989 there were only 10 visitors from Greece and 70 visitors from Spain. Look carefully at an atlas map to help you explain this.

4 Figure 2 describes the **impact** of tourism in the Algarve.
   a Describe the scene before the arrival of tourism. What were the traditional occupations of the local people?
   b Copy the outline from the figure and draw on to it the changes which have taken place. Label the new developments. Add a title.
   c In pairs or small groups discuss the changes. Have they been good or bad for the local people? Record your results.

5 Find the location of Venice on an atlas map of Italy and study the map in Figure 3. Describe the **site** of Venice. Remember the site is the place where a settlement is built.

6 a Draw a sketch from the photograph in Figure 3g. Use the map in Figure 3a to help you label:
   the Ducal Palace
   the Campanile
   St Mark's Basin
   a vaporetta (waterbus)
   b What evidence is there on the photographs to show how important water transport is?
   c What evidence is there that restoration work is being carried out?
   d Look closely at the photographs on page 147. Describe your feelings about Venice. Would you like to visit the city?

Figure 6

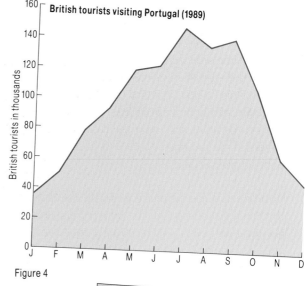

Figure 4

Visitor arrivals at Faro airport in June 1989	
The EC countries	120 793
Rest of Europe	9 584
Asia	138
North America	888
South America	88
Africa	121
Oceania	327

Figure 5

Green menace chokes Venice

by Tim Jepson

ROME

BESIEGED by tourists, swamped by the sea, Venice has been under attack from many quarters during its illustrious history, but to-day the city is facing a new twin peril ... insect life and its own seaweed.

Years of unchecked pollution and the nutritional effects of raw sewage have bred a glutinous mass of super seaweed – some specimens are the size of bedsheets – which threatens to choke the city's lagoon.

Last summer when the weed algae first entered the canals the stench of dead fish and decaying vegetable matter drove tourists from hotels and forced gondoliers to wear facemasks. This year the green menace is stronger than ever.

"We are on the brink of catastrophe," said the mayor, Antonio Castellati. "Almost the entire lagoon is covered. The algae are changing the whole environment, and I'm afraid I have little faith in the measures we are taking."

Regional Councillor Stefano Boato shares the general gloom. He said: "We are repeating the shambles of last year's clean-up – too little, too late. Come summer, the air will be unbreathable."

Venice, for all its splendid isolation, is ringed on the mainland by oil refineries and two vast chemical works. A million people live on the fringes. The resulting pollution is too potent for the sea – itself one of Europe's filthiest – to flush out the lagoon.

The sludge has made a remorseless advance, starving the water of oxygen and suffocating most other marine life. The lagoon, covering an area of 212 square miles, is becoming a swamp.

Fourteen boats have been sent into the fray, and in less than a month they have sucked up 40,000 tons of slime from the shallows near the city.

Rome has sent £6 million to help, but that is unlikely to be enough. Summer sun will send the already rampant weed into a frenzy of growth.

Alberto Bernstein, in charge of the operation is pessimistic. "These algae double in size every 15 days. It's simply a battle we cannot win."

Worse is in store, for the scum of mouldering seaweed is a perfect breeding ground for billions of tiny flies. Once hatched, they head for the lights of Venice.

Last year they descended on the city in a plague of biblical proportions. The city's airport was closed as carpets of insects made runways unusable and infiltrated aircraft engines. The railway station was cut off and street lighting obliterated.

Sunday Telegraph 18.6.89

7 Imagine that you are visiting Venice for the day with a friend. In pairs, plan your visit and tour of the city.
Use the information in the text and in Figure 3 to help you.
Produce as detailed an **itinerary** as possible for your day in Venice.
Include a map to show your tour.

8 Study the information about the problems of Venice. In pairs or small groups discuss the problems and possible solutions to them.
   a Copy and complete a table like the one below to record your results.

Problems	Solutions
Flooding	Tidal barrages
	Sea walls
	Abandon ground floor rooms

   b Design and draw a poster that could be used in the Venice in Peril campaign.
   c Is Venice worth saving? Or should it be left to rot and sink into the lagoon? Give two reasons for your answer.

12.5   Winter holiday – the Alps

The Alps and other mountain areas of Europe are popular winter holiday resorts because they have large amounts of snow, ideal for skiing and other winter sports. The tourist industry is very important to the countries in which the Alps lie. Have a look in your atlas. Which EC countries have a part of the Alps within them?

Many of the Alpine villages were small farming villages before the growth of winter holidays. The locals built hotels and chalets to accommodate the tourists. Ski-lifts, mountain railways, climbing huts and toboggan runs have all been built to cater for the visitors. Many of the locals are now employed in the tourist industry. There are jobs for ski instructors, guides, waiters, hotel owners, ski-lift operators and coach drivers. The busiest time of the year is February and March although the Alps attract visitors all year round for the spectacular scenery.

It is only recently that the Alps have attracted so much attention. Mountain areas were once thought to be dangerous, ugly and **hostile environments**. Today many people find the Alps inviting and beautiful. It is also much easier to visit these areas; new roads, railways, Alpine passes and airports make the Alps more **accessible**. But the Alps are being damaged by the huge numbers of visitors. The environment is fragile. Litter, noise and erosion are causing damage. Huge ski-lifts, modern hotels and car parks spoil the peaceful countryside and the beautiful Alpine forests and lakes are being damaged by **acid rain** (see page 26).

Activities

1 a On an outline map of Europe, mark on the extent of the Alps and label all the countries that contain part of the Alps. Label the UK. Colour in the countries of the EC in one colour and the non-EC countries in another. Add a key and title to your map.

2 Study all the information in this unit. Write a list of all the jobs that are available as a result of tourism.

3 a Describe the attractions of Les Deux Alpes for a winter holiday. Try to include some natural and man-made attractions.

 b Describe the location of the village.

 c What evidence is there that it is a modern resort?

 d How does the resort cater for skiers of different standards?

 e What different types of transport are available at the resort?

Off The slopes

Apart from the outdoor heated swimming pool and artificial ice rink (free to lift pass holders) there is a marvellous fitness centre. This offers jacuzzi, sauna, Turkish bath and a solarium. In Le Village there is a selection of shops, cafés and restaurants, plus the Sports Centre with squash courts, ten-pin bowling and swimming pool. The local bus and trains provide a good service to neighbouring areas such as Alpe d'Huez and Grenoble.

Après-Ski

The main street of Les Deux Alpes is lined with tea rooms, bars and cafés. Pub le Windsor and Mike's bar are lively meeting places. There are several discos – La Casa and L'Avalanch are both very popular.

Eating Out

There are a number of good restaurants in Les Deux Alpes offering a range of dishes, including fondue, raclette, crêpes and even couscous. La Patate has a very cosy atmosphere and is particularly good value. There are also a number of take-aways serving crêpes and brioches.

SKI FACTS

Approx. no. of snow cannons:	2
Approx. km artificial piste:	1.5km

Number of lifts:	66
Km of piste:	160km
Nursery slopes:	5
Number of easy runs:	49
Medium runs:	16
Difficult runs:	10
Off-piste skiing:	Limited
Longest runs:	13km
Slopes face:	SW.SE
Ski school Instructors:	170
English speaking Ski Instructors:	18
Usual hours of instruction: (09.30 – 12.30, 15.00 – 17.00)	
Cross country trails:	20km

SKI LIFTS

Lift No.	Name	Lift Type
1	Bons	Chair
2	Mont de Lans	Chair
3	Petite Aiguille	Drag
4	Le Floc	Drag
5	Le Vallée Blanche	Drag
6	Les Cimes	Chair
7	Pied-Moutet 1950	Chair
8	Pied-Moutet 2100	Drag
9	Les Cartons	Drag
10	Super-Venosc	Chair
11	La Village	Chair
12	Belle-Etolle	Drag
13	L'Alpette	Drag
14	Lutins/Cretes	Chair
15	Jandri I & II	Gondola
16	Jandri Express	Cablecar
17	La Rouge	Chair
18	Le Diable	Gondola
19	Les Vallons	Chair
20	La Girosp	Drag
21	Roche-Mantel	Chair
22	Le Signal	Chair
23	Le Puy-Salle I	Drag
24	Le Puy-Salle II	Drag
25	Le Dôme Sud	Drag
26	Le Sorelles	Drag
27	Les Belles-Combes	Drag
28	La Toura	Chair
29	Le Lac Noir	Chair

Figure 1

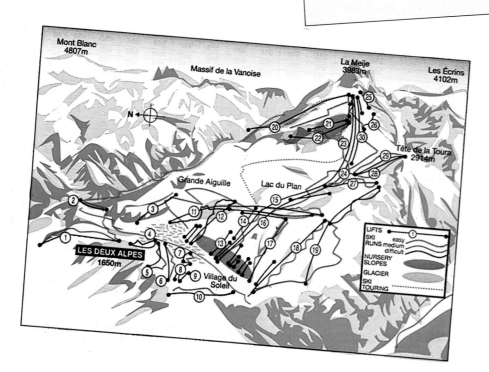

4 SKI TALK. *The tops and tails are all muddled up! Rewrite them correctly:*

cable car	pulls skiers up a mountain
white out	skiing downhill through poles
nursery slope	evening food and entertainment
piste	cabin on a cable which takes people up a mountain
powder snow	gentle slope used by beginners
slalom	prepared ski run
drag lift	fresh dry snow
après ski	loss of visibility through heavy snow

5 Study the text and the newspaper cutting in Figure 2 which talk about the problems in the Alps. Imagine that you live in a village in the Alps. There is going to be a public enquiry about developing the village into a skiing resort. In small groups choose one of the following roles and write a report to present to the enquiry giving your points of view.

- a farmer
- a hotel developer
- a keen skier who travels to the next village to instruct each day
- the local pub landlord
- a conservationist
- a young person who wants to move away to find work and more nightlife
- a forestry expert
- an architect who designs ski resorts.

a Hold a public enquiry; each group should present their report. Have a discussion and then vote as to whether the village should be developed or not.

b Consider all the points that were made in the public enquiry. Write a list of the advantages that tourism brings to the people and countries of the Alps. Write a second list of the problems of the Alpine areas.

6 You work for a local advertising company given the task of informing the public about the problems of the Alps and the ways to solve them. Either individually or in groups choose some of the problems of the Alpine areas and produce an action plan to prevent or reduce the problem. Either:

- Present one or more of your ideas as a poster which is to be distributed around the world.
  or
- Write the words for a song like the 'Band Aid' song passing on the message about the problems in the Alps. You may be able to set it to a familiar tune!

Produce a wall display in your work area with the posters and songwords.

Figure 2 *Independent* 16 January 1988

Turning the Alps into a Rocky Desert

The Alps are crumbling. Europe's most majestic mountain range, a symbol of unspoilt nature and paradise for holidaymakers is in grave danger.

The disease which is gnawing away at the Alps has many interconnected causes. But behind them all is one culprit – man. The fumes from factories, traffic and well heated homes is killing the forests. As roots weaken and trees fall, rain and snow sweep unhindered to the valleys, taking with them soil and vegetation and paving the way for more landslides. The forests also act as a filter for air and water pollution and many cities draw their water from the Alps.

The boom in winter sports and tourism is demanding yet more ski-runs, ski-lifts, hotels, roads and holiday homes, which mean yet more bulldozers tearing into the mountainsides and wrecking the fragile balance of nature. The bulldozers beat down the surface, making it harder and more impermeable so that the rain rushes straight downhill.

Alpine farmers, whose ancient way of life can hardly be sustained in modern economies, are moving down the valleys and abandoning their lovingly preserved pastures to the elements. The land is turning into scrub and forest. Some farmers have taken other jobs leaving the women to do the husbands' tasks. The women now work for up to 80 hours a week. At weekends the family is so tired that maintenance and drainage work does not get done. For centuries this work helped to prevent avalanches, landslides and erosion. For the young people, they earn more money in jobs elsewhere and not on the land. This creates tensions and resentment.

The air pollution and the traffic which pours daily across the Alps is mostly International, not from the 7 countries through which the Alps pass. The Brenner Pass from Austria into Italy carries 3,000 vehicles a day, including 1,000 lorries. There is much local resentment against the noisy, stinking traffic clogging the roads.

From now on, most experts and organisations agree the environment should be given high priority. One idea is 'soft tourism' where the tourist industry is secondary to the main activities of a mountain community rather than dominant. The tourists would have to fit into the community and not expect great luxury, elaborate ski lifts and entertainments.

A first priority has to be a drastic reduction in air pollution. A series of measures has been suggested to cut down the damage from car exhausts; this includes speed limits, a ban on all but lead free petrol, weekends without cars, traffic free regions and restrictions on air traffic over the Alps. No new roads should be built and as much traffic as possible, especially heavy goods, should be switched to new and existing railways.

But, of course the cost of saving the Alps is mind-boggling! In Austria alone it is estimated that £300 billion is needed just to rescue the forests. Are Europeans prepared to spend that kind of money to save their most beautiful mountains?

Independent 16.1.88

12.6   *European tourism in the future*

Tourism will continue to grow in the future. there are several reasons for this:

- people's wages continue to rise
- there are more package holidays and flights abroad from local airports
- people can afford more than one holiday a year and more people go on short-stay holidays and day trips
- more people want to travel further afield to see different cultures
- more advertising
- growth of self-catering holidays which can be cheaper e.g., camping, villas, time share
- encouragement by governments and the EC who give money to build resorts and facilities

Countries need to plan ahead to cater for the needs of the tourists. In France, they are developing their National Parks to take more visitors and new projects like Euro Disney are being built. Figures 1 and 2 give some more information about these tourist attractions. New European destinations may well grow in popularity as the countries of Eastern Europe become more accessible.

But the tourist industry is prone to all sorts of outside influences. In recent years some tour companies have gone bankrupt because they could not sell their holidays. Figure 3 explains why this has happened.

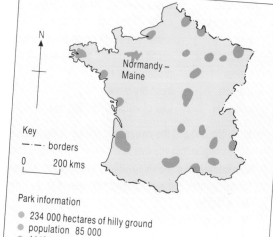

Key

-·-·- borders

0   200 kms

Park information

- 234 000 hectares of hilly ground
- population 85 000
- 44 184 tourist can be accommodated

second homes	20 655
hotels	4 716
rooms	8 674
youth hostels	659
camping/caravans	8 622
farms	910

- Bagnoles is the only real tourist centre although there are other small towns.
- In the area around St Leonard and Domfront there is spectacular scenery
- There are castles and chateaux and churches to visit
- The rivers are attractive for canoeists and fishermen as well as being pretty
- Tourism would help provide jobs in an area where people are leaving the countryside
- The farming is based on milk and meat, the cattle reared in small hedged fields

Figure 1a   National Parks in France

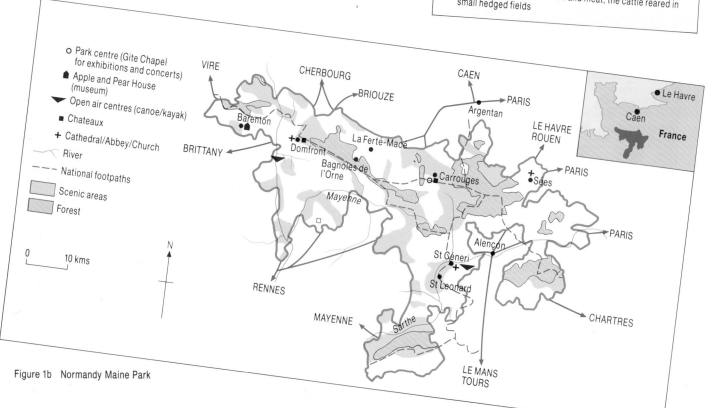

○ Park centre (Gite Chapel for exhibitions and concerts)
▲ Apple and Pear House (museum)
▼ Open air centres (canoe/kayak)
■ Chateaux
+ Cathedral/Abbey/Church
〜 River
--- National footpaths
▒ Scenic areas
▓ Forest

0   10 kms

Figure 1b   Normandy Maine Park

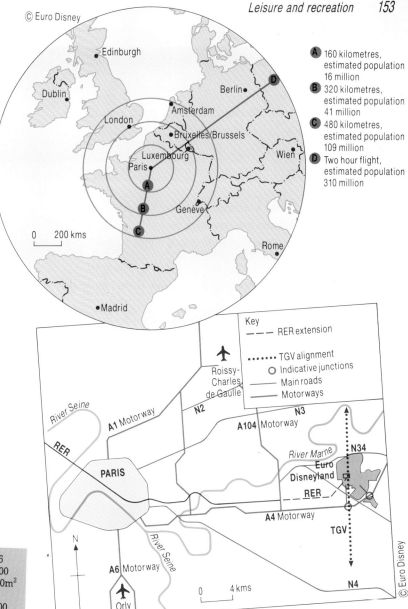

A) 160 kilometres, estimated population 16 million

B) 320 kilometres, estimated population 41 million

C) 480 kilometres, estimated population 109 million

D) Two hour flight, estimated population 310 million

0 200 kms

The scheme should be completed by 2017
The first phase is due to open on 12 April 1992
Cost of phase 1 is 22 billion French francs

The development programme (Master agreement over 30 yrs)

Theme Parks	2	Golf courses (halls)	45
Hotel rooms	18 200	Houses	5 500
Campgrounds (sites)	2 100	Shopping Centres	95 000m²
Entertainment centres	60 000m²	Water recreation area	1
Offices	700 000m²	Time shares units	2 400
Multipurpose corporate park	750 000m²		

Figure 2 Euro Disney

Key
--- RER extension
···· TGV alignment
○ Indicative junctions
— Main roads
— Motorways

Roissy-Charles de Gaulle

River Seine
A1 Motorway
N2
N3
A104 Motorway
RER
River Marne
N34
PARIS
Euro Disneyland
RER
A4 Motorway
N
River Seine
TGV
A6 Motorway
0 4 kms
N4
Orly

Figure 3 Why Holitours went bankrupt

Activities

1 Give one way each of the following have caused a growth in tourism:
- travel companies
- governments
- employers
- airlines

2 Study Figure 1 which gives information about French National Parks.
- *a* How many National Parks are there in France?
- *b* Find a map of France in your atlas. What sorts of area are they found in? (Hint – look at the relief of the land.)

3 Study the information in Figure 1 about the Normandy Maine Park. Work in pairs for this activity.
- *a* Discuss how you would cater for more tourists visiting the area. You need to provide:
  - accommodation for another 10 000 people
  - two more open-air centres
  - three more 'discovery routes' for ramblers, canoeists, pony trekkers or climbers
- *b* Use a copy of the map (Figure 1b) to show your plans.
- *c* Choose one of your ideas and describe why you chose the location.
- *d* Will your plan have any bad impact on the environment?
- *e* You need to advertise the park to attract the extra visitors.
  Either:
  - Draw a poster advertising the area
  Or
  - Write an interview to be broadcast live on the local radio advertising the area. If you can, record your interview and present it to the class.

  Using Figure 3, write a paragraph with the title 'Why Holitours Travel Company went bankrupt'.

4 Read Figure 2 about the new Euro Disney park near Paris.
- *a* How far from Paris will the new development be?
- *b* Describe the route a visitor arriving at Orly airport could take to reach Euro Disney.
- *c* How many people in Europe are within two hours' flying time of Euro Disney?
- *d* How many capital cities are within 480 kilometres of Euro Disney? Name them.
- *e* What facilities will be on offer ?
- *f* Work in pairs or small groups if you wish. Design your version of Euro Disney. Your final plan is to be used as a guide in the brochures that visitors will buy to help them find their way around.

  Draw a large copy of the outline of the site from the map in Figure 2 and include the transport routes. Add all the various facilities, the offices, shops and accommodation etc. where you think they should be. Make your plan as attractive and detailed as possible, but remember it must be clear and easy to follow. Not everybody is good at reading plans!

Dictionary

abroad   in another country
accessible   how easy it is to reach
destination   the end point of a journey

honeypot site   a place that becomes overcrowded by visitors
hostile environment   a place that repels people

itinerary   a plan for a trip or holiday
tourism   the industry which caters for visitors to an area

1:50 000

© Crown Copyright

ROADS AND PATHS
Not necessarily rights of way

VOIES DE COMMUNICATIONS VERKEHRSNETZ

Service area M 56 — Elevated — En Viaduc überhöht
Junction number 12
M 53

Motorway (dual carriageway)
Autoroute (chaussées séparées) avec aire de service et échangeur avec numero de l'échangeur
Autobahn (zweibahnig) mit Versorgungs - und Anschlussstelle sowie Nummer der Anschlussstelle

Motorway under construction
Autoroute en construction
Autobahn im Bau

Unfenced — Footbridge
A 41 (T) — Passerelle Fussgängerbrücke
Sans clôture — Dual carriageway
A 483 — Chaussées séparées Zweibahnig

Trunk road
Route de grande circulation
Fernverkehrsstrasse

Main road
Route principale
Hauptstrasse

Main road under construction
Route principale en construction
Hauptstrasse im Bau

Uneingehegt
B 5132

Secondary road
Route secondaire
Nebenstrasse

A 855 — B 885

Narrow road with passing places
Route étroite avec voies de dépassement
Enge Strasse mit Ausweich-Uberholstellen

Bridge Pont Brücke

Road generally more than 4 m wide
Route généralement de plus de 4 m de largeur
Strasse, Minimalbreite im allg. 4 m

Road generally less than 4 m wide
Route généralement de moins de 4 m de largeur
Strasse, Maximalbreite im allg. 4 m

Other road, drive or track
Autre route, allée ou sentier
Sonstige Strasse, Zufahrt oder Feldweg

Path Sentier Fussweg

Gradient: 1 in 5 and steeper 1 in 7 to 1 in 5
Pente: 20% et plus de 14% à 20%
Steigungen: 20% und mehr 14% bis 20%

Gates Road tunnel
Barrières Tunnel routier
Schranken Strassentunnel

Ferry P — Ferry V

Ferry (passenger) Ferry (vehicle)
Bac pour piétons Bac pour véhicules
Personenfähre Autofähre

PUBLIC RIGHTS OF WAY
(Not applicable to Scotland)

.... Footpath
— — — — — Bridleway
— · — · — · — Road used as a public path
—+—+—+—+— Byway open to all traffic

TOURIST INFORMATION

RENSEIGNEMENTS TOURISTIQUES DIVERS ALLGEMEINE TOURISTENANGABEN

Information centre
Bureau d'information
Informationsbüro

Parking
Parking
Parkplatz

Picnic site
Emplacement de pique nique
Picknickplatz

Viewpoint
Point de vue
Aussichtspunkt

Camp site
Terrain de camping
Campingplatz

Caravan site
Terrain pour caravanes
Wohnwagenplatz

Youth hostel
Auberge de jeunesse
Jugendherberge

Selected places of tourist interest
Endroits d'un intérêt touristique particulier
Ausgesuchte Orte, von Interesse für Touristen

Telephone, public/motoring organisation
Téléphone, publique/associations automobiles
Telefon, öffentliches/Automobilklub

Golf course or links
Terrain de golf
Golfplatz

Public convenience (in rural areas)
WC (à la campagne)
Toiletten in ländlichen Gebieten

ROUTE OF OFFA'S DYKE PATH
• WREXHAM
• Ruabon
Offa's Dyke Path (OD Path)

National trail
Sentier de randonnée national
Nationaler Wanderweg

RAILWAYS

Track multiple or single
Track narrow gauge
Bridges, Footbridge
Tunnel
Viaduct

Freight line, siding or tramway
Station (a) principal (b) closed to passengers
Level crossing LC
Embankment
Cutting

WATER FEATURES

Marsh or salting
Slopes
Cliff
High water mark
Towpath Lock
Flat rock
Low water mark
Aqueduct Canal
Ford
Lighthouse (in use)
Lake Weir Normal tidal limit
Sand Dunes
Footbridge
Bridge
Mud
Lighthouse (disused)
Beacon
Canal (dry)
Shingle

HEIGHTS

—50— Contours are at 10 metres vertical interval

•144 Heights are to the nearest metre above mean sea level

ROCK FEATURES

outcrop
cliff
scree

GENERAL FEATURES

Electricity transmission line (with pylons spaced conventionally)
Pipe line (arrow indicates direction of flow)
bruin Buildings
Public buildings (selected)
Bus or coach station
Coniferous wood
Non-coniferous wood
Mixed wood
Orchard
Park or ornamental grounds

Quarry
Spoil heap, refuse tip or dump
Radio or TV mast
Church / Chapel with tower / with spire / without tower or spire
Chimney or tower
Glasshouse
Graticule intersection at 5' intervals
(H) Heliport
△ Triangulation pillar
Windmill with or without sails
Windpump

BOUNDARIES

—·—+—·— National
—·—·—·— London Borough
National Park or Forest Park
NT National Trust

—— County, Region or Islands Area
——— District
NT open access
NT limited access

ABBREVIATIONS

P Post office
PH Public house
MS Milestone
MP Milepost

CH Clubhouse
PC Public convenience (in rural areas)
TH Town Hall, Guildhall or equivalent
CG Coastguard

ANTIQUITIES

VILLA Roman
Castle Non-Roman
⚔ Battlefield (with date)
☆ Tumulus
+ Position of antiquity which cannot be drawn to scale

🏛 Ancient Monuments and Historic Buildings in the care of the Secretaries of State for the Environment, for Scotland and for Wales and that are open to the public

The revision date of archaeological information varies over the sheet

---

1:25 000

ROADS AND PATHS
Not necessarily rights of way

M 1 or A6(M) Motorway
A 31(T) Trunk road
A 35 Main road
B 3074 Secondary road
A 35 Dual carriageway
Road generally more than 14ft wide
Road generally less than 14ft wide
Road generally less than 14ft wide, untarred
Other road, drive or track
Path

Unfenced roads and tracks are shown by pecked lines

RAILWAYS

Multiple track
Single track Standard gauge
Narrow gauge
Siding
Cutting
Embankment
Tunnel
Road over & under
Level crossing, station

PUBLIC RIGHTS OF WAY (Not applicable to Scotland)

— — — — Public paths { Footpath / Bridleway
—·—·—·— Road used as a public path

Information not available in uncoloured areas

DANGER AREA —
MOD ranges in the area
Danger!
Observe warning notices

Public rights of way indicated by these symbols have been derived from Definitive Maps as amended by later enactments or instruments held by Ordnance Survey on 1st Oct 1981 and are shown subject to the limitations imposed by the scale of mapping.
The representation on this map of any other road, track or path is no evidence of the existence of a right of way

BOUNDARIES As notified to 1- 2-73

— — — — Geographical County
— — — — Administrative County, County Borough or County of City
— — — — London Borough
— — — — Municipal Borough, Urban or Rural District, Burgh or District Council
— — — — Civil Parish*
— — — — Borough, Burgh or County Constituency

Coincident boundaries are shown by the first appropriate symbol opposite

*Shown alternately when coincident with other boundaries

SYMBOLS

Church / or / chapel with tower / with spire / without tower or spire
Y Glasshouse, Youth hostel
Bus or coach station
Lighthouse, lightship, beacon
△ Triangulation station
Triangulation point on { church, chapel, lighthouse, beacon, building & chimney
BP, BS Boundary Post, Stone
T, A, R Telephone, public, AA, RAC
P, MP, MS Post office, Mile Post, Stone

VILLA Roman antiquity (AD 43 to AD 420)
Castle Other antiquities
+ Site of antiquity
⚔ 1066 Site of battle (with date)
Gravel, sand pit
Disused pit or quarry
Chalk pit, clay pit or quarry
Refuse or slag heap
Sloping masonry
·W, Spr Well, Spring

Water
Sand, sand & shingle
Mud
Dunes
National Trust always open
NT National Trust opening restricted
NTS National Trust for Scotland
Electricity transmission line
pylon pole

VEGETATION Limits of vegetation are defined by positioning of the symbols but may be delineated also by pecks or dots

Coniferous trees
Non-coniferous trees
Coppice
Orchard
Scrub
Bracken, rough grassland
In some areas bracken (·) and rough grassland (..) are shown separately
Shown collectively as rough grassland on some sheets
Heath
Reeds
Marsh
Saltings

HEIGHTS AND ROCK FEATURES

50 · Determined by { ground survey
285 · air survey
Vertical face
Surface heights are to the nearest foot above mean sea level. Heights shown close to a triangulation pillar refer to the station height at ground level and not necessarily to the summit
Loose rock Boulders Outcrop Scree
Contours are at 5 metres vertical interval